National Geographic Society

LOST EMPIRES
LIVING TRIBES

LOST EMPIRES
LIVING TRIBES

Published by
The National Geographic Society

Gilbert M. Grosvenor
President

Melvin M. Payne
Chairman of the Board

Owen R. Anderson
Executive Vice President

Robert L. Breeden
*Vice President, Publications
and Educational Media*

Prepared by
National Geographic
Book Service

Charles O. Hyman
Director

Kenneth C. Danforth
Assistant Director

Anne Dirkes Kobor
Illustrations Editor

Staff for this book

Ross S. Bennett
Editor

Carol Bittig Lutyk
Assistant Editor

David M. Seager
Art Director

Linda B. Meyerriecks
Picture Editor

Robert Arndt
Edward Lanouette
David D. Pearce
David F. Robinson
Verla Lee Smith
Editor-Writers

Charlotte Golin
Layout Assistant

Orren J. Alperstein
Suzanne P. Kane
Melanie Patt-Corner
Susan Eckert Sidman
Penelope A. Timbers
L. Madison Washburn
Anne E. Withers
Editorial Research

Paulette L. Claus
Teresita C. Sison
Editorial Assistants

Robert C. Firestone
Production Manager

Karen F. Edwards
*Assistant Production
Manager*

Richard S. Wain
*Senior Production
Assistant*

John T. Dunn
Ronald E. Williamson
Engraving and Printing

Paintings by
Michael A. Hampshire

Maps and drawings by
Robert Hynes *and*
John D. Garst, Jr.
Peter J. Balch
Virginia L. Baza
Lisa Biganzoli
Patricia K. Cantlay
Jerald N. Fishbein
Gary M. Johnson
Susan M. Johnston
Alfred L. Zebarth
Geographic Art

Contributions by
Thomas B. Allen
Patricia Anawalt
Wayne Barrett
Patricia Corbett
Mary B. Dickinson
Diane S. Marton
Amanda Parsons
Maura J. Pollin
S. Jeffrey K. Wilkerson

Photographs by
Jaume Blassi
Lee Boltin
David L. Brill
David Hiser
Danny Lehman
Loren McIntyre
and others

George I. Burneston III
Michael G. Young
Index

Chief Consultants
George E. Stuart
Staff Archaeologist,
National Geographic Society

William H. Crocker
Curator,
South American Ethnology,
Smithsonian Institution
Washington, D. C.

First edition
375 illustrations, 17 paintings

Pages 2-3: Uxmal's Pyramid of
  the Magician
Pages 4-5: Fishing in the Amazon
Pages 6-7: Herding in the Andes

FOREWORD

Sun, corn, civilization. There was a mystic linkage in that trinity for the pre-Columbian Indians of Latin America. Corn was the stuff of life, and among their pantheon of deities of sun, rain, wind, and water the Indians often included a god of corn. In one instance, corn was even a part of Creation. The *Popol Vuh*, sacred book of the Quiché Maya, tells how the gods made the first mother and father: "Of yellow corn and of white corn they made their flesh; of corn-meal dough they made the arms and legs of man."

Centuries ago genius moved among the peoples of Mesoamerica and Peru. Without benefit of draft animals, iron tools, or the wheel they evolved sophisticated societies epitomized by the stone temples and palaces of the Maya, Aztecs, and Incas. Yet corn stands as their most enduring testimonial. They discovered it, developed it, domesticated it, and made it their lasting gift to the world. Long after the temples and palaces have crumbled, corn lives on to help feed all of humankind. Not only is it an adaptable cereal crop, it is also one of the world's most efficient in converting the sun's energy into food. It grows in the steamy lowlands of the tropics and on the windy slopes of the Andes, and each seed can produce 1,000 to 2,000 kernels. With such an amazing plant, the Indian was able to harvest the surpluses on which to build not just civilizations but empires.

Lost Empires, Living Tribes traces the rise and fall of those empire builders, and it also explores the fortunes of their progeny as well as less settled, less developed cultures. The "tribes" of the title comprise a colorful mixture of today's Indian groups, some large, some small, but all bound by a common heritage—descent from the first Americans. The location of the South American groups at time of white contact can be found on the foldup map that accompanies this book.

In total numbers the Indians of Latin America seem to have held their own, despite decimations following the Conquest. Estimates by scholars for the early 16th century range wildly—from 8 to 45 million. Today there are an estimated 30 million from Mexico to Tierra del Fuego. However, their distribution, viewed as a percentage of each nation's population, is dramatically uneven: 50-75 percent in Bolivia, 46 in Peru, 41 in Guatemala, 40 in Ecuador, 30 in Mexico, 5 in Nicaragua, 3 in Chile, 2 in Brazil and Venezuela, 1 in Colombia, and unknown fractions, if any, in the rest of Latin America.

Sad to say, there are lost tribes as well as lost empires, and some groups now struggling for survival may be fading into cultural oblivion as we go to press. Turn the page now to discover the past, present, and future of these determined and ingenious peoples.

George E. Stuart

Individual tiles in a Latin American mosaic, Indian faces represent today's living—and sometimes threatened—tribes. Top row: An Indian of San Juan Atitán, Guatemala, shows the Maya features of his people (left); a highland Peruvian woman takes part in Inti Raymi, *a sun festival (center); long hair—sometimes dyed or curled—distinguishes Ica men of northern Colombia (right). Center row: A young Yucatecan Maya attends a service for the* chacs *(rain gods) at Chichén Itzá, Mexico (left); beads, buttons, and tassels adorn a Quechua-speaking Indian in Peru (center); near Guatemala's Lake Atitlán, a teenage Maya girl carries her market bundle homeward (right). Bottom row: Wearing brass beads and a gold-colored sun disk, an Otavalan girl of Ecuador marches in the Yamor festival, a harvest celebration (left); the chief of an Achual-speaking group—Amazonian Indians of the Peru-Ecuador border region—wears a headdress of toucan feathers (center); determination marks the face of a Quechua-speaking man at Cuzco, capital of the Inca Empire (right).*

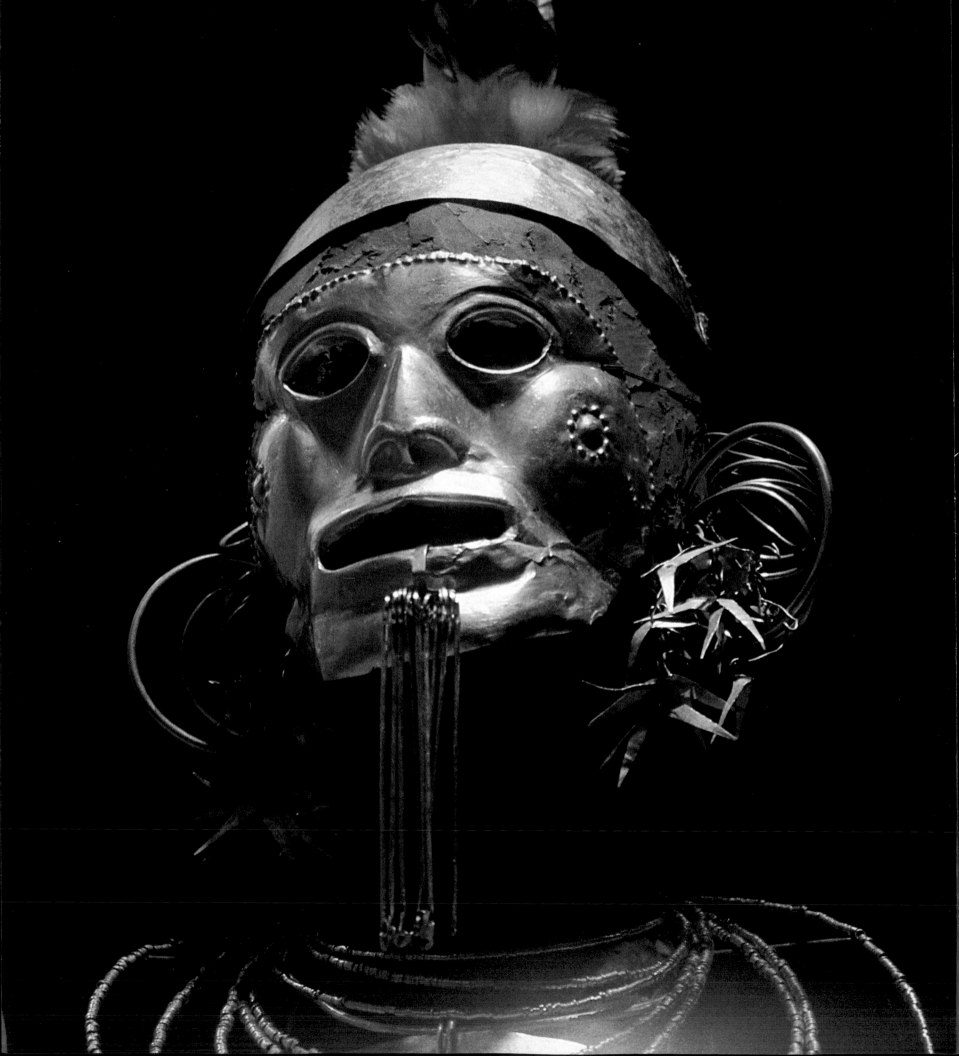

LURE OF THE PAST

Elizabeth P. Benson

I saw the things which have been brought to the King from the new land of gold, a sun all of gold a whole fathom broad, and a moon all of silver of the same size, also two rooms full of armour . . . and all manner of wondrous weapons. . . . All the days of my life I have seen nothing that has gladdened my heart so much as these things, for I saw amongst them wonderful works of art. . . ." So wrote the German artist Albrecht Dürer in 1520 as he marveled at the early evidence of great Indian civilizations hidden from Europe in unknown continents.

Something extraordinary had happened 28 years before. Christopher Columbus, seeking a new route to Asia, had stumbled upon a whole New World instead. Conquerors followed—and were followed in turn, over the next four centuries, by settlers, adventurers, priests, and in later years by archaeologists and anthropologists. Bit by bit the native peoples and their amazing histories began to come to light.

Reports of great civilizations came first from the conquistadores. One of them was Bernal Díaz del Castillo, a soldier who marched with Hernán Cortés in 1519 to conquer Mexico for the Spanish king. Years later, the old warrior wrote of his adventures and recalled the Spaniards' entry into Tenochtitlán, the great Aztec capital now in ruins and buried under modern Mexico City.

The Spaniards, who had traveled inland over rough terrain from the east coast, saw a great lake with cities and villages and connecting causeways. They spent the night outside the capital in a great town, Ixtapalapa, resplendent with spacious palaces made of handsome stone and the wood of scented trees, and awninged courtyards surrounded by a flower garden and orchard. The next day they were led onto a broad causeway into the capital, where they were greeted by chieftains in rich mantles and, finally, by Moctezuma himself.

The Aztec emperor was carried by great lords in a splendid litter beneath "a marvellously rich canopy" of green feathers with gold and silver embroidery, and a border of pearls and greenstones "which was wonderful to look at." Moctezuma, sumptuously clothed, wore sandals with precious stones and soles of gold. Nobles swept the ground and laid down blankets so his feet would not touch the earth.

Peering from a splendored past, a funerary mask of sheet gold—hammered and decorated from the back— recalls a forgotten Indian warrior. Mask and ornaments may have come from the Calima Valley in western Colombia, where Indians found and worked relatively pure gold.

"Gazing on such wonderful sights," Bernal Díaz reminisced, "we did not know what to say, or whether what appeared before us was real. . . . In front of us stood the great city of Mexico, and we—we did not even number four hundred soldiers!" (Other accounts say 600.)

Cortés with his hundreds would soon prove more than a match for the Aztec Empire with its millions. Armed with superior weaponry and helped along by restive chieftains and an incredible string of lucky coincidences, the conquistadores swept away in a few years a culture rooted in millennia, the final link in a great chain of preceding civilizations. Other chains had been forged in other places—the Maya in Middle America, the Inca in Peru—but these too would end in bloodshed and servitude, their cities in ruin, their treasures in Europe, their peoples in thrall to Spanish colonists who debated whether the Indian was even human. In a few tumultuous years, the glories of generations became but a dimly remembered dream.

In a poignant passage, Bernal Díaz had lamented that of all the wonders he had then beheld, "all is overthrown and lost, nothing is left standing." But he was wrong. Even four centuries later we stand awestruck amid the marvelous masonry of temples and pyramids. We study hieroglyphs carved in stone or pictures painted in a *codex*, an

In 1492 Christopher Columbus claimed the Bahamas for the Spanish crown, ushering in an era of New World discovery and conquest. Columbus's voyage embroiled Spain in a dispute with Portugal over Atlantic exploration rights. In 1494 Pope Alexander VI resolved the conflict with a line of demarcation, granting Spain lands west of the line and Portugal lands lying to the east of it.

Spanish navigator Vicente Pinzón (who sailed with Columbus) visited the coast of Brazil and explored the Amazon estuary in 1500. But because much of the territory lay east of the pope's line, Pedro Cabral was able to claim Brazil for Portugal later that year, and to this day Brazil is the only Portuguese-speaking nation in South America. Most of the rest of Latin America fell to Spain. In Mexico, Hernán Cortés crushed the Aztec Empire while Francisco Pizarro broke the back of the Incas in Peru. Pizarro lieutenants Diego de Almagro and Pedro de Valdivia extended Spanish rule south to Chile. Another of Pizarro's men, Francisco de Orellana, navigated the Amazon from the Andes to the Atlantic.

accordion-folded "book" with pages of soaked and pounded bark. In such glimpses of another world, another time, lies the lure of the past.

In that past we glimpse builders of mighty monuments, forgers of great empires, lowly farmers and busy merchants, fierce warriors and gifted artists. Each image is an elusive, incomplete portrait—but so it has been since Columbus's time. The Indians, for example, are not "Indians" at all. Columbus, after four voyages across the Atlantic, still thought that if only he could find a strait through Central America, he would be on the doorstep of the great cities of China and Japan. The word "Indian" comes from Columbus's belief that he had reached the Far East, perhaps the tip of Asia or India—the "Indies."

Ever since Columbus had seen gold nose ornaments on the natives of the island of San Salvador, his first landfall, the Spaniards had been obsessed with the quest for gold—so obsessed that the natives of Cuba, where the Spaniards were first based, thought the newcomers actually worshiped the yellow metal as a god. As Francisco Pizarro stormed through Peru ten years after Cortés had won Mexico, his secretary Pedro Sancho tallied up the ransom for the captured Inca emperor Atahualpa. He mentions vases and jars made of gold, and gold plaques weighing five to twelve pounds each that had been torn from the walls

Spaniards squabbling over tribute are rebuked by a Panamanian Indian: "Why quarrel and make so much turmoil about a little gold . . . ? Six days' march across [the] mountain will bring you to an ocean sea, like this near which we dwell . . . where the people eat out of vessels of gold. . . ." Thus came the first hint of the Pacific Ocean, which Vasco Núñez de Balboa reached in 1513.

of houses and temples. He describes a gold footstool and a fountain "all of gold and very subtly worked which was very fair to see as much for the skill of the work as for the shape which it had been given." All of these gold objects, Sancho tells us, weighed 2½ million ounces, "which, on being refined to pure gold, came to one million, three hundred and twenty-odd thousand" ounces. The treasures that Dürer saw were some of the very few metal objects that came to the Old World intact.

For most of the conquistadores, the Indians existed only to lead them to gold and to work on the estates that were granted to the Spaniards by the king. But the memoirs written by conquistadores do sometimes offer glimpses of ordinary Indians at the time of the Conquest. Pedro Pizarro paused in his eyewitness account of his cousin Francisco's triumphs in Peru to describe the *tallanos*, Indians who lived near the Pacific coast: "These tallanos wear shirts and mantles of cotton worked with decorations in wool; others wear scarfs about the head and under the chin with a trimming of fringe. The women wear long cloaks which fall from the throat to the feet. They have the lips bored near the chin, and in the holes they place round buttons of gold and silver which conceal the holes. They take them out and put them in whenever they wish to do so."

Pizarro's book also recounts briefly the history of the Inca Empire that the Spaniards destroyed—a history preserved by the Indians in an oral tradition, since the Incas had no writing.

Before the Conquest, the Indians of Peru and Middle America had a strong sense of their own history, although this history was often entangled with myth. They believed in previous creations and destructions of the world. Like their Christian conquerors, they thought the world had once been devastated by a great flood. In Maya lands, hieroglyphic inscriptions on monuments list mythical figures among the ancestors of great Maya kings. The deerskin picture books of the later Mixtec people of southern Mexico describe the exploits of their kings, and record the kings' genealogies. Aztec kings took the trouble to establish their descent from the Toltecs, whom the Aztecs thought were the most cultured people of the past.

Spanish interest in the Indians' history and culture rose sharply when priests followed the conquistadores to the New World. Some of the Spanish priests considered the Indians "beasts" or "natural slaves," but Bartolomé de las Casas, a Dominican missionary who was a boy in Spain when Columbus returned there from his first voyage, defended the Indians against "all the wickedness, injustice, violence and tyranny which the Christians have done in the Indies. . . . More than twelve

Molten gold quenches a Spaniard's thirst for loot (foreground) while his companions suffer a fate scarcely more enviable. Such tales, often exaggerated by 17th-century artists' imaginations, helped to promote a New World aura of riches, savagery, and cannibalism.

15

million souls, men, women and children, have perished. . . . After they have killed off all those who could long or sigh for liberty, that is to say, all chiefs and warriors, they oppress those that remain, being commonly only children and women, with the most horrible and relentless and pitiless slavery to which ever men or beasts were put."

Among his proofs the outraged friar cited the *requerimiento*, an order to be read to the Indians "bidding them come to the true faith and do homage to the Kings of Castile." Failure to comply meant death or slavery. But in greedy hands the requerimiento became a handy excuse to pillage. De las Casas tells of a raiding party that halted to read the requerimiento in Spanish well outside an Indian town, then stormed in to slay the Indians in their sleep.

The question of the Indians' humanity had arisen because the Spaniards, like other Christians of the time, believed that every human being was descended not just from Adam and Eve but from Noah and his family, the sole survivors of the biblical flood. How could the Indians of the New World claim such descent? Theories about their origin were many: They were one of the lost tribes of Israel; they were refugees from one of the sunken continents, Atlantis or Mu; they had come from Scandinavia, or Scythia, or Carthage, or Egypt, or Phoenicia; they were descended from the survivors of a lost fleet of Alexander the Great—or from Alexander himself.

One author suggested that the Indians had come from Asia in a long overland migration. He was José de Acosta, a Jesuit who served in Peru and Mexico in the 1570s and 1580s, and whose *Natural and Moral History of the Indies*, published in Spain in 1590, is an important early source of information about the Indians. Later writers—and still later scientists—came to the same conclusion as Acosta, and today it is generally believed that the American Indians migrated from Asia over a long period via a land bridge that then crossed the Bering Strait.

De las Casas knew nothing of such matters—of Ice Age glaciers perhaps a mile thick that lowered sea levels and exposed the Bering Strait's floor. But he knew his conscience. And through the force of his words he was largely responsible for a declaration by the pope, in 1537, establishing that the Indians were truly human.

Spanish missionaries, having decided that issue, set about to convert the Indians to Christianity. To succeed in their work of salvation, the missionaries had to learn something of the Indians' beliefs and way of life. Columbus had thought that the Indians had no religion, but the missionaries found complex religions and rituals. Some of the churchmen, like de las Casas, who became bishop of Chiapas, seem to

Face embedded in his chest, a headless horror from Guiana stalks the pages of a 16th-century travel book. Fanciful illustrations such as this and the giant Patagonians (opposite) published two centuries later fed an insatiable European appetite for news and views of New World wonders. Huge footprints left by the Patagonians' hide shoes probably contributed to the erroneous impression of their size—and led to their Spanish name, Patagones: Big Feet. Later travelers reported tall, but not gigantic, Indians in Patagonia.

have had a genuine interest in the subject, almost like that of a modern anthropologist or ethnographer.

In mountainous central Mexico, Friar Bernardino de Sahagún compiled an illustrated manuscript that describes not only the Aztec religion but also craft techniques—how gold was cast, how feathers were worked into cloth—and the plants and animals of the area. But even in the "natural history" section, mythical elements raise their heads. A page of the manuscript shows all the different species of snakes in central Mexico, each realistically drawn—and among them is a feathered serpent, a creature of Indian mythology.

Sahagún's manuscript is one of the most important sources on Aztec customs for modern scholars. Another missionary, Diego de Landa, performed as great a service by describing the Maya Indians of the Yucatán Peninsula. Landa, a Franciscan who was sent to Yucatán in 1549, became fluent in the Mayan language. Excessive in his zeal to convert the Indians, Landa burned all the Maya books he could find, for they contained Maya religious material, which he believed to be the work of the devil. Recalled to Spain, he wrote his *Relation of the Things of Yucatan* there, around 1566. It describes Maya customs in detail, opening up the everyday lives of a people just then coming under the weight of an alien civilization.

"The Indian women," wrote Landa, "put the maize [corn] to soak one night before in lime and water, and in the morning it is soft and half-cooked . . . and they grind it upon stones, and they give to the workmen and travelers and sailors large balls and loads of the half-ground maize. . . . And of that they take a lump which they mix [with water] in a vase made of [the shell of a gourd-like fruit]. And they drink this nutriment . . . and it is a savory food and of great sustaining power. From the maize which is finest ground they extract a milk and they thicken it on the fire, and make a sort of porridge for the morning. And they drink it hot and over that which remains from the morning's meal they throw water so as to drink it during the day; for they are not accustomed to drink water alone. They also parch the maize and grind it, and mix it with water, thus making a very refreshing drink, throwing in it a little Indian pepper or cacao [chocolate]."

Landa also described the ruins of Chichén Itzá, well known to visitors to the Yucatán Peninsula today. His book was one of the few early works to reflect any interest in Mexican archaeological remains. Landa was, as well, the first outsider who tried to understand Maya hieroglyphic writing; his work was the basis of attempts at decipherment by later scholars. Like many other early writings on the

Colombia's Quindío Pass, in the Andes' Cordillera Central, was sketched around 1800 by German naturalist Alexander von Humboldt during his five-year exploration of the Americas. His expedition launched modern scientific study of the New World.

Indians, Landa's manuscript went unpublished for many years—in Landa's case for almost three centuries, until 1864.

Like their compatriots in Mexico, Spanish missionaries in Peru wrote about Indian life in the decades after the Conquest. There are also accounts written by Spanish-born soldiers and civil servants who traveled widely over the coastal desert and in the high Andes. Agustín de Zárate, sent to Peru in 1543 by King Charles V of Spain as a general inspector of accounts, described the impressive Inca road system and the lives of coastal fishermen. His book reveals traces of Indian resistance to the Spaniards, even after the Conquest was complete. He writes of Indian rafts big enough to hold 50 men and three horses, "although it has happened that, when Spaniards have sailed on those rafts, the Indians subtly have undone the ropes wherewith the timber was bound together, causing the pieces suddenly to separate from each other, by means of which many Christians have perished, and the Indians saved themselves, for they can swim exceeding well."

By late in the 18th century, with the conquest of Peru and Mexico more than two centuries old, many of the Indians' beliefs were no longer preserved in living traditions, but only in archaeological remains. Two of the most spectacular were discovered in 1790 in the

heart of Mexico City, near the 16th-century cathedral on the great plaza, or Zócalo. One, the gigantic Sun Stone nearly 12 feet across, shows the anthropomorphized face of either the sun god or the earth god, surrounded by figures that tell of the coming destruction of the world. The other is a great sculpture—eight feet high—of Coatlicue, found during drainage work. Coatlicue was the earth goddess who gave birth to the sun-war deity, Huitzilopochtli, tribal god of the Aztec people. Her head is composed of two serpent heads; her shoulders also are serpents; her skirt is woven of smaller snakes entwined. And on her throat she wears a necklace of cut-off hands and hearts with a skull pendant. Both carvings are showpieces of the National Museum of Anthropology in Mexico City.

When the Coatlicue was found, it was immediately removed to the National University, where Antonio de León y Gama—who has been called the first Mexican archaeologist—drew a picture of it. But then the sculpture was reburied. When Baron Alexander von Humboldt, the German naturalist, explorer, and statesman, asked to see the sculpture in 1803, it was dug up for him and promptly buried again. Even in the 19th century, Coatlicue may have been thought to recall too much of pre-Christian belief. The sculpture was exhumed for good in 1824.

Camped on the windy plains of southern Argentina, Tehuelche Indians huddle amid skin tents called toldos. *Spaniards brought misery, but they also brought the horse—soon to become a companion essential to the Tehuelche. Horses were used to hunt the llama-like guanaco, whose hides provided shoes, clothing, and shelter. Later Tehuelches decorated saddles and bridles with silver studs, and were so constantly on horseback that one traveler believed they had "almost lost the walking capabilities of other men." When a Tehuelche died, his possessions were burned and all his horses strangled with lassos or killed with bola blows. The horsemeat was distributed to his relatives.*

Von Humboldt contributed to the new surge of archaeological interest by publishing, in 1810, a book called *Views of the Cordilleras, and Monuments of the Indigenous Peoples of America*. Scattered among drawings of Latin American mountains and volcanoes are pictures of Aztec, Maya, and Inca ruins and a number of sculptures.

It was not until late in the 18th century that some of the most important Maya ruins—those at Palenque—became known outside their own immediate vicinity. The story of Palenque's spreading fame illustrates how interest in Indian antiquities slowly blossomed.

A priest had been told about the "houses" at Palenque by a schoolmate who had lived in a village near the ruins. In 1773 the priest organized a small expedition to the site and found a Maya city on a deeply forested hillside; trees and vines were tearing at the elegant ruined buildings. The priest reported his find to the governor, who later sent a local official, José Antonio Calderón, to investigate.

Calderón spent three days at the site in 1784 and decided that the Romans had built Palenque. He counted 215 "houses" and a palace, which "from its size and style could have been nothing less."

The king of Spain ordered further exploration at Palenque, and in 1786 a Spanish army captain, Antonio del Río, was sent to the site. His visit was brief and he accomplished little by the standards of modern archaeology. But in his report he claimed to have left no "window nor adobe wall, no chamber great or small, passage, courtyard, tower, chapel or basement where we have not dug and delved." Fortunately, del Río did not do nearly as much damage as his report suggests.

In 1805 a retired captain of Mexican dragoons, Guillermo Dupaix, received a commission from the king to spend three years investigating "all the monuments of this kingdom which could exist from the time before its conquest." His travels included Palenque; Dupaix thought it had been built by citizens of Atlantis.

Yet another theory of Palenque's origins came from the colorful Jean Frédéric Maximilien, Comte de Waldeck (a title undoubtedly granted by himself). After traveling widely, Waldeck came to Mexico and illustrated the first publication, in 1822, of Captain del Río's report on Palenque. Waldeck imagined that the original builders of Palenque were Chaldeans from ancient Babylon, but he proposed that the bulk of the population was Hindu.

All of this activity stirred the imaginations of two world travelers, John Lloyd Stephens, a New York lawyer, and Frederick Catherwood, an English artist. The two men set off for Middle America in October 1839. Getting to Palenque in those days was not easy. They climbed

Amazon warriors stamp out a war dance in a George Catlin painting titled "Tapuya Encampment." Already famous for his portraits and sketches of North American tribes, Catlin traveled to South America in the 1850s. Here his subjects wave bows and arrows more like those in North America. But the style of feathers and body paint resembles that of Indians who lived along the Ucayali River in eastern Peru. "Tapuya" provides no tribal clue—it means any enemy of the Tupí, large Indian language group in Amazonia.

Workers clear jungle growth in front of
the Castillo at Tulum, on the eastern
coast of Mexico's Yucatán Peninsula.
The main temple of this important Maya
center, the Castillo stands on a high cliff
overlooking the ocean. Even before the
coming of Cortés, Spaniards had seen it
from seaward, bright stone amid the
jungle growth. American adventurer
John Lloyd Stephens and English artist
Frederick Catherwood visited Tulum in
the 1840s on their second trip to Middle
America. Their best-selling books
introduced an eager public to the Maya
and prepared the ground for modern
archaeology in the region.

narrow mountain trails on muleback in stormy weather. Descending into the lowlands, they followed a track through a dark forest thick with undergrowth. Sometimes the mud was so deep that the mules were mired. It was hot and humid.

When they arrived in Palenque, Stephens was ill with malaria. There were no inns, so they set up housekeeping in the ruins.

"We had reached the end of our long and toilsome journey," Stephens wrote, "and the first glance indemnified us for our toil. For the first time we were in a building erected by the aboriginal inhabitants, standing before the Europeans knew of the existence of this continent, and we prepared to take up our abode under its roof. We selected the front corridor as our dwelling, turned turkey and fowls loose in the courtyard, which was so overgrown with trees that we could barely see across it."

Stephens's *Incidents of Travel in Central America, Chiapas, and Yucatan*, with Catherwood's illustrations, was published in 1841. Stephens wrote the first vivid descriptions of a number of Maya sites, and Catherwood's drawings were the most careful that had yet been made. Catherwood drew the unfamiliar sculpture and architecture without reading into it the artistic conventions of other lands. Stephens wrote clearly and objectively. He had studied the early literature as well as contemporary writings. He recognized that all of the Maya sites were the work of people who shared the same culture, and he concluded that the buildings had been made not by exotic foreigners but by the ancestors of the Indians he found living near the ruins.

Stephens and Catherwood's book and their account of a later journey, *Incidents of Travel in Yucatan*, were so popular that they quickly went through numerous reprintings. They produced a real change in attitudes toward American antiquities.

In 19th-century Peru, as in Mexico, soldiers and priests were no longer in the forefront of investigations of the Indian past. Serious amateur archaeologists were revealing more and more of the culture of the ancient Americans.

At about the time that Stephens and Catherwood were in Mexico, the Swiss naturalist Johann Jakob von Tschudi was traveling in Peru. He eventually published *Travels in Peru during the Years 1838-1842*, a book with pictures of ancient ruins, pottery, gold, and mummies, as well as descriptions of sites and accounts of his travels. Von Tschudi visited and mapped Chan Chan, the enormous capital of the Chimú people on the north coast. The site consists of nine high-walled compounds, most of them now named for archaeologists who worked

In a self-portrait, artist Frederick Catherwood measures the Temple of the Frescoes at Tulum. His experience with Middle Eastern antiquities helped him realize that the Mexican ruins were "erected by the Indian tribes in possession of the country at the time of the Spanish conquest," and not by Chaldeans, Atlanteans, or Egyptians. His painting of Yucatecans (opposite) captures the struggle to survive dry seasons in a region where surface streams are rare and water had to be carried from cenotes, or wells.

there; one is called Tschudi. Von Tschudi also went to Tiahuanaco, a site with impressive monumental sculpture; it lies south of Lake Titicaca on the desolate altiplano, some 12,000 feet above sea level, that stretches from Bolivia into Peru. An urban center in its heyday around A.D. 700, Tiahuanaco was later known to the Incas as a sacred place.

It was not just the travelers who were writing about the Indian civilizations. Though near-total blindness confined William H. Prescott to his study in Boston, this devoted scholar knew the work of his contemporaries, and, corresponding with a broad network of them, he located previously unknown archival documents related to the Conquest. His success—and the intensity of the reading public's interest then in Mexico's past—carried his 1843 treatise, *Conquest of Mexico*, through 22 printings in less than 10 years. This and his 1849 *Conquest of Peru* are still in print more than a century later.

Today museums in the Old World and the New have become increasingly active in preserving Indian handiwork and studying its meaning. Scholars have excavated historic sites, translated ancient manuscripts, and worked on deciphering the Maya hieroglyphs. Excavations are under way even in the center of Mexico City, uncovering the foundations of the ancient capital of the Aztecs.

In the eye of the archaeologist, few artifacts can match the allure of the humble potsherd. For ancient people made pottery in almost unbelievable quantities, using it for cooking, eating, storage, ceremonies, burials. And they made it in different styles and of different materials at different times and places. Today the simple sherd of a broken pot is the keystone of the science of archaeology, for as the scholar digs he can trace the changes in an ancient civilization, and even date those changes, by the changing fashions in its pottery.

Until the beginning of the 20th century, archaeological reports were largely descriptive; the archaeologists told what they had found, but it was difficult for them to establish a chronology for the different objects at a site. Then Max Uhle in his 1903 report on Pachacamac, a pre-Inca city near Lima, told of finding Inca potsherds on the surface of the ground; beneath them, covered by earth, he found sherds similar to some he had found at Tiahuanaco, the ancient ceremonial center. He found a third style at Pachacamac, and he placed it in time between the other two styles. Potsherds had given him a chronology—and a breakthrough in the study of Andean prehistory.

Archaeology has borrowed this study of layers, or strata, from geology. Geologists have also contributed to archaeology by naming the sources of stones used by ancient sculptors. Astronomers can determine

Alfred P. Maudslay works on a drawing in Chichén Itzá's Nunnery—so called because of its many cell-like rooms. Drawn to American antiquities by John Stephens's books, the English scholar became, in the late 19th century, the leader of Maya archaeology's second wave: those whose documentation and study began to wring information from the ruins their predecessors had discovered. Accurate and detailed, Maudslay's five-volume Archaeology *still ranks as a standard reference on Middle American antiquities.*

Lured by legends of ancient Maya rites and treasures, American archaeologist Edward Thompson set out in 1904 to probe the sacred well at Yucatán's Chichén Itzá—site of human sacrifice. With dredge (above) and diving suit he plumbed the depths, retrieving relics—pots, tools, figurines—and the bones of men, women, and children. His finds shed new light on old myths.

Feathered serpents garland this four-foot stone ring (left), target for teams vying on the ball court at Chichén Itzá. Myths linked the strenuous game to death and the underworld; at some stages in its history it included human sacrifice. Played in much of the New World, the ball game was pictured in Indian codices—in one drawing with death standing between the players.

that buildings have been oriented toward certain stars. Zoologists can tell what kinds of animals inhabited the ancient world and which animals the people ate. Botanists can tell what crops ancient farmers grew. Linguists can reconstruct ancient languages. Physicists, using a variety of techniques with such names as thermoluminescence and obsidian hydration, can test objects to determine how old they are.

Despite archaeology's new scientific precision, the romance has not entirely gone out of the field. Some 20th-century discoveries have been spectacular. Tomb 7, a particularly rich one at Monte Albán in Mexico, yielded dazzling cast-gold necklaces, pendants, and ear and nose ornaments. Because the tomb was found by archaeologists, and not by the conquistadores or modern-day looters, its precious ornaments are now safe in museums.

Modern archaeologists, of course, are lured to the past not by treasure but by the possibility of reconstructing and understanding a lost way of life. And they know that there is still much to learn. The Amazon Basin in South America, long considered a region peripheral to the great civilizations, has attracted attention in recent years, because people living there today have customs and beliefs that may be remnants of religious ideas that once were widespread. The Amazon

Basin may shed light on the origins of South American civilizations, for some scholars believe that New World civilization may have had its beginnings along its edges. Ancient peoples in the Andes and Middle America shared many of the same ideas about the creation of the world, about what was important ritually, and about what should be depicted in art. These basic unities of thought and custom throughout the area point toward a possible common origin for the different Indian cultures.

In the modern equivalent of the Atlantis theory, some suggest that ancient astronauts brought civilization to the New World. But there is no need to explain, for example, the earthwork designs on the Nazca Plain of Peru as landing strips or markings for astronauts. The ancient Indians were excellent astronomers, and sky deities abounded in their mythology. They developed the building techniques they needed, and they had plenty of labor to accomplish their tasks. They achieved great things, and they alone deserve all credit for them.

Now most of those achievements lie in ruins. The silent stones seem almost to echo a passage from the epic *Popol Vuh:* "Fallen then were the towns of all the tribes." Fallen too, perhaps, are the great and powerful gods who gave the Indian rain and crops and writing and art. But the Indian endures. And so does the lure of his fascinating past.

Gaunt bones of a city in stone "fairly took my breath away," wrote explorer Hiram Bingham after his 1911 Yale University expedition discovered Machu Picchu deep in the Peruvian Andes. Vines and thickets choked the ruin he thought was Vilcabamba, last refuge of the Incas now known to lie some 50 miles west. Then what was Machu Picchu? Scholars still ponder its mysteries. Even its name is lost; Bingham named it for the mountain it adorns—Old Mountain in the Quechua tongue. Secure in its isolation, fed by terraced gardens and watered by a web of aqueducts, the citadel sheltered perhaps 8,000 people.

QUEST FOR EARLY MAN AND AGRICULTURE

Richard S. MacNeish

With daggerlike claws, a 10,000-pound giant sloth flails at Ice Age hunters who crept into its Andean den. Propped by a short thick tail, the ground-dwelling sloth stripped leaves from trees with its long tongue. Early man may have trapped and stabled the now-extinct beasts in caves for future slaughter.

P ressed against the wall of a huge cave, a small band of Ice Age hunters, spears at the ready, creep toward an elephant-size ground sloth. Just out of reach of its massive claws, the men attack. The sloth rears up and lashes out at the puny creatures. With determined fury, they hurl and jab their spears again and again deep into its heart, neck, and stomach. At last the sloth staggers and falls dead. Soon come the women, hesitantly at first, to butcher the tons of meat with crude stone knives and hand axes. After eating their fill of roasted sloth, the group—made up of two or three families—settles down to live off the mass of rotting flesh.

The cave echoes with the laughter of children playing or imitating the work of their elders. Women scrape the skin with sharpened rocks or sloth rib bones, then tailor clothing with bone awls and needles. Men make knives by chipping stone with pebble hammers and then flaking the edges sharp. One day men will make scalpels of fine surgical steel, but the edges will not be as sharp as some of these knives.

Millennia earlier the Asiatic ancestors of these Ice Age hunters had trekked across a vast land bridge then spanning the shallow sea between Siberia and glacier-gripped North America. Generations later their descendants, mingling with a steady stream of newcomers, had peopled the vast reaches of two continents, from Alaska to Tierra del Fuego.

Because the first Americans left no written records of their travels, modern scientists have had to sift telltale bits of evidence from layers of earth and time, patiently piecing together fragments of tools, chunks of charcoal, and the bones of extinct animals. Searching out the story of man's rise from big-game hunter to village dweller seems a never-ending quest, for two key parts of the puzzle have long eluded archaeologists: When did humans first set foot on American soil? Where—and when—did they cultivate the first American crops? The latter was particularly significant. Their domestication of more than 300 plants—including corn, beans, squash, and potatoes—helped to create and feed New World civilizations. This cornucopia of crops still sustains Latin American economies and nourishes more than half the world.

Archaeologists have long disputed the antiquity of man in the New

34

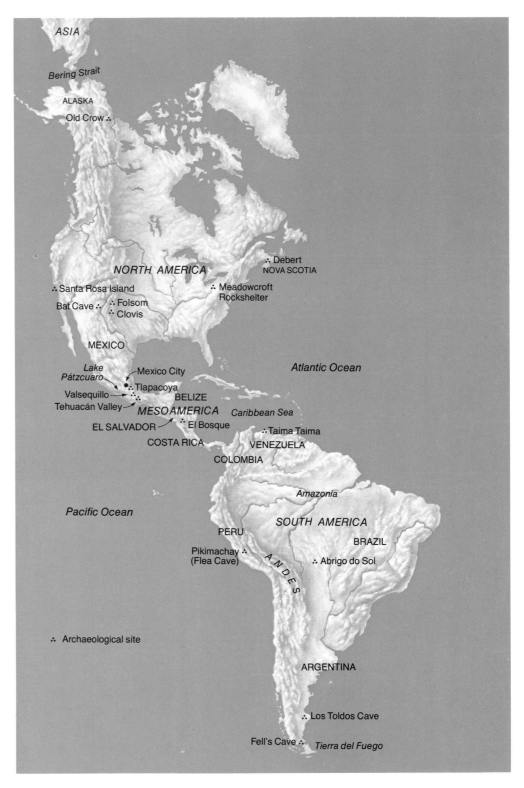

ASIA

Bering Strait

ALASKA
Old Crow ⁘

NORTH AMERICA

⁘ Debert
NOVA SCOTIA

⁘ Santa Rosa Island
⁘ Meadowcroft
Rockshelter
Bat Cave ⁘ ⁘ Folsom
⁘ Clovis

MEXICO

Lake
Pátzcuaro — Mexico City
⁘ Tlapacoya
Valsequillo
Tehuacán Valley — BELIZE
MESOAMERICA Caribbean Sea
EL SALVADOR — ⁘ El Bosque

COSTA RICA ⁘ Taima Taima
VENEZUELA
COLOMBIA

Atlantic Ocean

Amazonia

Pacific Ocean SOUTH AMERICA

PERU BRAZIL
Pikimachay ⁘
(Flea Cave) ⁘ Abrigo do Sol

A
N
D
E
S

⁘ Archaeological site

ARGENTINA

⁘ Los Toldos Cave

Fell's Cave ⁘ ⁘ Tierra del Fuego

A vanished people and a vanishing skill: A Héta Indian of southern Brazil shapes a stone ax the way his ancestors did millennia ago. After pecking, grinding, and polishing the stone blade for days, he used a tapir bone to chisel a hole in the wooden handle for the ax head.

Ancestors of today's Indians trekked across the Bering land bridge from Asia and peopled the New World when tundra, plain, and forest teemed with oversize mammals. Stone and bone projectile points tipped the spears of big-game hunters from Old Crow to

Fell's Cave. Artifacts tell of mastodon kills at Taima-Taima and El Bosque, the slaying of giant ground sloth at Pikimachay, and the appearance of Clovis points around 10,000 B.C. Some 5,000 years later, domesticated crops appeared in the Tehuacán Valley.

World. For years many scholars regarded 10,000 B.C. as the earliest date. But I believe humans first crossed the Bering Strait at least 40,000 years ago. I base that belief in part on digs in the mountain-ringed Ayacucho Valley of highland Peru, where I found the oldest evidence of man's presence in South America at Pikimachay (Flea Cave).

In 1969 I led an archaeological-botanical team here in a search for clues to early man's development from nomadic hunter to settled farmer. One day a couple of workmen came to me, talking excitedly about *huesos de vacas gigantes*—bones of giant cows. My first glance at a large forelimb bone and rib convinced me that these were the bones of an enormous extinct animal. The men had unearthed a ground sloth that once stood as tall as a giraffe. I guessed that the bones might be about 14,000 years old—a date later confirmed by carbon tests.

The next morning a student supervisor showed me several large, crude stone tools from the same level as the sloth bones. I began troweling a small section. An hour later I uncovered five or six more bone fragments; one lay next to a stone flake struck from a man-made tool. The flake and bones were lying on top of another artifact—a crude scraper fashioned from volcanic rock. Any doubts I might have had about associating the tools of man with the bones of the sloth vanished.

During our second season at Flea Cave, we dug up tools and animal bones dating back to about 18,000 B.C. Now I knew that man had arrived in the Americas long before 10,000 B.C. Considering the vast distances between Alaska and Peru and the wandering nature of early man's movements, I think that at least 40,000 years ago is a reasonable estimate of human entry into the New World.

Although the dates are often disputed, clues left along the way indicate the north-to-south movement of the first immigrants. On an island off the California coast, Paleo-Indians slaughtered and roasted bull-size mammoths some 40,000 years ago. At Tlapacoya in the Valley of Mexico, big-game hunters manufactured crude stone implements about 22,000 years ago. Around the same time at nearby Valsequillo, ancient butchers carved up a mastodon, and artists incised Ice Age mammals on one of its bones. Bits of charcoal, rock carvings, and stone tools testify to human presence at the southern rim of Amazonia at least 9,000 years ago. Hunters were slaying sloth, horse, and guanaco at the southern tip of South America 11,000 years ago.

A hunter's paradise awaited the first Americans. Woolly mammoths, mastodons, horses, camels, giant sloths, and other mammals furnished humans with virtually all their material needs. Meat and marrow fed them, skins provided their clothing and covered their simple dwellings,

Meaningless graffiti or religious symbols? Puzzling petroglyphs at Abrigo do Sol tell of human presence at Amazonia's edge some 9,000 years ago. Ax-sharpening may have formed the deep cuts. Triangular symbols of female fertility have been found worldwide.

36

dung fueled their fires, bones became their tools and weapons.

As big-game hunters exploited the bountiful Ice Age landscape, they developed an arsenal of specialized spearheads. In the pine-cloaked Valley of Mexico, hunters armed with leaf-shaped points chased mammoths onto the marshy shores of a shallow lake, where the men risked impalement on the formidable tusks of the mired beasts. Slayers of giant bison on the grassy plains chipped grooved, or fluted, points that could easily be withdrawn for repeated stabbings. Spearpoints used to kill smaller game, however, remained embedded in the flesh. Sharp-shouldered points felled camel and deer in northern South America and the Andes, while hunters who knapped fishtail-shaped points stalked horses and guanacos as far south as desolate Tierra del Fuego.

Since the earliest Americans must have spent a lot of time in unsuccessful pursuit of big game, they had to supplement their diet: trapping rabbits in group drives on the grasslands of central South America; collecting shellfish along Peru's sandy coast; gathering grasses, seeds, prickly pear leaves, mesquite pods, and wild avocados in the highlands of Mexico. Life was relatively easy.

Then, between 11,000 and 9,000 years ago, disaster struck: The beasts that man had stalked for so long vanished at the end of the Ice

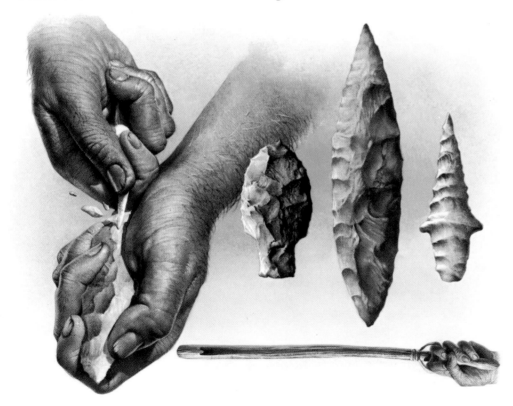

Out of the hand of Ice Age man came an arsenal of specialized weapons. With the tip of a sharp bone, ancient toolmakers sharpened flakes hammered off larger pieces of stone. Hunters lashed the finished spearpoints to wooden shafts, and threw them with lethal force from a short, hooked stick. Known today by the Aztec word atlatl, this revolutionary device gave the thrower more leverage, and enabled him to hurl a spear without getting too close to his prey. A Tarascan duck hunter on Mexico's Lake Pátzcuaro demonstrates this all but vanished skill.

From the shadows of snowcapped Andes to the forested fringes of Tierra del Fuego, big-game hunters also preyed on the rangy guanaco. Both South American camelids and Old World camels evolved from a jackrabbit-size ancestor in North America. Once numbering in the millions, the 250-pound guanaco provided early man with meat, hide and fleece for shelter and clothing, and sinew for sewing. Although more than 30 species of supersize mammals vanished at the end of the Ice Age, guanacos survived as the tallest of South America's wild animals. As the big-game supply dwindled, early man began to cultivate the soil.

Staff of life for ancient farmer and modern Indian, cultivated corn sustained pre-Hispanic cultures and today ranks as one of the world's most productive food plants. In highland Peru an Indian girl spreads corn to dry; later it will be ground into flour, or toasted, or fermented into beer.

Age. Some scientists theorize that they died out because of overkill. Others believe that the onset of a warmer, drier climate turned lush grazing lands into desert waste. Whatever the reason, early man had to adapt to radically changing conditions, or he too would die.

Fortunately, humans had already laid the foundation for a new way of life based on plants that could be domesticated—brought into controlled cultivation to grow and grow again. Just when and where this took place involved another quest, and discoveries clarifying the origins of corn agriculture resulted from years of detective work by a botanist, Dr. Paul C. Mangelsdorf, and me. Our great corn hunt began in 1951.

Studies indicated that the remains of corn's ancestor, probably a highland desert grass similar to pod popcorn, would be found in dry caves between Chiapas and the Valley of Mexico. Careful examination

of climate, rainfall, topography, and geology revealed the most likely area: the Tehuacán Valley, about 150 miles southeast of Mexico City.

After I had inspected more than three dozen caves in the cactus- and scrub-covered valley, the prospect of finding remains of early corn seemed dim. One day, after a long, dusty walk, I arrived at the 39th site, Ajuereado Cave. After a week of digging, my guide uncovered a tiny, dried-up corncob no longer than a thumbnail. Only half believing, I took his place at the bottom of the pit. Carefully troweling and dusting away the dirt with a paintbrush, I excavated two more well-preserved specimens. In our hands we held the oldest corncobs ever found, the possible ancestors of modern domesticated corn! Carbon-14 tests later revealed that these tiny cobs were 7,000 years old.

To re-create a complete sequence of ancient cultures and environments in the Tehuacán Valley, I drew on the work of many scientists—botanists, geologists, paleontologists, zoologists, even atomic physicists. Slowly cutting through layers of earth at dozens of sites, we brought to light the lost, broken, outworn, or discarded treasures of nearly ten millennia, including a quarter of a million artifacts of clay and some 13,000 of stone. These artifacts—clay heads with slit eyes and high turbans, crude flint scrapers, fine obsidian blades, stone palettes for grinding paints—are very sensitive indicators of cultural change. Each fragmentary clue shed light on the transition of the valley's residents from nomadic hunters and collectors of wild foods to food producers dwelling in villages.

As the Ice Age waned, nomadic families in the Tehuacán Valley gradually shifted from hunting all year long to a seasonal round of hunting and gathering. Around 7000 B.C. they began to settle down. Small groups still hunted during the dry season. But when the summer rains filled meadows and ravines with flowers and grasses, small bands gathered to consume the lush vegetation, and then moved on.

This new way of life witnessed a gradual transition from seed collecting to seed planting—the first halting steps toward plant cultivation. During this remote epoch, some 4,000 years before the building of Egypt's first pyramid, the Tehuacaneros began planting seeds at the spring campsite. Later they came back to harvest the crop. As families returned each year, they cleared the area, removed weeds, enriched the soil with refuse, and improved the habitat of certain fruits and seeds. Man was probably still the hunter and woman the collector; her occasional selection of larger fruits and seeds led to genetic changes in the size of the fruit and seeds. Over the centuries this process led to the annual planting of corn, avocados, squash, and other crops.

First European illustration of corn (above) mistakenly labeled the plant as Turkish in origin. The quest for corn's ancestors eventually led to a tiny, 7,000-year-old cob (below) in the Tehuacán Valley. Plant sleuths debate whether teosinte, a tasseled weed, is the ancestor of corn—or vice versa. Or are both cousins descended from the same wild grass? The thin husk of wild corn opens and spills the kernels on the ground to germinate. But the thick husk of cultivated corn must be peeled by man so its seeds can be removed and planted.

The beginning of horticulture, or growing plants in gardens, fostered the crafts of settled life. Men whittled fire tongs, dart shafts, and spring traps for catching food. Women wove baskets from grass stalks, agave fibers, or palm strands; from cotton or cornhusks they made cord.

Between 5000 and 3500 B.C. sedentary life slowly took root. The valley dwellers probably lived in patrilineal bands—a number of families whose male members were related and who traced their ancestry through the male line. Men very likely married women from unrelated bands. Usually led by a male—the oldest, wisest, or strongest hunter—each band exploited its own territory. Burials showing human sacrifice, infanticide, corpses with heads switched, and slain family groups point to religious ceremonies.

In the middle of the third millennium before Christ, the Tehuacaneros shifted toward a female-oriented society with organized religion. Richly furnished female burials hint that kinship and property rights may have had a female bias. Greater dependence on agriculture and rainfall undoubtedly strengthened the power of the *shaman*, or witch doctor. He played a major role in birth and death ceremonies, medicine, and planting and harvesting rituals.

Very slowly the valley's inhabitants took the final steps toward true agriculture by growing enough food so they could live in one place all year round. Some groups congregated along river terraces in permanent hamlets of small, oval pit houses roofed with poles, brush, and twigs. With more stable food supplies, populations swelled; the weak no longer died off as they had during the tough seasonal migrations. To supply the growing demand for containers, the Tehuacaneros shaped clay to imitate stone bowls and baked it. Dating

Indians of highland Peru freeze-dry potatoes in age-old ways. On the coldest nights of midyear they soak small potatoes in a stream or lake, then spread them on the ground to freeze overnight and thaw in the morning. The Indians then mash them with their feet until the moisture squirts out. Spread to dry again, the potatoes become chuño, *a chalky substance that keeps for months. During famine or war the Incas relied on surpluses of dehydrated tubers. The potato originated in the Andes, where early farmers terraced mountainsides and cultivated the starchy staple destined to feed huge populations.*

to about 2000 B.C., this is the oldest pottery yet unearthed in Mexico.

By 900 B.C. full-time shamans held considerable power as new deities came into prominence: gods that controlled rain, the bounty of crops, the fertility of man and beast. Day after day, farmers walked to their fields and, with digging sticks and stone tools, planted, cultivated, and harvested their crops. They lived in wattle-and-daub huts in villages of 100 to 300 inhabitants. Stable food production and surpluses eventually gave rise to the making of clay figurines and the building of pyramids.

Recent investigations suggest that the lowlands of Mexico and Belize followed a pattern very different from that of the highlands. At the end of the Ice Age, lowland hunters and gatherers began to exploit the bounty of tropical jungle, shoreline, and sea. By about 3500 B.C. stable villages—with no agriculture—had popped up along the coast. Burgeoning population may have forced them to borrow domesticated crops and cultivating techniques from the highlands and to develop some of their own. Farming villages and pottery appeared a thousand years later, leading to the first stirrings of Maya culture.

In Peru the development of village agriculture in the lowlands also contrasted sharply with that of the highlands. With the extinction of big game, coastal dwellers survived by gathering plants and trapping animals in the hills during the wet season. In dry months they collected protein-rich foods from the sea and riverbanks. By 4400 B.C. hamlets of pit houses existed year round without benefit of agriculture. As villages prospered and populations grew, the inhabitants supplemented their food supply with plants domesticated in the highlands. Once again, as in the Mexican lowlands, village life preceded agriculture.

In the Andean highlands, village agriculture laid the foundation for pre-Inca societies. At the end of the Ice Age a seasonal round of hunting and plant collecting evolved. Eventually, as in the Tehuacán Valley, the highlanders domesticated the same plants—but added an important one of their own, the potato. By growing hardy potatoes and by freeze- and sun-drying foods, farmers mastered the lofty Andes. The pattern of development in highland Mexico and the Andes—both centers of village agriculture and later of empires—looks much the same.

In the tropical lowlands of Costa Rica and El Salvador, domestication may have started with such easily prepared root crops as sweet manioc and yams. Since they can be eaten raw, roasted over coals, or steamed in shallow pits, no equipment was needed for threshing or grinding. Perhaps hunters and fishers of Colombia grew starchy root crops in their spare time, thus adding carbohydrates to a high-protein diet.

The story of the peopling of the New World and the beginnings of agriculture is incomplete. Painstaking research, even to examinations of ancient human teeth, is providing us with more clues about the origins and movements of Ice Age hunters. Different patterns of agricultural development are still emerging from the past, for plants were domesticated in many places in various ways. But one thing is certain: Stable food supplies and surpluses set the stage for the flowering of the Maya and Aztecs in Mesoamerica and the Incas in Peru.

MESOAMERICA

For the anthropologist, Mesoamerica begins in north central Mexico as a broad hilly plateau and swings southeastward to the jumbled peaks of lower Central America. In this highland heart edged by coastal lowlands, nature created a landscape of almost infinite variety—from dense rain forest to stark desert plain, from steamy marshes to snowy peaks. These contrasts helped mold spectacular cultures that rose and fell between 2000 B.C. and the 16th century A.D., when the Spaniards came and extinguished the bright flame of the civilization they found.

In the Archaic period (7000-2400 B.C.), Mesoamerica's first farmers domesticated corn, beans, squash, and other plants—and laid the foundation for a settled way of life. The emergence of farming villages united by trade networks ushered in the Preclassic (2400 B.C.-A.D. 300). Gulf coast Olmec bequeathed a pantheon of gods and perhaps writing and the calendar to later Mesoamerican civilizations.

During the Classic period (A.D. 300-900), religion inspired spectacular advances in art and architecture under the patronage of the elite classes. Teotihuacán, the New World's first true city, left its imprint throughout Mesoamerica. Ceremony, writing, astronomy, and calendrics reached their peak in the eloquent and literate Maya. But widespread migration and violence, triggered by invasions of outsiders and accelerated by economic collapse, snuffed out this golden age. From the remains of Classic cities arose the commercial and militaristic world of the Postclassic (A.D. 900 to the Conquest). With the collapse of Toltec rule in the 12th century, small city-states competed against one another until the Aztecs forged Mesoamerica's last great empire.

Even after the arrival of Hernán Cortés in 1519, the Indians preserved many traditional ways. They still speak more than 60 languages, yet are otherwise bound by thousands of years of common heritage and interaction. Many highland Indians still plant once a year and live in compact villages, while their lowland cousins usually plant twice a year and dwell in settlements of loosely clustered houses. Although these Indians are relentlessly subjected to change, their way of life provides a glimpse of pre-Hispanic Mesoamerica.

Above: Classic Maya jade chest ornament, Guatemala, A.D. 700-900.
Opposite: Maya embroidered weaving, Guatemala.

CHILDREN OF TIME

George E. Stuart

A richly coiffed and bedecked noblewoman in this stone carving from Yaxchilán epitomizes Maya ideals of beauty. The Maya prized faces with a long, thin look. Heavy jewelry pierced and distended the earlobes. To achieve the sloping, elongated forehead, Maya mothers clamped the pliable skulls of their growing infants between boards. A ball of pitch suspended from a thong tied around the baby's forehead dangled between its eyes, making it cross-eyed.

Late August, A.D. 792. The sudden and brief downpours of summer have begun in earnest. The rain forest glistens and steams as Lord Sun makes his afternoon journey across the Maya sky toward the western entrance to the underworld and the sojourn into night. In the stifling air of a dark chamber inside a stone temple, a slightly built artist, clad only in loincloth, hunches on a scaffolding of tied poles and paints bold black lines on a freshly stuccoed wall. Large bolts of light-colored cloth are carefully arranged on the floor and bench below to diffuse the sunlight that enters the room.

With the confidence of long practice and the help of charcoal guidelines, the painter outlines two captives on the giant steps of a stone platform. Above them stands the imposing figure of the local ruler, Chan Muan. Flanked by richly dressed attendants, he is bedecked in jade and full royal costume: jaguar-skin tunic, sandals, and a headdress topped by a sweeping fan of quetzal feathers.

Satisfied with the composition, the artist dips his fine brush in a paint pot made from a small conch shell. Deftly he outlines another seated captive with bleeding hands and with mouth opened in a silent scream of pain that will echo across the next 12 centuries.

What the anonymous artist painted during that summer so long ago depicts the climax of a series of dazzling ceremonial events that took place at or near the Maya city of Bonampak in the Mexican State of Chiapas. There, hidden by a mantle of jungle, a crumbled stone temple containing the paintings remained undiscovered until 1946, when filmmaker Giles Healey stepped through a vine-clogged doorway and beheld the astonishing panorama. For me, Bonampak evokes many of the images associated with the ancient Maya and their land: a ruined city in forsaken jungle, the splendor of proud rulers in jaguar skins and jade, the obsession with astronomy and time itself, and—somewhat jarring to those who see the Maya as a gentle people—the vivid scenes of war and cruelty that attended mass sacrifice.

From the very beginning the Maya owed a great cultural debt to their predecessors. By 1500 B.C. small farming settlements—clusters of about five to a dozen thatched houses—dotted Preclassic Mesoamerica.

50

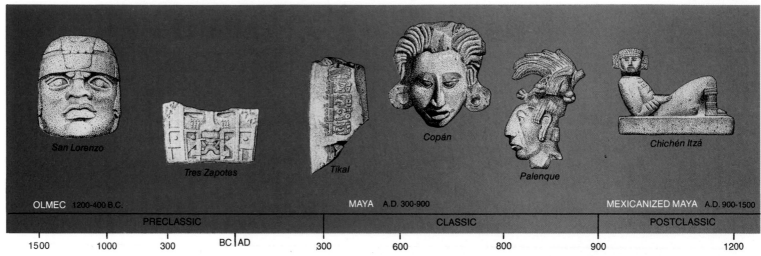

San Lorenzo

Tres Zapotes

Tikal

Copán

Palenque

Chichén Itzá

OLMEC 1200-400 B.C.	MAYA A.D. 300-900	MEXICANIZED MAYA A.D. 900-1500
PRECLASSIC	CLASSIC	POSTCLASSIC

1500   1000   300   BC | AD   300   600   800   900   1200

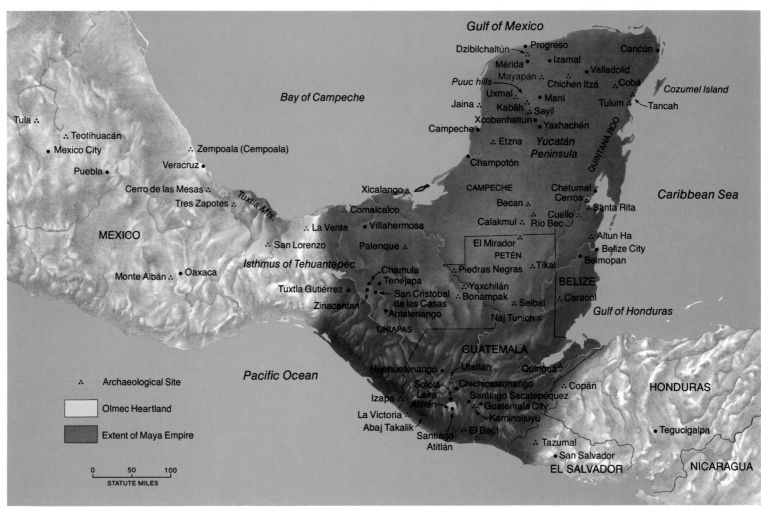

Precursors of the Maya, the Olmec flourished for nearly a millennium along Mexico's Gulf coast. Many elements of their culture would later appear in Classic Maya civilization: monumental art, ceremonial ball games, and bloody religious ritual. The Maya built massive stone pyramids, wrote in hieroglyphs, studied astronomy, revered numbers as gods, and marked time with a calendar. During the Postclassic period, Mexican motifs appeared at many Maya sites, reflecting the expanding power of militaristic cultures from the west.

Then as now in rural Mexico, Belize, and Guatemala, the predawn silence was broken by the waking barks of dogs, movement and murmuring behind the pole or mud house walls, and soon the scraping of handstones on *metates,* or grinders, as women ground soaked corn kernels into dough for food that the men would take along for their day of labor in nearby cornfields. In low-lying coastal lagoons, men in dugouts fished, while in the forest others hunted with dogs. Women and children, knee-deep in mud at the water's edge, groped for shellfish to put in the baskets on their backs.

From such ordinary farming settlements along Mexico's Gulf coast a new kind of society emerged around 1200 B.C. The enigmatic and energetic Olmec possessed a dark, pervasive religion centered on "were-jaguars," half-human, half-jaguar forms with snarling feline features. At least ten other major deities filled the Olmec pantheon, some of them direct ancestors of the gods of later Mesoamericans.

The Olmec created Mesoamerica's first recognizable art style—jade figurines and ornaments, and monumental basalt sculptures of altars, human and animal figures, and the famed colossal heads. So far, 20 of these massive stone heads have been recorded; the largest one, ten feet high, weighs about 20 tons. Although the Olmec vanished abruptly around 400 B.C., their distinguishing traits would be inherited by others, including the Maya.

Links between the Olmec and the Maya are reflected in the remains of Izapa, a cluster of some 80 mounds near the Pacific coast of Chiapas which dates between 400 B.C. and A.D. 300. Carvings on 50 *stelae*—upright slabs of stone—reflect the Olmec art style: storm gods gathering water, gods riding in canoes, and a warrior brandishing a severed head. Similar Izapan-style monuments—in the Olmec heartland itself, along the narrow coastal lowlands of Guatemala, and in the highlands immediately to the north—give us our first tantalizing glimpses of two innovations in the Western Hemisphere that were uniquely Mesoamerican: the calendar and hieroglyphic writing. Both appear on the stelae of Abaj Takalik, a huge site whose dirt mounds dominate several coffee plantations in southwestern Guatemala.

The great highland site of Kaminaljuyú may help explain the spread of Maya civilization to the lowlands far to the north. Grassy mounds occupy a pathetically small part of the original site, now largely obliterated by housing developments in suburban Guatemala City. Despite this, archaeologists have found not only sophisticated Izapan-style monuments bearing hieroglyphic inscriptions, but incredibly rich tombs of elite dead, buried on litters surrounded by slain retainers and

The brightly colored quetzal, now endangered by hunters and a shrinking habitat, was sought by Mesoamericans for its three-foot-long tail feathers. Only nobility wore its flowing plumes, plucked from live birds. Any commoner who killed the regal bird faced death.

OVERLEAF: *Tree-ringed* cenote, *a limestone sinkhole at the ancient Maya city of Dzibilchaltún, holds secrets of the past. Modern divers have brought up jade ornaments, flint tools, pottery, and the bones of people who probably fell in by accident and drowned.*

hundreds of splendid pottery vessels. More than any other known site, Kaminaljuyú shows us the kind of cosmopolitan and literate society that helped set the mood for Classic Maya development to the north.

The Maya heartland, centered in northern Guatemala, is a limestone shelf blanketed with rain forest and occasional stretches of savanna. This region, called the Petén, stretches westward to the Usumacinta River—and the famed Maya ruins of Palenque, Yaxchilán, and Bonampak. To the southeast the lowlands give way to parallel ridges that end in the hills of western Honduras, locale of the great center of Copán.

From the Petén northward, the forest diminishes in height. By the time it reaches the northern coast of the Yucatán Peninsula, it has become a monotonous, scrubby thorn forest. Here there are no rivers, only occasional *cenotes,* natural sinkholes where the limestone ground has collapsed to the water table. Many centers—among them Chichén Itzá and Dzibilchaltún—were built around these sources of precious water. Others, like Uxmal, Kabah, and Sayil, situated on higher ground, relied on large cisterns to catch the bounty of the rainy season. Rare lakes glimmer in the canopy of higher forest around Cobá. Tulum, Tancah, and other ruins line the coast where the limestone shelf drops suddenly into the uncanny turquoise waters of the Caribbean.

When did people first come to this land? We don't know for sure. Our best evidence for the oldest habitation of the area comes from Belize. Along the shores and rivers of the southern coast, archaeologists have begun to explore dozens of preceramic sites that appear to date between 9000 and 2500 B.C. Beginning around 2000 B.C., farmers at Cuello in northern Belize made pottery, grew corn, and built thatched houses on low platforms of stone and clay—dwellings much like those still used in the area. Around 1500 B.C. the people of Cuello began to trade with the Olmec and other Mesoamericans, importing jade beads and obsidian blades from the highlands.

By the time Cuello faded into oblivion in the third century A.D., other centers had arisen. At Cerros, near the Belize-Mexico border, a massive stucco pyramid-platform bears enormous painted masks. Deep in the desolate northern Petén, incredibly large mounds dominate El Mirador, which once may have been the largest—and earliest—city in the Maya area. The volume of one of these huge mounds may be the greatest of any structure in ancient America. Strategically located as if for defense, El Mirador is partly enclosed by a masonry wall some 15 feet high and 9 thick. The city inexplicably declined between A.D. 300 and 500, the precise time span that saw the rise of the first great Maya city 40 miles to the southeast: Tikal. (Continued on page 69)

Masterpiece of Olmec art, this 26-inch basalt sculpture may portray an athlete in a ritual game played with a rubber ball. The Olmec—or Rubber People—dwelled in humid lowlands where rubber trees later supplied the Maya with waterproofing for their capes.

Carved from a block of basalt by the Olmec, who had no metal tools, this 20-ton head (opposite) from San Lorenzo is among the largest of 20 found on Mexico's Gulf coast. The Olmec rafted and dragged colossal boulders 60 miles from quarries in the Tuxtla Mountains.

Olmec offertory grouping from La Venta (above) still baffles archaeologists decades after its discovery. Against a palisade of polished stones, a coarse-skinned figure faces long-headed men of jade and tawny serpentine. Scholars suggest the scene may represent a sacrificial victim facing death, a prisoner about to be executed, or a priest addressing a crowd.

Matthew W. Stirling (left), a pioneer in Olmec studies, measures a stone head at Tres Zapotes in 1938. Workers cross-section a temple mound (right) on his 1946 San Lorenzo expedition.

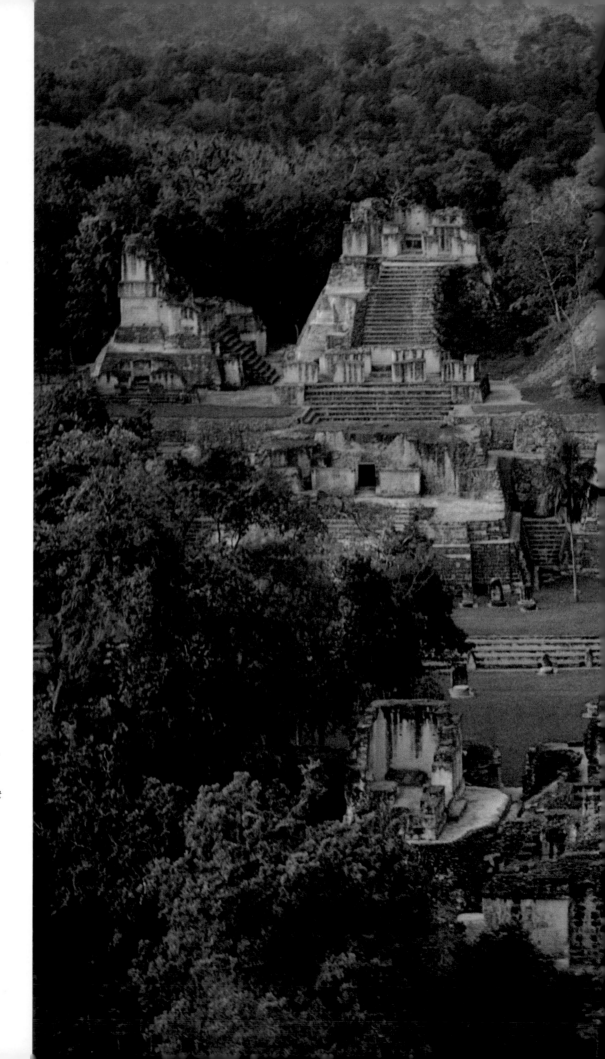

Man-made mountains soar free of the Guatemalan jungle's suffocating embrace at Tikal, one of the largest Classic Maya cities. The Temple of the Giant Jaguar, named after one of its carvings, dwarfs visitors to the three-room shrine on its crest. Beneath the pyramid, archaeologists discovered a vaulted tomb containing pottery, jade, seashells, pearls, alabaster—and the skeleton of Double-Comb, a ruler of Tikal. Years of excavation have reclaimed only a fraction of Tikal—most of its 50 square miles still lies unexplored beneath a canopy of green.

THE MAYA

Rulers of Tikal and other Classic Maya cities commissioned monuments to proclaim and legitimize their rule. Intricately carved slabs of limestone, called stelae, usually depicted the ruler, richly dressed and ornamented, along with columns of hieroglyphic dates and text. Stela 31 (left), dedicated on October 17, A.D. *445, depicts Stormy Sky, a Tikal lord who came to power in the fifth century. In his belt he wears the heads of the Maya sun god and the jaguar god of the underworld.*

More than two centuries later, Double-Comb, who traced his lineage to Stormy Sky, took the throne on the anniversary of his ancestor's accession and proclaimed himself inaugurator of a new cycle of history. To emphasize this change he had the old stela moved. Workers, using log skids and ropes, and water to reduce friction, dragged it up the steps of the steep pyramid. At the top they wrestled the stela into the temple, where it was ceremonially burned and laid to rest. The temple was then sealed and another built over it. The Maya built three temples here.

Marketplace and ball court, temple and causeway pulsate with brightly attired Maya in this bird's-eye view of Copán. Nestled in a long, narrow valley high in western Honduras, Copán has long fascinated explorers and archaeologists with its intricately carved monuments.

Until recently, scholars knew little about who built and supported this Classic Maya city. Recent excavations suggest that more than 10,000 people—from priests and artisans to farmers and merchants—lived here. The wealthiest families, whose compounds often included well-made temples, inhabited the densely settled areas northeast and south of the main plaza. Elsewhere, settlement was less dense—a mixture of masonry buildings for the rich, pole-and-thatch houses for servants or the poor. Across the Copán River, fields of corn, beans, and other crops fed the thriving population of the valley.

A Ball Court
B Hieroglyphic Staircase
C Temple dedicated in A.D. 773
D East Court of the Acropolis
E Residence of last known ruler of Copán
F Ruler's minor temple
G Ruler's minor temple
H West Court of the Acropolis
I Ruler's major temple
J Residential compound of powerful lineage
K Residential compound of less powerful lineage
L Residences for male ritual seclusion
M Four-staircase temple for community ceremonies
N Stelae erected by 13th Ruler of Copán, 18 Rabbit
O Temple erected by 18 Rabbit
P Young men's dormitory and education building?
Q Temple
R Auxiliary building to P
S Causeway
T Residential compound
U Elevated walkway
V Marketplace in Great Plaza
W Copán River
X Scattered residential compounds
Y Foothills of the Copán Valley

66

Maya priests inside the Palace of the Governors at Uxmal take measurements and consult planetary tables as they watch Venus rise at dawn. Once every eight years the planet rose on the horizon at a point aligned with the center door of the palace. Later that morning Lord Chac, for whom the ornate palace was built, ascended the platform of the double-headed jaguar throne (right) to celebrate the planet's appearance. Calculations by priests enabled the Maya to link planting, harvesting, and celebrating with propitious astronomical events.

Tikal has always overwhelmed me. Its great temple-pyramids seem to possess a steeper angle than most and soar to greater heights; the very stones seem larger and darker, giving the buildings such a forbidding aspect that I feel hesitant to approach—a feeling akin to entering the most sacred place connected with an alien religion, a sense of not quite knowing when to genuflect. Tikal sprawls over some 50 square miles, forming a city that once may have housed 40,000 people.

Standing on the now carefully manicured Great Plaza, the visitor to Tikal finds himself at the center of a stage surrounded by a panoramic backdrop that is distinctly Maya. The slanted stone walls of a ball court embrace a small rectangle of ground where the pompous and padded elite played the ritual game with a hard rubber ball. The monumental stairway that forms one entire side of the plaza rises majestically in four great stone steps that lead into the North Acropolis. Here remnants of the first known occupation of Tikal, around 600 B.C., lie deeply buried beneath the successive plaster floors and masonry pyramid-temples of the next 1,500 years. Across the top and along the bottom of the wide stairway are 70 stone stelae and "altars" carved with the portraits of many Classic-period rulers of Tikal and with hieroglyphs proclaiming their dates, ancestry, and exploits. Some stelae are badly eroded, for they have stood in place from the fifth century B.C. onward. The altars are drum-shaped stones upon which various kings of Tikal probably stood during elaborate ceremonies. Dominating the whole plaza are two soaring pyramid-temples, the largest built in A.D. 700 as a memorial to a dead ruler whose tomb lay beneath it.

Only now are we beginning to see the complexity of the society that built Tikal and other Maya cities. Farmers sustained the dynamic

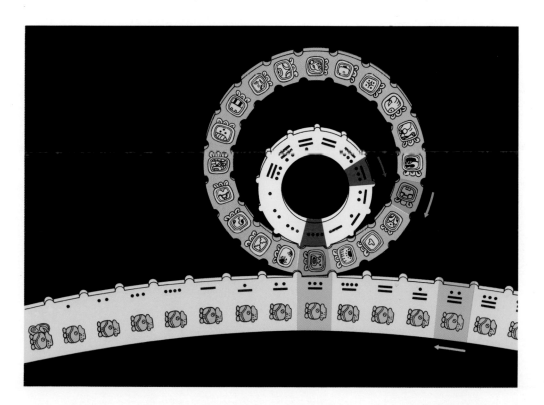

Obsessed with time, the Maya perfected intricate methods to record its passage. Priests may have charted the heavens from observatories like this one at Chichén Itzá (opposite). Ancient sky-watchers perfected an accurate calendar based on sophisticated mathematics. In the calendar's two meshing, repeating cycles (left), a dot equals one, a bar five. The sacred calendar lasted 260 days, with a sequence of 13 numbered days on the inner wheel meshing with 20 named days on the outer wheel. A section of the larger wheel below them represents the secular calendar of 365 days—18 named "months" of 20 days each, followed by five evil days. The dates in the diagram, 4 Ahau 8 Cumku followed four days later by 8 Kan 12 Cumku, would not come around again for about 52 years. Two fragments of a stela (above) from Tres Zapotes bear one of the New World's earliest recorded dates—31 B.C.

civilization by growing corn, beans, squash, and chili peppers in a harsh and capricious land. Ever at the mercy of erratic rainfall, encroaching jungle, or indifferent soils, the Maya proved no less innovative than their counterparts in the Fertile Crescent, Egypt, and other settings where intensive farming and high civilization went hand in hand. At Etzna in Campeche, Maya farmers maintained a huge irrigation channel, while others engineered a network of canals and built "raised fields" with the rich mud taken from waterways stretching across much of the Petén. When necessary, farmers built terraces to catch and hold water, or carried vessels of water to pour on elevated fields. From the jungle they cut huge fields, then worked nearly full time to keep the forest at bay. With huge populations to feed, the Maya also relied on groves of breadnut trees and on deer, wild turkey, and other game.

It appears likely that the Maya were ever conscious of their debt to their land and its bounty. In a Bonampak mural of a young heir to the throne being presented to distinguished lords and emissaries, a figure in a lower register of the painting holds an ear of corn. He has pulled the green husk back to reveal yellow kernels at the very moment of the presentation of the child—a metaphorical reinforcement of the link between planting and harvesting and the cycle of rulership.

Cycles. In retrospect, Maya timekeepers seem to have been obsessed with them. Nowhere is this more obvious than in the use of the calendar inherited from their Preclassic forebears. Maya astronomer-mathematicians continuously sought to reconcile the harmony of the moving universe with the eternally recurring cycles of time.

Calendar specialists worked with two ancient kinds of years. One, a year of 365 days, was much like our own, except that it had no built-in leap year correction. It consisted of 18 "months" of 20 days each, plus a short 5-day period. The other "year," apparently a ritual period, consisted of only 260 days—itself a blend of two smaller cycles of 13 numbers and 20 different day names. These two kinds of years ran concurrently, locked for all time into a greater cycle of 18,980 days—about 52 years—when the designations for any given day would repeat.

The Maya recorded the passage of days by using what we call the Long Count, usually a five-place positional notation involving the concept of zero, also inherited from their Preclassic forebears. The Classic Maya, however, were not content with these mere numbers. They made each a god and conceived of them as an endless procession on the trail to eternity. Each number, bent beneath the load of its tumpline, carried animals or birds, who were gods and patrons of individual days or multiples of days. Stations along this trail formed

Timeless beauty of Classic Maya ceremony unfolds in this copy of a mural from Bonampak. White-robed lords stand pompously while the "Bonampak Band" plays in the lowest section. Scenes in other temple rooms depict a raid, sacrifice, and celebration dance.

dates where the procession of gods would pause to rest, sometimes to be immortalized on the great monuments of the Classic period. We Mayanists could not have asked for a better system. By multiplying the numbers—whether simple combinations of bars and dots or complex portraits of number gods themselves—by the accompanying animal gods, we can calculate any date recorded in the Long Count. We know its beginning to have been August 10, 3114 B.C.—and this was merely the end of another cycle that had begun earlier!

Classic Maya priests at Tikal and elsewhere directed human participation in the bewildering realm of the supernatural. The Maya cosmos was based on the notion that people lived in a giant square of earth centered around a giant ceiba tree; its foliage soared to the heavens and its roots twisted deep into the underworld. Each of the corners and cardinal directions had its own gods and associated colors. The east, the prime direction, was red; the west, black; the north, white; and the south, yellow. And the center was called *yax*, the Maya color for something between green and blue.

The Maya heavens were arranged in thirteen layers terraced like a giant Mesoamerican pyramid, six steps up and six down, with the highest unit in the center of the sky. Each layer was also occupied by gods mainly associated with good. Below, the underworld comprised nine layers, four steps down, the bottom, and four steps up. The earth upon which man lived was held up by giant beings who stood at the four corners of the underworld. The heavens, in turn, were supported by gods who stood on earth. Each day, the celestial universe would pass through this cosmos: The sun would begin in the east, proceed through the thirteen layers of heaven, and in the west enter the dread world below and begin its harrowing journey through the night sky.

Our most complete and vivid description of the Maya underworld comes from the *Popol Vuh*, the sacred book of the Quiché Maya written down sometime in the mid-16th century. According to the epic, the dread patrons of Xibalbá, the cave of the underworld, lured two brothers into their lair, for their noise while playing ball had disturbed the evil gods below. The brothers descended, failed certain trials, and were sacrificed. Later, the heroes of the narrative, Hunahpú and Xbalanqué, twin sons of one of the hapless victims, determined to avenge the death of their father and their uncle. These precocious young lords happened to be magicians as well.

Intentionally provoking the gods of hell, Hunahpú and Xbalanqué are summoned below, as were the original brothers. Descending, the twins cross a river of blood and abomination on rafts improvised from their

Figurines up to 12 inches tall

Lifelike portraits fired in clay illustrate Classic Maya costumes and customs—and may depict individuals buried on Jaina. From this island cemetery off Yucatán's west coast have come thousands of molded figurines. Many hollow-bodied statuettes, including the old man embracing a girl (opposite), served as ritual whistles or rattles. Feathers cloak the shield-wielding Fat God in a conical headdress and a paunchy nobleman wearing a tasseled loincloth. Ceremonial finery also garbs a bearded man on a throne (left).

74

blowguns. The lords of death challenge them with seemingly impossible tasks. Undaunted, the Hero Twins endure the House of Darkness, the House of Knives, where they are threatened by the gnashing of sharp stone blades, the House of Cold, and the House of Killer Bats. The twins also play ball with the gods—and lose. Sacrificed, they miraculously reappear. Soon they perform their greatest trick: They cut one another into pieces, then reassemble each other. Enthralled, the evil lords ask that the twins do the same to them. You know the ending: This time the twins cut the evil ones into pieces but do not restore them to life. The Hero Twins emerge, triumphant from the underworld, in a great act of resurrection and conquest of evil.

Recently my son David and I visited this evil realm—or at least a version of it—in Naj Tunich, a newly discovered cave in the southeastern Petén. During the eighth century, Maya had penetrated its limestone depths and painted the empty white walls with long hieroglyphic texts and scenes of dwarfs, ball games, and bloodletting.

As we sat resting ourselves and our flashlight batteries in the velvet blackness of one of the cave passageways, I reflected on the paintings we had seen. Ball-game scenes evoked memories of the Hero Twins. Dwarfs, I knew, had some connection with celestial gods. Suddenly a glint of Maya consistency appeared in my mind's eye—a rare moment of revelation perhaps evoked by the long, twisted tunnels and their ancient ghosts. The icons of the cave had linked underworld and sky as interrelated opposites. The bloodletting scenes recalled that Maya nobles, sometimes shown dressed as females, performed these rites to "nurture" the gods, much as a mother nurtures her children. And the cave itself, an ultimate symbol of water by virtue of actual pools and symbolic limestone formations, was a place of life and death. In Naj Tunich these motifs had come together. I was so awed by this revelation that I would not have been surprised had one of the ancient artists stepped out of the darkness brandishing his flaming torch.

Artists and many other specialists filled the ranks of Maya society. High on the scale were the master architects. The invention of the corbel arch (the Maya never developed the true arch) allowed architects to build great stone rooms, which were adorned with mosaic facades or with carved and painted stucco.

Maya painters and sculptors created one of the great art styles of the ancient world. Since few murals have survived, the greatest body of painting lies in the thousands of graceful cylindrical vases that served as funerary offerings in elite tombs. These vases often depict scenes of the underworld and the mythical realm. Some show ball games, others

Copán's deserted ball court once echoed with the whack of a solid rubber ball against stone walls, the thud of colliding bodies, and the cheers of spectators. Before starting the fast-moving game, teammates purified themselves in ritual sweathouses and chanted spells. To keep the ball in motion, players could bounce it only off the hips or buttocks. Though padded for protection (left), players often died from internal injuries. If the ball dropped to the paved floor and "died," so sometimes did the losing team's captain. Gambling onlookers wagered houses, jewels, cornfields, and even themselves or their children as slaves. The large, round eyes of the macaw-head goal markers may have evolved into the stone hoops of Postclassic ball courts. The player who knocked the ball through the ring won the game for his team and collected the spectators' jewelry and clothing.

throne scenes with retinues of Classic rulers. Still others present worlds so obscure that we can perhaps never know their full meaning.

No less important were the scribes—guardians of the knowledge of ancient America's most highly developed writing system. Perhaps, too, they knew the calendar and composed the hieroglyphic texts on carved monuments, painted pottery, engraved shells, and murals.

In the rich panorama of Classic Maya society the rulers themselves played the dazzling lead role. Indeed, they appear as the principals in virtually all surviving Maya sculpture and painting. On the great stone stelae they stand solemnly, covered with ornaments of jade and clothing of jaguar skin—the ultimate symbol of Maya royalty. Stelae probably functioned as public posters, depicting rulers in official regalia with texts proclaiming their ancestry and, thus, their right to rule.

From hieroglyphic texts Mayanists have recovered dates—birth, accession, and death—of Maya lords and have reconstructed many royal histories. We can now speak of Maya rulers much as we do of Egyptian pharaohs or Roman emperors, for now we have names, or at least nicknames—Bird Jaguar of Yaxchilán, Sunrise of Copán, Lord Chac of Uxmal. We can also glimpse into their lives, such as that of Pacal the Great of Palenque. We know his face well. A stucco portrait head from

Clutched in death's stony grip, the dead ruler of Palenque sinks into the jaws of an underworld monster. But, like the rising sun, Pacal the Great will ascend into the heavens. This bas-relief, carved on a five-ton limestone sarcophagus lid, eluded discovery until 1952, when a Mexican archaeologist excavated a rubble-filled stairway and reached a dark crypt 80 feet below the Temple of the Inscriptions. Here in A.D. 683, Maya buried Pacal with sacrificial victims and lavish jade treasures, then painted the royal tomb with red cinnabar—symbolic of the east, the rising sun, blood, and resurrection. Nearby, the unique four-story Palace tower (below), which may have been an observatory or lookout post, watches over the ruins of the once-dazzling city and the Gulf coastal plains.

the late seventh century reveals a slender face with high cheekbones, thin lips, and the long sloping forehead artificially flattened after birth to produce the graceful profile prized by Maya nobles.

Pacal was born on March 26, A.D. 603, the child of Kan Bahlum Moo and Lady Zac Kuk, of the Palenque royal family who traced their ancestry deep into the past and the realm of the gods. Twelve years later, on July 29, Pacal was formally inaugurated as ruler of Palenque. We can imagine much of this ceremony, for depictions of Pacal and the events of his life still grace the buildings that dominate Palenque's grassy plaza. In the hallway of a palace corridor we can even see the young ruler seated on a stone jaguar throne as he receives the headdress of royal office from his mother. One can easily visualize the brightly dressed dignitaries who must have crowded the small private patio to witness this all-important ceremony.

Under Pacal's 70-year reign, one of the longest known during the Classic period, the town of Palenque grew into a proud and beautiful city. We can only guess that these visible remnants of Pacal's greatness were matched by an enormous prosperity—the collective contribution of everyone, from farmers to masons and artists.

Pacal's death on the last of August 683 must have been viewed by the Maya of his city as an extension of his long life—for his stone tomb forms a fitting threshold from the living world of Palenque to the realm of the afterlife. His sarcophagus bears portraits of his ancestors arranged so that Pacal himself, when laid to rest in the hollow slot of the great stone, was surrounded by his ancestral cosmos. There his body lay with a superb death mask of green jade, a necklace of giant jade beads interspersed with finely carved fruits and vegetables—again the homage to agriculture that is often seen even in the most noble settings—and a tiny carved image of the sun god whose trail Pacal would trace through the underworld to triumphant resurrection and eternal life.

The century following Pacal's death proved a dark one for the Classic Maya of the Petén and its reaches. The inscriptions tell us when disaster struck: At Palenque the last date was carved in 799; at Bonampak, 800; and at Tikal, 869. Temples fell into disuse, occasionally inhabited by squatters who used them as simple dwellings. The old monuments fell, and their very purpose soon became unknown to the Maya of succeeding generations. At Tikal and Cobá, broken stelae or parts of the carvings were re-erected, sometimes upside down, in a pathetic attempt perhaps to recapture some of the lost pomp and glory.

We don't know exactly what took place, but whatever happened was so disastrous that it led to a demographic catastrophe of the first order.

Women grind corn and cook, men with digging sticks in hand trudge to the fields, slaves tote goods on their backs. This mural from the Temple of the Warriors at Chichén Itzá bustles with the humdrum of everyday life in a Postclassic Maya village. In canoes, six dark-skinned conquerors—Toltec warriors from the central Mexican highlands—skim across waves dancing with sea creatures. With the invaders came their omnipresent god, the feathered serpent, which wriggles around the green-roofed temple.

Some archaeologists suspect natural disasters, earthquakes, or diseases as the cause. Others cite the possibility of peasant revolts or foreign invasion by Mesoamericans outside the Maya area.

Though no single factor probably caused Maya society to crumble, the most likely explanation is economic collapse. Even at its greatest height, Maya civilization maintained a precarious balance between successful agriculture and the harsh environment. Perhaps a minor fluctuation in the climate increased the imbalance until salvation was beyond reach. Related to this decline was the delicate trade network that had brought the Maya articles from outside their virtually resourceless area—metates made of volcanic stone, jade and obsidian for luxury goods. The main Maya stock in trade appears to have been ideas that, once transmitted, stimulated other burgeoning civilizations in Mesoamerica. But the exotic temple-cities deep in the jungle had little relevance to the commercial orientation of the Postclassic.

Whatever happened, the population of the central Petén dropped by what some archaeologists estimate to be as much as 80 percent in less than a century. Tikal, Copán, Palenque, Bonampak, and dozens of other sites gradually disappeared under the very jungle that had spawned them. When the Classic period died, the Long Count calendar

died too, for it dealt with eternity. To the Postclassic Maya the very idea of eternity must have been a mockery of what had gone before.

But in the north, Dzibilchaltún, Uxmal, and other Yucatán sites endured the Classic-Postclassic transition. Exotic art motifs—skulls and crossbones, feathered serpents—and unusual architectural elements mark the presence of outsiders and of change. At Chichén Itzá, once a city of Classic Maya facades, rain god masks, and lintels and door jambs bearing hieroglyphic dates, the change is startling. The architectural monuments of the Postclassic incorporate great columns carved in the shape of feathered serpents, one of the trademarks of the cultures of central Mexico far to the west. How did these come to the Maya area? Part of the answer may lie in colonial chronicles, recollections of history written down after the Spanish Conquest.

One of the most intriguing stories revolves around Quetzalcóatl, a priest-king who, tradition says, ruled at the central Mexican city of Tula in the tenth century. Renowned for his kindness and wisdom, he advocated only the sacrifice of snakes and butterflies to the gods. Quetzalcóatl, however, was threatened by Tezcatlipoca, or Smoking Mirror, one of whose aspects stood for all that was dark and evil. Legend says that he tricked Quetzalcóatl, usurped the throne, and

In a Chiapas marketplace a Maya vendor slices salt disks from cylindrical loaves, formed by drying damp crystals in small straw bags. The salt comes from a local brine well exploited by the Maya since pre-Conquest times. To make sal cocida—*cooked salt (opposite, top)—a Salvadoran pours salty estuary water into a shallow pan atop an adobe oven. The ancient Maya made salt the same way, using large clay caldrons, and traded it within their lands and beyond. Salt-loving microorganisms color the brine mauve in modern evaporation ponds (opposite, bottom) in Yucatán— the same solar-powered process used by the Maya 2,000 years ago. Salt had ritual importance to the ancient Maya; their descendants still use it for curing and divination, as well as in food.*

82

expelled the loser and his retinue from Tula. Sadly the group made its way southward and eastward toward the Gulf coast. Finally reaching the water, Quetzalcóatl turned to the land he was leaving, promised to return someday, and sailed east with his followers on a giant raft.

Some versions of the story say the raft rose to the sky, turned into fire, and became the planet Venus. Others claim that Quetzalcóatl, the feathered serpent, sailed to a land of the red and black, which may have been Yucatán. At this time, around A.D. 1000, feathered serpent motifs appeared suddenly at Chichén Itzá, and Maya life throughout northern Yucatán reflected a "Mexicanization" influence. Chichén Itzá flourished for some two centuries, then lost its power and was partially abandoned, never to thrive again.

Around A.D. 1200, Mayapán, a shabby and clumsy imitation of Chichén Itzá, rose to prominence 60 miles to the west. The fact that this once-crowded capital city was enclosed by a massive stone wall with few gates reflects the turbulent times. Mayapán did not even survive to the Conquest. A fire in the mid-15th century hastened its fall. Thus, nearly a century before the Spaniards arrived, Maya civilization had essentially died, or become hybridized beyond recognition.

Nowhere is this more evident than at Tulum, now a lovely ruin on the east coast of Yucatán. One can see something about Tulum which is Maya—the layout of its hallways, the construction of some of its vaults. But most of it is simply Postclassic Mesoamerican—crude masonry evened out with massive globs of stucco, buildings painted brilliant colors, a high wall protecting it from the trackless interior.

The Postclassic Maya of Yucatán clung to an abbreviated version of the old calendar, counting in units of 20 years, the katuns, named for their last day, Ahau. This "Short Count" became the basis for marking time in the Postclassic period, for telling history, and for predicting the future. In these troubled times, history and prophecy became confused. After all, the Maya were firm believers in cycles. If a Katun 6 Ahau had been a time of drought, then the *next* Katun 6 Ahau—260 years later— would also be one. So convinced were they of this that they let history overrun their own future. This fatalism contributed to the ease with which they and other Mesoamericans were conquered.

It may have been from Tulum in a Katun 8 Ahau, a traditional time of doom and foreboding, that Maya looked east one morning in February 1517 and, mystified, beheld the silhouettes of large wooden ships. They were gazing at Spaniards in an initial confrontation that would forever end a kind of life that had endured for some 1,500 years—and in a manner more drastic and disastrous than they could imagine.

Early morning light wakens the "city of dawn." A mariner's landmark perched high above the iridescent Caribbean, Postclassic Tulum watched over traders gliding by in huge dugouts loaded with feathers, jade, wax, salt, cotton, and honey. Its high, thick fortification walls bespeak local feuds; squat limestone buildings reveal shoddy workmanship; plumed serpent columns and elaborate murals tell of foreign intrusion. Last citadel of a fading civilization, Tulum was sighted by the Spanish in 1517. Fifty years later the city lay silent.

THE ENDURING MAYA

Louis de la Haba

L orenzo Beh and I sat within the charred walls of his partially rebuilt house on the edge of Xcobenhaltun, a backcountry Maya village in Mexico's State of Yucatán. Broken household goods and scorched remains of clothing littered the ground around the house. Although new beams and rafters were in place, nothing impeded the view of massive gray clouds scudding overhead on the wings of a chilly north wind. Lol—Lorenzo's nickname—said he had no money to buy palm thatch for the new roof. Beyond Lol's backyard, with its flimsy chicken coop and pigsty, stretched the rolling bush country where the Maya Indians of the Yucatán Peninsula—*mazehualob*, as they call themselves—scratch an uncertain living from the thin, stony soil.

Lol told me how three months earlier he had been cruelly burned from ankles to knees in a fire that destroyed his house. Since then, he had been unable to work, though he was now almost fully recovered. He agreed readily to act as my guide and interpreter, and for more than a week he and I traveled through the Maya country around the Puuc hills. We visited ancient Maya sites with their pyramids and massive buildings, and the vast underground galleries of the caves at Loltún, where Lol had played hide-and-seek as a boy. Lol told me that it was said that in the "old days"—the time of the ancients—people were stronger and the stones were lighter in weight, and thus was it possible to erect the imposing structures. He had friends and acquaintances everywhere, and we frequently stopped to chat with them.

Lol spoke to me in Spanish, but most of his friends preferred Maya, and Lol would translate their words. I found I could understand an occasional phrase, for Yucatecan Maya, as it is spoken today, is riddled with words of Spanish origin, including numbers. Ironically, the ancient Maya, ancestors of today's Yucatecans, were master mathematicians who perfected one of the most accurate and complex calendars known until modern times. A version of the old Maya calendar is still in use in parts of the Maya highlands for ritual and agricultural purposes. Yet today's Maya find it handier to use Spanish words for numbers.

About 20 Mayan and Mayan-related languages are spoken in the area stretching from the Yucatán Peninsula southward into Belize, parts of

Mists enshroud the Puuc hills of Mexico's Yucatán Peninsula while a Maya farmer gathers his treasured harvest of corn. For today's Maya, as for their ancient predecessors, corn remains a primary source of sustenance and a mystical entity venerated in daily use and occasional ritual.

Honduras, the jungle lowlands and volcanic highlands of Guatemala, and the mountains of Mexico's State of Chiapas. Some are mutually intelligible, others not. But the fact that they persist after nearly five centuries of Westernization is one of the identifying hallmarks of the various Maya groups. There is some erosion, however, and in Yucatán, for example, people in large cities or in the coastal fishing villages of the west and north, perhaps because of their greater contact with mainstream Mexican life, speak Spanish almost exclusively.

One day Lol invited me to lunch at the house he and his family were sharing with his mother. When we arrived, his wife Conchita and his elderly mother were sitting in the kitchen by the *xcoben*, the three-stone fireplace typical of Maya houses. They were slapping flat tortillas out of handfuls of moist cornmeal and cooking them on a flat iron *xamach*, or griddle. Conchita bade me sit at a tiny wooden table and served me a bowl of bean-and-beef stew and a stack of warm tortillas.

A round-faced, plump woman of about 40, Conchita had an easy laugh and a shrewd sparkle in her eyes. It was easy to see that she was the driving force in this family, even though among the Maya, generally, the male reigns supreme. When I first visited Lol's house in the company of a woman teacher *(Continued on page 91)*

With reverent word and gesture, a Maya ritual expert prays for rain near the 1,000-year-old ruins of Chichén Itzá. Behind the kneeling h-men, an assistant wigged in wispy sisal fibers represents a rain god; food offerings bedeck the temporary altar.

Wind-fanned flames burn off weeds and stubble from a field in preparation for planting. This Yucatecan farmer uses the ancient slash-and-burn method to plant his milpa, *or field, for as long as three years; then it must lie fallow, and he will have to clear a new plot.*

Atop an ancient pyramid, once the site of a temple to the Maya sun god, Yucatecan pilgrims end a trek to Izamal and light candles to the Virgin. Elsewhere at this ancient ceremonial center dedicated to Itzamna, greatest of the Yucatecan Maya deities, Spanish priests had the Indians build a great church and convent on the leveled top of another pyramid during the mid-16th century. The construction of Roman Catholic structures on pagan foundations, common in Mesoamerica, once evoked the comment from a bishop that "It is wonderful to see and a scandal to allow!" Such juxtapositions of colonial and Maya religious architecture reflect a prevailing Maya cosmic view. Outwardly and sincerely Christian, the Maya are inwardly and enduringly anchored to a traditional system of pagan religious beliefs.

and her visiting woman friend, only one chair was brought out—for me. Women are expected to bear the children, keep house, and tend the household garden. And though they work hard making preparations for certain pagan rituals, they are excluded from many of them.

Conchita had been dubious about Lol working for me. She felt he had not recovered sufficiently from his burns.

"What do you want with him?" she had asked.

I explained that I wanted Lol to accompany me for a few days, and she asked what sort of work I did.

"That is all you do? You write?" She seemed incredulous when I told her about my work.

Slightly abashed, I asked Conchita what she considered work.

"Work," she proclaimed without hesitation, "is making *milpa*— cutting down trees with an ax, cutting bush with a machete, planting corn. That is work." And she agreed that being with me would not tax her husband excessively.

After I finished my meal (the family ate separately), Conchita showed me some of her needlework—attractive flower embroideries cross-stitched in bright-colored threads on strips of gauzy material. She had no pattern to follow; it all came out of her head. The embroidered strips, she said, she would sell to a seamstress who would sew them on the necklines and hems of the long, white cotton *huipiles* that are the traditional dress of Yucatecan women.

Conchita's mother-in-law demonstrated how she split palm leaves with her fingernails, then with gnarled but deft hands wove them into a long, seven-part braid that she would sell to a hatmaker. It takes a strip of braid about a hundred feet long to make a single hat, she informed me. Such hats are sold in town as ordinary wear and also offered to tourists in Mérida, capital of the State of Yucatán.

Thus occupied, the two women earned enough to keep the three adults and three children in the family supplied with life's necessities— corn, beans, an occasional piece of beef, and wood for the family fire. In the garden around the house, Lol had planted bananas and plantains; there were a few orange trees and a couple of papayas in fruit. Half a dozen chickens and a few small turkeys pecked at the ground.

Since his accident, Lol had not worked his milpa, the plot he had cleared near Xcobenhaltun where he grew his annual crop of corn and beans. The accident had been a misfortune not only for Lol and his family but for the entire community as well, since Lol was the one there who knew best how to operate the village tractor. The machine had been the gift of evangelical Presbyterians (Continued on page 97)

Trained from an early age, girls cheerfully help their mothers with daily chores. With ropes and pulleys, they lift water from a well in the Yucatecan town of Maní. Cenotes, or natural wells, have supplied the inhabitants with water since the time of the ancient Maya.

THE LACANDON MAYA

Long-haired Lacandon, wearing the traditional white tunic of his tribe, paddles a dugout cayuco *across a forest stream. Only about 350 Lacandon remain in the forested lowlands of Mexico's State of Chiapas. Originally a seminomadic people, the Lacandon have lost much of their territory to encroaching farmers of Chol and Tzeltal Maya and now live in scattered settlements. Increasing contact with outsiders, government agencies, and missionaries has dramatically changed their lives, though many still farm and fish as in the past. Logging concessions for mahogany and other tropical hardwoods bring them some revenue, and many have become accustomed to Western clothing and to such modern artifacts as radios and tape recorders.*

Squatting Lacandon burn pungent copal incense in honor of old gods that still affect their lives. A housewife (opposite) prepares her family's meal—thick corn tortillas cooked on a clay griddle. An elderly woman smokes a cigar, a custom enjoyed by children as well as adults.

who had also built a modest hospital at Xul, a town near Xcobenhaltun. Doctors and other professionals would go there to give low-cost care. One Sunday I saw more than a dozen pregnant women lined up for prenatal checkups, something they had never had before and which they welcomed eagerly, given the high rate of infant mortality.

The Maya appreciate their children and treat them well and rather permissively. At Xcobenhaltun I attended a crowded service in the little palm-thatched Presbyterian chapel to celebrate a boy's first birthday. It was a moving moment when the child's mother stood up before the congregation and thanked God for her child's good health.

From an early age, little girls help their mothers in the house and kitchen. Boys, from what I have seen, have more freedom; but I have also seen them working with their fathers and struggling up steep mountain trails bent over under the weight of bundles of firewood.

In the interior of Yucatán, where water is scarce and irrigation difficult or nonexistent, and in other lowland regions, as well as in the highlands of Chiapas and Guatemala, most Maya make their living on rainfall-dependent milpas. Some work on cattle ranches and on the vast plantations of fiber-producing henequen, which may be privately, communally, or publicly owned. But henequen, though it provides employment, has been a mixed blessing for the Maya. When the bush country was cleared for the plantations, so was the cover for game— deer and other meat animals—on which they had depended for extra protein. The lack of vegetation even altered the local climate so there was less rainfall. Semiarid Yucatán became even drier.

Land here produces crops, at best, for two or three years. Then a *milpero* must select a piece of unworked bush from his village's

Trial by fire purifies Maya elders as they dash across burning thatch during carnival rites in the town of Chamula. The elders hold religious offices, or cargos, *in the autonomous community, one of about a hundred Tzotzil Maya* municipios *in highland Chiapas. Some of the men carry banners with flower designs that symbolize the gods. Thatch-roofed houses (above), in a style unchanged for millennia, overlook rugged mountain forest. Tzotzil Maya of Tenejapa (right) share a ritual drink of* pox, *a home-distilled cane liquor.*

communal holdings. In January or February, the beginning of the dry season, he fells trees and scrub, then leaves the cut vegetation to dry until spring. Just before planting time, he sets the milpa afire. In springtime throughout the land of the Maya, the air is filled with smoke and the pungent odor of burning bush and forest. When the vegetation has been reduced to ashes, the milpero punches a hole in the earth with a metal-tipped digging stick called a *xul*, drops in seed corn, measures off a pace, punches another hole, and drops in more seed. Yucatecan cornfields look sparse and lack the visual lushness of those in grain-growing areas of the more fertile highland regions.

At various stages in the agricultural cycle, prayers are offered to the Christian God and to various ancient Maya deities. Before clearing the land, the milpero asks the blessing of the guardians of the bush—the *kuil-kaaxob;* when he burns the brush and dead trees, he prays to the *cichcelem-yum* for wind to fan the flames so the milpa will burn cleanly; before and after planting, he invokes the power of the *chacs*, the rain gods, to send timely rain so the crop will flourish. Other ceremonies, usually presided over by cult specialists called *h-men*, include the *primicias*, offerings of the earliest-maturing crops, and the *u-hanli-col*, a thanksgiving service after the harvest is in.

These rituals, some simple, some elaborate, vary from place to place and go by different names in the Maya area. But nearly everywhere the Maya dwell, the age-old links between religion and agriculture persist.

On a stony road that wound its bumpy way through dense bush near the village of Yaxhachén, Lol and I met a man who was carrying a bundle of freshly cut palm fronds. Like most of the Maya men traveling in out-of-the-way places, he also carried an antique shotgun cradled in his elbow, just in case he might run across an armadillo, a wild turkey, or some other small game to supplement the next day's dinner.

The palms, he told us, were intended to decorate an altar for a *chachaac*, a rain ceremony. We were in the middle of the dry season, with the milpas cut and drying, and I asked Lol why anyone would be praying for rain at this time. Lol told me about the *cabañuelas*.

This is a period that comprises the first 12 days of the year, days that supposedly represent the 12 months to follow in terms of expected weather and rainfall. That day was January 8, the equivalent of August, and though clouds had flown overhead almost daily, no rain had fallen since the New Year. The milperos were worried, and so the chachaac.

Lol described the ceremony, one for which a milpero must hire the services of a professional h-men. Although women take part in the preparations for the chachaac, usually only men may witness the actual

Festive huipiles *like this may dress up a bride on her wedding day in Zinacantan, another Tzotzil Maya community in Chiapas. Chicken feathers and a geometric design adorn the hem of the long, blouselike dress. The weaver works with a backstrap loom on the hard-packed dirt of her yard. A sacred peak punctures the sky above San Lorenzo (right), one of three Catholic churches in Zinacantan Center. Residents pray not only at the church, but also atop the holy mountains that surround their highland village.*

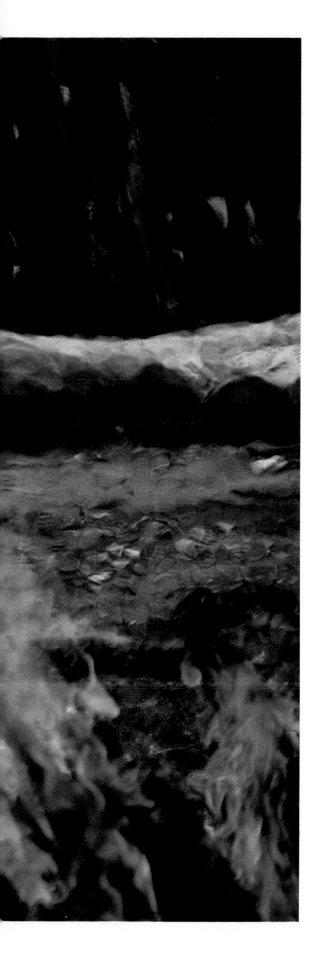

event. Food offerings include thick corn cakes stuffed with squash seeds; *atole*, a cornmeal gruel; and *balché*, a slightly intoxicating and, some say, mildly hallucinogenic beverage made from the bark of a tree and the fermented honey of a stingless bee.

The altar for the chachaac is a rough wooden table set out in the milpa. On it the h-men arranges the food and a few candles. Four young boys are seated under the table, one by each leg. The four legs represent the points of the compass and the directions of rain-bearing winds. As the h-men prays, he sprinkles ashes from the milpa, seeds, water, and drops of honey on the boys' heads. Then he bids them, "*Kayeex! Kayeex!*—Sing! Sing!" And the children croak like a chorus of frogs to attract the rain.

Familiar as he was with the ritual, Lol spoke of it disparagingly, dismissing it as superstition. Lol is a Presbyterian convert and, though illiterate, considers himself a modern man, above such foolishness.

Since the Spanish Conquest, the Maya of Yucatán have been traditionally Roman Catholic, actually practicing the pagan-Catholic admixture common in Mesoamerica. Protestantism has made some inroads, due to the efforts of missionaries and to the mazehualob's innate distrust of the white and mestizo power structure that has ruled their lives. In the mid-19th century, weary of this domination, the mazchualob rcbcllcd in a prolongcd and bloody uprising that locked them in savage conflict with the whites. Beginning in Quintana Roo in 1847, the flames of revolt soon engulfed the whole peninsula. The mazehualob marched on relentlessly, picking up supporters, killing whites, and destroying haciendas and churches.

Reaching Mérida, where the whites feared an unspeakable slaughter,

Near her Amatenango home, a woman fires her pottery without using a kiln by burning branches piled on a heap of jars and bowls. The heat removes moisture from the clay and hardens it, turning it into earthenware. In Amatenango, women make the pottery, while men farm, gather wood for fires, and take the pots to market in other Chiapas communities. Floral patterns decorate the rims and sides of the distinctively styled pots and jars (left). The work of women potters accounts for some 20 percent of Amatenango's income.

the Indians suddenly stopped in their tracks and then withdrew. It was the time for planting. The inexorable call of the land and the corn had to be heeded, and the mazehualob returned to their fields. They still controlled eastern and southern Yucatán and continued to do so for many years, but the back of the rebellion had been broken—of its own accord. Today, the War of the Castes—as it came to be called—is vividly remembered in Yucatán; some of its tangible consequences—the burned-out hulks of colonial churches and former estates—are plainly visible in the rural countryside.

Because the British from neighboring Belize—then British Honduras—helped provide arms for the Yucatecan Maya during the war, and because the United States had been at war with Mexico just before the uprising, the mazehualob came to believe that the British and the Americans were natural allies who would help liberate them. Even now, the Yucatecan Maya think of the rest of Mexico as a foreign country. And to this day, the English language is highly prized.

While in Yucatán, I met a young anthropology student who had been living in one of the more remote villages as part of her research. Wanting to help her hosts in some way, she decided to organize a program to teach illiterate adults to read and write.

"But do you know what they wanted? They wanted me to teach them to read and write in English! They didn't want Spanish at all."

For nearly half a millennium, whether in the lowlands or the highlands, whether in Mexico or Guatemala, the Maya have never become fully integrated into their countries' social and economic structures. One result has been their continuing status at the bottom of the economic and social scale. This has been partially due to their continued domination by the more advantaged classes. But to a large extent, it has been due to the profound sense of Maya cultural identity, their sense of "separateness," or "otherness," that has kept them aloof from outside influence and resistant to change.

Even Lol, the modern man, told me about a government agricultural agent who suggested that he plant his corn two or three grains to a hole and that he place the holes close together in order to increase his crop. Lol, perhaps more aware than his adviser of the thin soil and sparse rainfall, told me, "It is not my custom to do it that way. I plant as I always have—one kernel to a hole and not too close together."

For the Maya of the highlands of Guatemala, who live in fertile valleys and slopes among the towering peaks of the country's volcanic backbone, change comes ever so slowly. In mountain towns and villages the people, especially the women, wear distinctive costumes of

OVERLEAF: *Wreathed in a halo of clouds, 10,300-foot-high Tolimán Volcano rises in somber splendor above Lake Atitlán. In towns and villages scattered throughout Guatemala's highlands dwell three million Maya— about half the country's population.*

103

Flickering candles and smoky incense surround Maximón, a Maya idol worshiped by Tzutuhil Indians of Santiago Atitlán, Guatemala. Dressed in layers of clothing, the idol contains a carefully guarded inner core. Maximón's ties with Mam, an ancient Maya god, inspire fear and hope of favors among its followers. Hidden most of the year, Maximón makes a public appearance during Holy Week. A Quiché Maya burns incense at a Catholic church in Chichicastenango (right) and prays to Christian saints and pagan deities.

brilliantly colored designs that go back to the early days of the Spanish Conquest. It is still possible to tell where a person comes from—even in the big market in Guatemala City—by the design and color of the clothes he or she wears. In other places, however, first the men, much later the women, have traded traditional garb for factory-made clothing.

This kind of change has become increasingly evident in the Pacific coast area, where few people wear traditional clothing or pursue age-old occupations. But the process can best be seen, perhaps, in the region around Guatemala's magnificent Lake Atitlán, a mile-high sapphire mirror surrounded by the immense conical peaks of four dormant volcanoes. The tallest, Atitlán, reaches 11,604 feet above sea level. Lake Atitlán is a place of dreams—of clouds, of sudden, violent windstorms, of spectacular red and orange and pink sunsets, and of cool, gray misty mornings. A dozen villages of the Tzutuhil and Cakchiquel Maya surround the lake.

Not much more than three decades ago, the people of these communities lived in almost total isolation, harvesting their milpas and their gardens and orchards luxuriant with every kind of vegetable and fruit. Some worked on coffee plantations, others fished in the lake or collected the plentiful reed, called *tul*, from which they wove mats.

Some of this still goes on, of course, but in towns like Panajachel, on the north shore of the lake and just off the tourist artery of the Pan American Highway, change has come with a vengeance in the form of tourist hotels. The people, naturally, have become tourist-minded to a high degree. Other villages around the lake, not so readily accessible, have managed to keep some degree of seclusion.

When I first went to Santiago Atitlán a dozen years ago, the lakeside

A plume of water scooped from an irrigation channel nurtures a crop of beans in Sololá, a mountain village overlooking Lake Atitlán. Beans, corn, and squash are the staples of Maya agriculture now as in the past. Rich volcanic highland soils produce a variety of crops both for family consumption and for sale in the market. Sololá women dressed in huipiles and wraparound skirts bring a rooster and garden vegetables to the Sololá market.

town was a quiet place with a few stores, a market, a big whitewashed church overlooking a terraced main square, and a small pension and restaurant. During Holy Week each year, the town still comes alive with religious fervor and festivities that include Christian celebrations and the annual appearance of a closely guarded pagan idol called Maximón. This idol, which is regarded with considerable awe and reverence by many of the Tzutuhil Maya and even by people from other parts of the nation, has many ties with the ancient Maya god Mam, a powerful and evil deity that in pre-Conquest times ruled over the *uayeb,* the five unlucky days at the end of the Maya ritual calendar.

Today, Maximón rules over the five days of Holy Week leading to the end of the Christian ritual year. The idol is dressed in colorful finery donated by his cult followers and is taken to a special chapel near the Catholic church. Pilgrims and petitioners come to pray, to light candles in his honor, to burn pungent copal incense, and to bring various offerings of tobacco, liquor, and money in order to procure his favor.

I went to Santiago Atitlán again almost a decade after my first visit, and Maximón was still there. By now, however, many things seemed different. Shops selling tourist goods lined the town's main street. There was a new hotel and restaurant, both full of tourists. There was even a small radio station, broadcasting locally in the Tzutuhil language.

Change, indeed, had come. Some of the townspeople had been quick to take advantage; others, more tradition-bound, were striving to keep their old customs. I felt heartened one day when I watched a girls' outdoor basketball game between the local school and one from Patzún, a larger, less traditional town more than 30 miles away, but on the main route to Guatemala City. The girls from Patzún wore green, knee-length jumpers and white, short-sleeved blouses; the girls from Santiago Atitlán played spiritedly, but somewhat clumsily, hampered by their ankle-length Tzutuhil skirts. Later on, as I walked along a street, I saw a young man approach a pretty teenage girl. As he passed her, he quickly took hold of one end of her *faja,* the long woven sash the women of Santiago Atitlán wear around their waist, and tugged on it. The girl remonstrated and tugged back, but then she laughingly followed the youth around a corner. The old courtship etiquette, I was amused to see, was still in force.

I left the land of the Maya with a concern for the future of the people I had come to know, but also with hope and a measure of confidence: hope that the change that will inevitably come will bring real improvement to their daily lives; confidence that their deep-seated cultural integrity will enable them to maintain their Maya identity.

Like fragile flying saucers, gigantic tissue-paper kites take wing above the hilltop cemetery in Santiago Sacatepéquez. Bachelors in the highland Guatemalan town build and fly circular kites to impress the señoritas on the feast days of All Saints' and All Souls'.

The painstakingly built creations are often 20 feet or more in diameter. During these festivals the Maya of Sacatepéquez scatter marigold petals on their doorsteps and place bouquets of the pungent flowers on doors and windows and on cemetery graves.

SONS OF HUITZILOPOCHTLI

Ignacio Bernal

Like the mosaic of cultures that made up the empire, this Aztec mask, inlaid with shell and turquoise, gleams with beauty and mystery. Does it represent Chalchiuhtlicue, goddess of water, or Quetzalcóatl, the powerful feathered serpent? No one really knows.

To 16th-century conquistadores marching into the Valley of Mexico, the Aztec capital of Tenochtitlán appeared as an "enchanted vision." Brilliantly hued towers and pyramids seemed to hover above shimmering waters, for the city rose out of an island in Lake Texcoco 7,000 feet above sea level. In the circling distance, wooded mountains and snowcapped volcanoes towered above the valley floor.

Streams of people—peasant and pilgrim, craftsman and noble, warrior and slave—crowded the causeways leading to the island, some headed for the Great Temple dedicated to Tlaloc, god of rain, and to Huitzilopochtli, god of war. Palaces of stone told of Aztec wealth and power. Merchants back from exotic lands poled canoes along the network of canals past thatch-roofed huts, adobe houses, and lush *chinampas*—plots of landfill planted in corn and other crops. Cargoes of rare spices, cacao beans, gems, feathers, skins, and finely worked gold jewelry found their way to the north side of the island, where, Spaniards would later report, as many as 60,000 people jammed the great marketplace of Tlatelolco, once an independent sister city. Cacao and feathers were luxuries highly prized by the thousands of people crowding the metropolis. But it was the gold that would whet the appetite of Hernán Cortés and his small force of weary soldiers.

At its founding early in the 14th century, Tenochtitlán comprised little more than a few reed huts on some marshy mud flats at the site of present-day Mexico City. Now in 1519 on the eve of its destruction by the Spaniards, it ruled millions of subjects in an empire that stretched 700 miles from sea to sea across southern Mexico.

Who were these empire-building Aztecs? To understand their cultural origins we must reach back to the second millennium before Christ. By then, dwellers in the Valley of Mexico had become sedentary agriculturalists. Here in the fertile basin fed by mountain streams, they lived in scattered villages around five small lakes, the largest called Texcoco. They knew how to make excellent pottery, fashion beautiful clay figurines, and carve stone implements. They ritualistically buried their dead; magic prevailed, but as yet there was no real religion.

Around 500 B.C. the first ceremonial monuments were constructed in

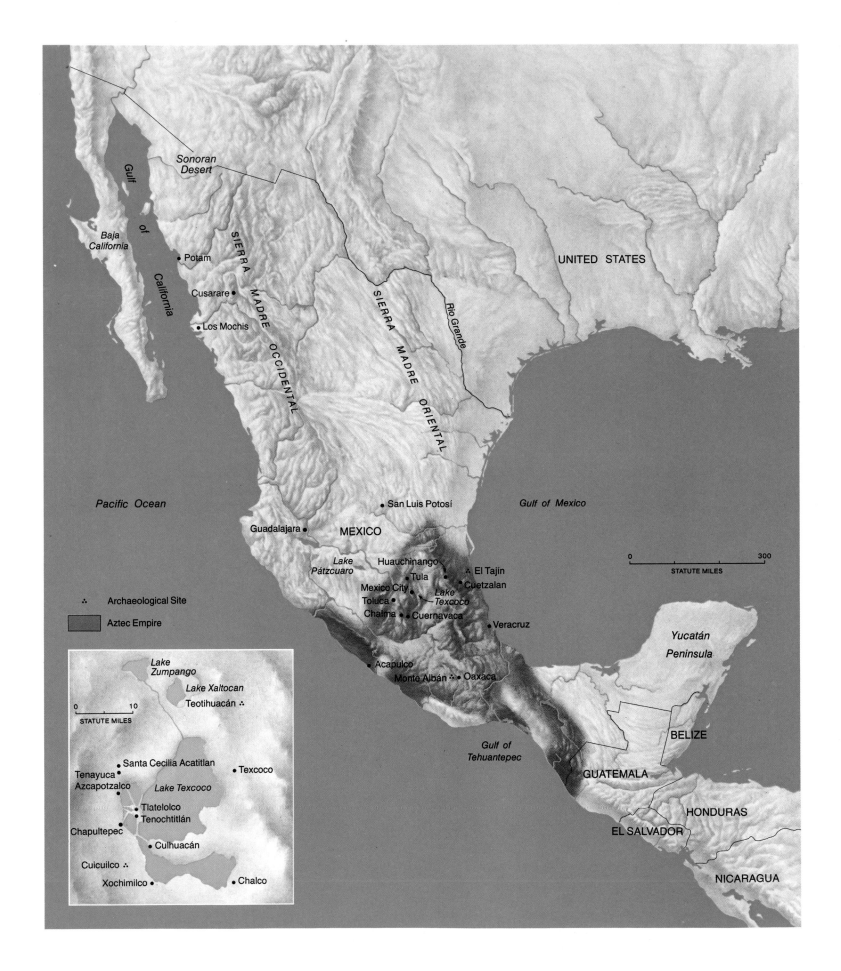

Sonoran
Desert

UNITED STATES

Gulf
of
California

Baja
California

Potam

SIERRA MADRE OCCIDENTAL

SIERRA MADRE ORIENTAL

Rio Grande

Cusarare

Los Mochis

Pacific Ocean

San Luis Potosí

Gulf of Mexico

Guadalajara

MEXICO

Lake
Pátzcuaro

Huauchinango
Tula
El Tajín
Cuetzalan
Mexico City
Lake
Texcoco
Toluca
Chalma
Cuernavaca
Veracruz

∴ Archaeological Site

Aztec Empire

Acapulco
Monte Albán ∴ Oaxaca

0   300
STATUTE MILES

Yucatán
Peninsula

Gulf of
Tehuantepec

BELIZE

GUATEMALA

HONDURAS

EL SALVADOR

NICARAGUA

Lake
Zumpango

Lake Xaltocan
Teotihuacán ∴

0   10
STATUTE MILES

Santa Cecilia Acatitlan
Texcoco
Tenayuca
Azcapotzalco
Lake Texcoco
Tlatelolco
Tenochtitlán
Chapultepec
Culhuacán
Cuicuilco ∴
Xochimilco
Chalco

the highlands. One of these, at Cuicuilco, appears to have been most important. It had a circular stone pyramid surmounted by a temple roofed with thatch. The presence of a statue of Huehuetéotl, Old God in Nahuatl, the Aztec tongue, attests to an emerging religion. But during the second century before Christ, Cuicuilco drowned under the lava from a volcano near the site of Mexico City's national university.

During this period a number of villages had grown in clusters in the northeastern reaches of the Valley of Mexico. The area proved particularly suited for agriculture, for its rich alluvial soil and freshwater springs freed farmers from the uncertainties of rainfall. The region also possessed an enormous deposit of obsidian. A volcanic glass easily flaked to make spearpoints and cutting tools, it would play an important role in the early stages of economic growth.

Slowly the isolated settlements prospered, spread out, and finally merged into the first metropolis of ancient America—Teotihuacán. Commanding an easy route through the mountains, it extended its influence and by A.D. 500, under the dual leadership of priests and war chiefs, had achieved supremacy throughout the highlands. Instrumental in this growth must have been the long-distance merchants, who embarked on expeditions to the coastal lowlands to bring back tropical feathers, animal skins, jade, and seashells. Since there were no beasts of burden, porters carried these cargoes on their backs, supported by tumplines around their foreheads.

The period of expansion coincided with the arrival and probable settlement inside the city of groups from Veracruz along the Gulf coast and Zapotecs from Oaxaca to the south. An outstanding example of such integration is the "Oaxaca barrio," where not only numerous small

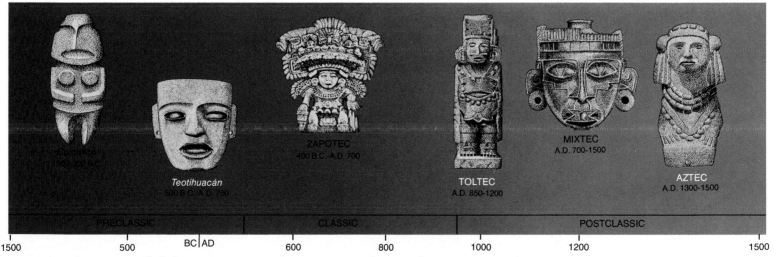

ZAPOTEC
400 B.C.-A.D. 700

Teotihuacán
500 B.C.-A.D. 750

TOLTEC
A.D. 850-1200

MIXTEC
A.D. 700-1500

AZTEC
A.D. 1300-1500

PRECLASSIC · CLASSIC · POSTCLASSIC

1500 · 500 · BC|AD · 600 · 800 · 1000 · 1200 · 1500

Dynamic cultures preceded the Aztecs. City-states, scattered in time and space across Mesoamerica's central plateau (opposite), varied in size, power, and religious zeal. Mystery shrouds the demise of Teotihuacanos and Toltecs, but their artifacts show great artistry.

The Aztecs came from Aztlan—Heron Place—but the birds (upper) have kept secret the location of that legendary homeland. Huitzilopochtli, the Aztecs' tribal god, led them to their new home, Tenochtitlán in Lake Texcoco (inset opposite), the heart of their empire.

artifacts but also a complete tomb in Oaxaca style have been discovered. It is unique in a city where crypts for the dead were not usually built.

Visitors were, and still are, impressed by Teotihuacán's grandiose layout. The broad main avenue, the Street of the Dead, lies athwart the valley on a north-south axis, so that east-west travelers were bound to pass through the city. Massive public buildings rose on either side. At the center stood a triumph of religious architecture, the Temple of Quetzalcóatl, god of wind, the bringer of learning and of civilization. His image as a plumed serpent, intricately carved in stone, still adorns the facade of the pyramid row upon row. In Nahuatl, *quetzal* refers to the beautifully feathered birds of the forests and *coatl* means serpent. Like any dual entity, the quetzalcóatl held great magic.

At the height of its power, Teotihuacán probably required few defenses, since no enemy would dare mount an attack against its brilliant regime. But eventually political decay set in and weakened its prestige and social fabric. By 750 the city lay helpless before the repeated onslaughts of fierce nomadic peoples on its frontier. Charred timbers tell of the devastating blazes that finally consumed the splendor of Teotihuacán toward the end of the Classic period.

Teotihuacán's fall created a power vacuum in the highlands until the 10th century. Then, storming into the Valley of Mexico mainly from the west or northwest, came a semibarbarous, warlike people known as Toltecs. One of their leaders, a chief named Mixcóatl, became the first real flesh-and-blood figure in the history of the highland Indians. Mixcóatl took a group and established a base at Culhuacán in the south, a site now on the southern edge of Mexico City. It was near Cuernavaca, legend says, that Mixcóatl met and wed a woman named Chimalman. Shortly thereafter a captain assassinated Mixcóatl and usurped the throne. Chimalman fled back to her family, where she died giving birth to a son, who was named Ce Acatl, One Reed. The boy grew up among his mother's people, who still worshiped Quetzalcóatl, the old god of Teotihuacán. Ce Acatl became the high priest of this cult and, as customary, took the name of its god. As a young man he vanquished his father's murderer, recovered the throne, and moved his people north of Lake Texcoco to Tula.

It was Quetzalcóatl's intent to create a regal metropolis. Because the northern Toltecs were still subjected to barbarian influences, he imported artists and builders from neighboring regions. Both city and builder would grow in legend. Wondrous gifts were attributed to Quetzalcóatl. He stole corn from the god of the underworld and gave it to man. He determined the reckoning of time according to a fixed

Pyramids to the sun (215 feet high), right, and the moon (150 feet high), top, awed the thousands who thronged ancient America's great city, Teotihuacán. It covered 8 square miles and spanned a millennium. A glimpse of change comes from anthropologist Warren Barbour,

who studies fingertip imprints on clay relics. From 200 B.C., women crafted most pottery. About A.D. 350, male prints predominate, suggesting the craft had gone commercial. As the culture began to crumble, around 700, the prints again become female, the craft domestic.

calendar, introduced the study of medicine, mathematics, and astronomy, and devised the rituals for ceremonies. We know that this knowledge existed long before his time. But we also know, from legends that survived into Aztec times, that Quetzalcóatl and the Toltecs together came to be regarded as the one great civilizing force in Mesoamerican history.

With the Toltecs the Nahuatl-speaking people came to power, and their language, still spoken in central Mexico today, would become one of the identifying features of the Aztecs. The Toltecs also created a new type of militant society, with human sacrifice increasing in importance.

It was this question of sacrifice, legend says, that led to Quetzalcóatl's exile. Several tribes inhabited Tula and most worshiped Tezcatlipoca, the supreme, terrifying god ever hungry for human sacrifices. Quetzalcóatl opposed the practice and tried to convert the people, declaring that he desired only snakes and butterflies as offerings. But Tezcatlipoca's priests plotted against Quetzalcóatl and finally succeeded in driving him out. He left Tula with his followers, wandered the highlands, then journeyed to the Gulf coast, where he sailed away toward Yucatán, promising to return in the year Ce Acatl.

The legend that grew around Quetzalcóatl—he had light skin, wore a

"Precious butterfly" motifs filigree pillars of a Teotihuacán palace (opposite) and endow it with a name—Quetzalpapálotl. Located near the Pyramid of the Moon, it might have housed a priest. Workers grouped by crafts lived in one-story adobe apartments facing a patio.

Plumed priest of the rain god Tlaloc peers from an ancient mural near the Pyramid of the Sun. Teotihuacán painters used patterns to duplicate images. Clay figurines shaped by hand, like this one dating from A.D. 150-250, were later made from molds.

120

beard, and left crosses wherever he went by piercing trees with arrows—would help doom the Aztecs 500 years later. Cortés, coming from the east with men bearing crosses, was white, wore a beard, and landed at Veracruz in the year Ce Acatl. In the mind of the Aztec king, Quetzalcóatl had returned—and it was useless to fight a god.

As the Toltecs extended their domains and established cities around the lakes, more foreign groups settled in Tula, some of them dislocated perhaps by an extended drought in northern Mexico. Bitter rivalries and intrigue resulted, setting the stage for the fall of the city and the collapse of the empire. Early in the 13th century, nomadic tribes pushing down from the cactus wastelands to the north overran the capital. These desert barbarians, called Chichimecs, were a hardy breed who wore the skins of the deer they hunted with bow and arrow.

Several groups made up the Chichimec hordes, but one quickly emerged as the most powerful, the people led by Xólotl. Settling for a while at the Toltec city of Tenayuca on the west side of Lake Texcoco, these erstwhile nomads built a pyramid upon which they placed two temples, one to Tezcatlipoca and the other to the rain god Tlaloc, whose powers they sought with increased devotion as they adopted a limited agriculture. The pyramid, its base decorated with protruding stone-carved serpents, stands on the northern outskirts of Mexico City.

Still seminomadic, the Chichimecs moved on and conquered much of the Valley of Mexico, with Xólotl establishing power bases in the decadent Toltec cities around the lakes. To the Tepanecs, an Otomí-speaking people from the Valley of Toluca to the west, he gave the Toltec city of Azcapotzalco just south of Tenayuca. The Tepanecs would build a kingdom and become part of a future Triple Alliance.

In the 14th century Xólotl's Chichimecs finally ended their migration and allied themselves with a group of much-harried Toltecs on the east side of Lake Texcoco. Exchanging their armed protection for Toltec culture, they took up farming, made pottery, and built a powerful city-state, Texcoco. Infusions of even more refined culture from Mixtec peoples to the south introduced them to the art of painting *hieroglyphs*, or pictorial characters, and the working of gold and silver.

Another group also held power in the basin. After the fall of Tula, a Toltec prince had led his people southward and revitalized the city of Culhuacán. Here they built their prestige on a claim: In their veins flowed the only legitimate royal blood of the Toltec kings. It was a claim recognized by Chichimec cities cropping up around the lake, and Culhuacán spread its influence by marrying off its royal daughters to Chichimec rulers seeking Toltec ties.

Still standing guard at Quetzalcóatl's Pyramid at Tula, these 18-foot-high stone columns represent richly arrayed Toltec warriors. Military might spread the Toltec Empire over the Valley of Mexico, providing the security in which to develop its legendary high culture.

No group was more eager for these ties than a small band of Chichimecs who had wandered far from a fabled island home called Aztlan. From that name we derive the word Aztec.

Notoriously cruel but supremely tough and quick to learn, these early Aztecs probably served as mercenaries in the Toltec armies and may have helped bring down the city of Tula. Yet they had cleverly established a link to the Toltec dynasty. A myth related how a devout Toltec widow, the mother of a daughter and 400 sons, was sweeping the temple one day when she picked up a bunch of feathers, stuffed them in her bosom, and became pregnant. Thus dishonored by their mother, the children plotted to kill her. As her sons approached, a new son was born on the spot, full grown and fully armed with shield, spear-thrower, and a divine new weapon, the "serpent of fire," a lightning flash.

Monte Albán perches high above the Valley of Oaxaca. Zapotecs built the city, but an earlier people carved the danzantes *(opposite)—not dancers perhaps, but shamans or captives. Goldsmith's fine work (left) attests to later Mixtec occupation of the area.*

This was Huitzilopochtli, the sun, who would become the Aztec god of war. With the serpent of fire he beheaded his sister, the moon, and dispersed his brothers, the stars. He vanquished them just as the rising sun vanquishes the light of the moon and the stars. His mother would become Coatlicue, the Aztec earth goddess.

By transforming the sun into their tribal god, the Aztecs thus acquired the protection of the most important force in nature. But with that acquisition came fearsome responsibility. They believed that the sun had been created and destroyed four times and that to create the Fifth Sun—the one that still shines—two gods at Teotihuacán had committed sacrificial suicide by throwing themselves into a fire. Now, as new representatives of the Fifth Sun, the Aztecs were duty-bound to keep it alive with human hearts and blood.

Led by four priests bearing their god in the form of a statue wrapped in a bundle, the Aztecs left the ruins of Tula around 1168 and headed south. Speaking through the priests, the god directed his people in every move they made, told them to call themselves Mexica, and promised to find them a home—where an eagle perched on a cactus. The journey would take 150 years.

The trek was not a happy one. Quarrelsome and treacherous, the Aztecs were thoroughly despised by every neighbor. Driven from one settlement after another, they finally found a temporary home in the shadow of Chapultepec, Grasshopper Hill. It jutted into Lake Texcoco south of Azcapotzalco and lay in territory ruled by the Tepanecs. At its base gushed sweetwater springs. But as the Aztecs grew in numbers and strength, their fearful overlords attacked and drove them from this place also. The bulk of the survivors gave themselves up to the lords of Culhuacán, who settled them on a snake-infested lava bed at Tizaapan northwest of Cuicuilco. There, the Culhua chiefs believed, the Aztecs would die. But they ate the snakes and grew strong.

For a generation the Aztecs served their new masters so well that they won the right to intermarry with the Culhuas. But once again their audacity uprooted them. A legend says they requested from a Culhua lord his daughter to wed their god. The Aztecs took the princess back to Tizaapan, flayed her, and then invited her father to attend the ceremony. When he discovered a priest wearing her skin, the outraged lord called for war. Once again the Aztecs were scattered. The few survivors fled out into Lake Texcoco and huddled on an island. It was here that Huitzilopochtli directed them to found their capital, Tenochtitlán. According to one tradition, the year was 1325.

It was a miserable way to start an empire, hiding in the reeds, eating

Toylike treasures of coastal Veracruz recall a Classic culture—centered on the city of El Tajín—that flourished between the fall of Teotihuacán and the rise of the Toltecs. Ceramic fawn wears wheels, though wheeled vehicles were unknown in Mesoamerica until the Spaniards arrived. Howling coyote ranked with the jaguar as a totemic animal. Smiling caricature of a Veracruz villager (opposite), with turban, necklace, bracelets, and earplugs, may represent any of several deities, including the god of alcoholic pulque.

tadpoles and marsh scum, and enduring repeated humiliation. As part of their tribute to the Tepanec overlords who owned the island, they had to deliver ducks that laid eggs at the moment of arrival at Azcapotzalco. But from the first, the Aztecs realized the site's advantages. No power in the area wanted the place, and even if it did the island was easily defended. They also saw its virtues as a commercial center. In a region lacking beasts of burden and the wheel, their canoes could provide rapid transportation. For the first time the Aztecs had achieved a small degree of independence.

With single-minded devotion to their god, the Aztecs made their first act the building of a rustic temple to Huitzilopochtli. Then they turned to the heroic task of creating a city. Weaving reed mats on which they piled mud from the lake bottom, they anchored them in the shallows with poles. On these plots, or chinampas, they planted crops, adding more land as the population increased. Shoreline cities must have watched in awe as this creation of the chinampas, carried on decade after decade, extended the boundaries of the Aztec capital.

We will speak of Tenochtitlán as if it were a single city. But in the early days two separate Mexica groups developed their own communities, Tlatelolco on the north side devoted to commerce and the canoe, Tenochtitlán on the south dedicated to warfare. The cities elected their own kings, but in time Tenochtitlán would dominate and finally annex Tlatelolco in a fratricidal battle so savage that even women fought beside the men.

For a century after the founding of their capital, the Aztecs lived mainly as mercenaries and tributaries to the powerful Tepanecs. It was only between 1428 and 1433 that they *(Continued on page 136)*

Famous Sun Stone, 26-ton basaltic disk 12 feet in diameter, represents the Aztec cosmos as their seers re-created it. Day-signs (numbered 1-20, right) misled scholars, who first called it a calendar. Square panels (A-D) represent the dates when four previous creations, or suns, perished. The fifth was created in 13-Reed (E), perhaps A.D. 1011; its predicted date of destruction was 4-Movement, whose abstract symbol (F) outlines the central figures. Deity at center (G) is either the sun god, Tonatiuh, or the earth god, Tlaltecuhtli, with a sacrificial knife (H) protruding from his mouth. On either side of the deity, claws (I) hold human hearts. Two fire serpents (J, K) encircle the sculpture, their tails meeting at the creation date (E).

For the Aztecs, each of their 20 calendar days combined with a glyph, or named sign, and a patron deity. Progressive pairings augured good or evil for a child born on that day. The Sun Stone combinations follow.

1 - Crocodile
2 - Wind
3 - House
4 - Lizard
5 - Serpent
6 - Death
7 - Deer
8 - Rabbit
9 - Water
10 - Dog
11 - Monkey
12 - Grass
13 - Reed
14 - Jaguar
15 - Eagle
16 - Vulture
17 - Movement
18 - Flint Knife
19 - Rain
20 - Flower

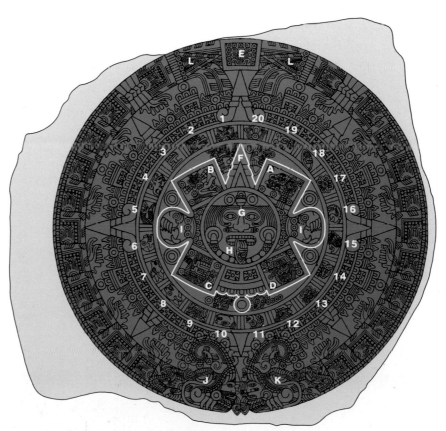

THE AZTECS

Sun-splashed Tenochtitlán spreads a patterned cloak across Lake Texcoco. Laced with canals, checkered with flat-roofed villas and "floating gardens" called chinampas, *the Aztec capital awed conquering Spaniards in 1519. Hernán Cortés dubbed it "the most beautiful city in the world." He marveled at causeways "as broad as a horseman's lance" and spliced with movable bridges. A masonry aqueduct (lower left) funneled fresh water from a mainland spring. Above the island city a nine-mile-long dike held back brackish water and controlled flooding.*

Dredged from marshes, this New World Venice grew to encompass both Tenochtitlán and sister city Tlatelolco (island's left arm), an area of some 4 square miles. At the center of each city gleamed palaces and towering pyramids. Paved plazas hummed with commerce. Cortés found Tlatelolco's vast market "completely surrounded by arcades, where every day there are more than sixty thousand souls who buy and sell."

Black-sooted priests, lean from fasting, haunted Tenochtitlán's religious quarter. There loomed the dual-shrined Great Temple, scene of human sacrifice.

Bearing gifts, Moctezuma and his nobles attend the mountaintop sacrifice of a child to the rain god Tlaloc, whose effigy sits at left just inside the temple. The Aztecs believed Mount Tlaloc, where this ceremony took place, was a divine source of life-giving rains that nourished crops. In a few moments, hidden from view, the six- or seven-year-old child in the sling will be slain to the tune of trumpets, conch shells, and flutes. The more that people cried during the sacrifice, said the priests, the greater the rainfall would be.

OVERLEAF: *In a reach for territory, costumed Aztecs clash with cone-helmeted Huastecs in Veracruz. Knowing their foes are fearless fighters, the Aztecs have resorted to a ruse: Corps of seasoned eagle and jaguar knights hide in the grass on a hill, while the main Aztec force feigns retreat below, luring the enemy into a trap. Seeking escape, the Huastecs race up the hill, only to be butchered or taken captive. Burning the Huastec temple in the distance will signal victory and the impotence of the local god. Such conquests enabled the Aztecs to exact tribute of vanilla, jade, and parrots from the lowlands of Veracruz.*

134

Grotesquely costumed in "garments of
gold," the yellowed skin of slain
captives, Aztec priests mock-fight at the
foot of Tenochtitlán's Great Temple. In
grisly rites of spring, they impersonate
Xipe Tótec, "our lord the flayed one"
and god of renewal. Prisoners taken in
battle were painted chalk white and
crowned with tufts of down, then led—
or dragged—one by one to the summit
of the pyramid. While five priests bent a
victim backward over a sacrificial stone,
a sixth wielding a chert knife cut open
his chest and ripped out his beating
heart. This "precious eagle-cactus fruit"
the executioner held high and offered to
the sun before tossing it into a gourd or
stone vessel. The bleeding body tumbled
down the pyramid, splattering the
stairs, and was seized by other priests
who flayed it. They gave the flesh to the
captor's family for a ceremonial meal.
The head of the victim, beaded onto a
rod, joined thousands more in a massive
skull rack—ghoulish witnesses to the
voracious appetite of the gods. During
the festival, Aztec nobles sniffed flowers
to mask the stench of the dead.

managed to achieve real independence. Led by a brilliant chief named Itzcóatl, they allied themselves with the Chichimec king of Texcoco, Nezahualcóyotl, and defeated the Tepanecs. Out of this war grew the Triple Alliance, with most of the power in the valley shared by Tenochtitlán and Texcoco, and the remainder left to Azcapotzalco.

In 1440 the death of Itzcóatl brought to the throne Moctezuma I, who found a friend and mentor in Nezahualcóyotl. The latter was a genius— poet, philosopher, engineer. He had codified Texcoco's laws, founded a library, and turned the city into an American Athens. He had even started a zoo and botanical garden. From him Moctezuma drew the inspiration that caused Aztec power to soar and culture to flower. Importing artisans, Moctezuma began construction of the Great Temple and built a dike east of the city to control flooding and keep out brackish

water. From Chapultepec he extended an aqueduct to bring fresh water to the city. To obtain sacrificial victims, he stepped up the "flowery wars," a Tepanec custom of ritualistic battles with neighboring states. And he began the expansion of the empire by sending armies south into Oaxaca and east to the Gulf coast.

City after city fell into the Aztec orbit. The procedure was ritualistic. Ambassadors marched into a city and demanded tribute, trade, and worship of the Aztec god. If the city agreed, it became a tributary. If it refused and chose to fight, it was given two more chances, and token weapons were presented to the leaders so they could defend themselves. Then the Aztec army, stiffened by elite corps of eagle and jaguar knights armed with spears, bows and arrows, and obsidian-bladed clubs, slashed through the defending warriors, burned the city's

A rare book showing religious rites and a catalog depicting booty help scholars piece together aspects of the Aztecs' complex civilization. The Tribute Roll of Moctezuma *(below) lists items of tribute paid to the rulers of Tenochtitlán.*

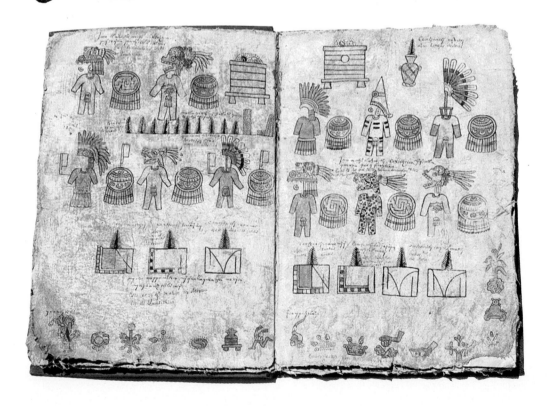

Elegant battle dress, feathered shields and headdresses, bolts of cloth, and bins of exotic foods were distributed to priests and warriors. Quantities—in units of 20 and 400—are indicated by banner- and pine tree-like symbols. The Codex Magliabecchiano—*a picture-history book completed after the Conquest in the mid-16th century—graphically shows human sacrifice (opposite). Most early codices were destroyed by missionaries, who thought them the devil's work. Sacrificial knife (above)—its handle a mosaic rendering of an eagle knight—evokes the harmony of beauty and death in Aztec society.*

temple, took prisoners, killed the chief, and installed an Aztec governor. The resulting flow of tribute soon turned Tenochtitlán into the wealthiest and most important capital of Mesoamerica.

In 1455 Moctezuma celebrated the beginning of a 52-year cycle, the New Fire Ceremony, on Cerro de la Estrella, a sacred hill near Culhuacán. All over the valley, people extinguished their fires as the previous cycle came to an end. To forestall the end of the world, priests at midnight of the last day sacrificed a high-ranking captive and built a fire on his chest. From this blaze, runners carried the new fire to all the temples, where the people came to relight their fires.

The reign of Axayácatl, Moctezuma's successor, saw the subjugation of Tlatelolco, ostensibly the result of a personal insult. Moquihuix, the king of Tlatelolco, had taken as his wife one of Axayácatl's sisters. She bore the name Little Precious Stone, but she had grown ugly and "her teeth emitted a great stench, for which reason the king could never take pleasure in her." He made her sleep in the kitchen, and when her brother sent her fine cotton blankets, Moquihuix gave them to his concubines. Axayácatl's patience finally ran out, and in 1473 he marched across town, defeated the Tlatelolcans, and threw Moquihuix to his death from the top of Tlatelolco's main temple.

Emperor Ahuítzotl enlarged Tenochtitlán's Great Temple in 1487, sacrificing at its four-day dedication hundreds of victims. Under this dreaded conqueror the empire extended its reach to Guatemala.

By the beginning of the 16th century the Aztecs had surpassed the dominions of ancient Tula, and Tenochtitlán had been transformed into a city nearly four square miles in size. Causeways connected the city to the shore, and canals provided easy access to every quarter. The administrative and ceremonial structures stood closely grouped in the center, just as they were at Teotihuacán: the main temple complex, a vast plaza, the imperial palaces, a marketplace.

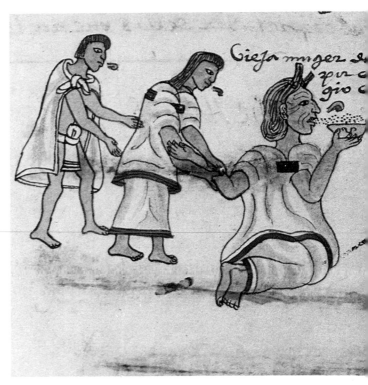

Aztec society had now matured into a clear-cut, though flexible, class system: an upper strata of priests, nobles, and officers, and a lower strata of artisans, vendors, soldiers, and farmers. The great merchants formed a powerful intermediate class, guiding the economic destiny of the empire and collecting tribute from vassal states. Nobility was hereditary, but it could also be attained through valor in battle. Slavery, on the other hand, was not an inherited condition and resulted from crime, debt, or capture in war. Slaves could own property and have slaves of their own. In the market at the time of sale, a slave might break loose and race to the king's palace. If he reached it before being caught—and only the buyer could chase him—he went free. In hard

A farmer with his burro gathers juice from the maguey plant for fermenting into pulque, *potent nectar of the Aztecs, who restricted its use to rituals, medicine, and celebrations. Only the aged were allowed to overindulge, like the old woman in the* Mendoza Codex *(right) drinking another bowlful. Leaves of the maguey supplied thorn needles and stringy fibers for weaving before the introduction of cotton. Thatch-topped corncrib in Morelos (above) also echoes Aztec times. Tapered wall funnels grain—and foils hungry rats.*

times people sold themselves or their children into bondage, but they could be redeemed later by repayment.

In urban areas, land was held communally by clans residing in their own districts and governed in local matters by a tribal council. Common laborers lived in one-room mud huts, craftsmen and merchants in adobe houses with rooftop flower gardens, nobles in multiroomed whitewashed stone palaces close to the main plaza.

Around the age of eight, most boys went to school to learn to be warriors and some to be priests. Novices were taught to read and write, make herbal medicines, interpret omens and the heavens, and reckon the calendar. Since they had no alphabet, they wrote by painting hieroglyphs on paper made from tree bark soaked in water and pounded into sheets. Stuck together in strips and folded like a screen, the sheets became a *codex*, or book, used to record lists of tribute, feast days, and history. Only a small number of these beautiful books have survived. Most of them come from the Mixtec area in Oaxaca, where the best book painters were to be found.

Aztec laws were strict and harsh. Drunkenness, except for people more than 52 years old, and certain sexual sins were capital crimes. A thief caught stealing in the market was judged by a court that sat there and, if found guilty, was stoned to death on the spot—and everyone was expected to participate. The death penalty extended even to the dress code. Peasants had to wear a plain cloak made from rough maguey fiber. Only the higher classes could wear cotton garments, and rank was distinguished by designs of flowers, birds, and geometric patterns. Warriors and nobles adorned themselves with ear, nose, and lip plugs of gold and precious stones.

Most resplendent of all was the emperor, who held the offices of war chief and high priest. By the time of Moctezuma II's ascension in 1502, the emperor presided over a court of almost Oriental splendor and despotism. No ordinary citizen could touch him or even look upon his person. Moctezuma had been a valiant soldier, but as emperor he became obsessed with religion. While his armies marched through the empire conquering new provinces and putting down rebellions, he spent his days in Tenochtitlán serving the gods. Strange omens, increasingly reported throughout the land, alarmed him; one year a comet appeared in the eastern sky.

Then in 1519 word came of Quetzalcóatl's return: Cortés had landed at Veracruz. Appalled at the fulfillment of a 500-year-old prophecy, Moctezuma tried magic and persuasion to make Quetzalcóatl depart. He invoked sorcerers and all the gods, and sent embassies to Cortés

Quiet waterways carry a farmer to his chinampa near Mexico City. The garden plots, built of lake-bed mud and held in place by trees and stakes, enabled the early Aztecs to enlarge their island home and create farmland from lakeshore shallows. Planted in corn and other crops, which helped anchor the soil, the compost-fertile chinampas yielded such abundant harvests they freed manpower for wars of conquest. The major chinampa zone followed a line of freshwater springs from Xochimilco (left) 12 miles east to Chalco.

142

with gifts and powerful religious emblems decorated with gold. The tactic, of course, had the reverse effect. Hungry for more gold, Cortés marched to the gates of Tenochtitlán, his troops augmented by thousands of Indian warriors from vengeful vassal states.

On November 8, Moctezuma went out to meet Cortés and welcomed him into the city, but the emperor's indulgence of the visiting god soon split the people into two parties, one for war and one for peace. As tensions grew, Cortés put Moctezuma under palace arrest for his own protection. A short time later the Spaniards, fearing an uprising during a rain dance in the plaza, attacked the performers and butchered nearly a thousand unarmed Indians.

The Spaniards had now precipitated the very thing they feared and soon found themselves besieged in the palace complex. They held out for a month, but with food running low they tried to steal out of the city. Halfway along the western causeway on the night of June 30, 1520—forever after known as Noche Triste, Night of Sorrow—they were discovered and set upon.

The Aztecs had removed the bridges over the canals that cut through the causeway, leaving watery gaps in the road to freedom. Some of the Spaniards escaped by clambering over the floating bodies of fallen comrades and making their way around the lakes to friendly territory. Some made a last stand atop the Great Temple but were overpowered and sacrificed to the gods. Spanish accounts say that it was there that Moctezuma received a mortal wound from a slingstone as he exhorted his subjects to honor their god. The Indians claim Moctezuma was strangled by the Spaniards.

The following year Cortés returned with more troops and even greater numbers of Indian allies. He cut the aqueduct and, after a two-month siege supported by a blockade with specially built boats, broke into the city, slaughtering thousands of people. The battle ended August 13, 1521, in the marketplace of Tlatelolco as Cuauhtemoc, the last Aztec king, stood in his war canoe offshore, lowered his weapons, and surrendered. The Aztec Empire came tumbling down that day, and with stone from the toppled structures the Spaniards began to build a new society. Out of the rubble would rise one of the largest metropolitan areas in the world, Mexico City, enfolding the few ruins of Tlatelolco in the Plaza of the Three Cultures.

The arrival of the conquistadores extinguished the last of the great pre-Columbian civilizations of Mesoamerica. But Mexico, inheriting not only its ruins but many of its ancient traditions, gave birth to a distinct new culture, a rich mixture of the Hispanic present and the Indian past.

The sun sets on Santa Cecilia Acatitlán Pyramid near Mexico City. Rebuilt from rubble according to clues provided by other monuments, it bears the most complete copy of an Aztec temple. Sculptures studding the elevated roof may represent Tenochtitlán's skull rack.

THE VARIED WORLD OF THE MEXICAN INDIAN

Amanda Parsons

The sacred Lenten ceremonies, I had been told, "set the Yaqui apart." They symbolize the territory, customs, and traditions which these Indians have fought for centuries to maintain.

To get to Yaqui lands, my Volkswagen bug and I pounded past bullying produce trucks with cargoes of lettuce, tomatoes, and strawberries from northwest Mexico's Sonoran Desert. Routing directions took me "to the end of the road," over the barren square that was the town's core, and on into the dank two rooms of the *comunila*, or town governor's office.

The bold black letters of the white sign projected from walls of luminescent blue: "Office of the Yaqui Tribe. Potam—Second Headquarters of the Eight Villages."

The town appeared little more than a saucer of dust. The spirit of the people who live here is another matter. These are people who endure heat and leaching salt to keep their communal lands productive. A bumper sticker on a white camper truck expressed it best: "I Am a Yaqui Indian . . . And Proud of It."

The governor's chandelier was a single light bulb. A political poster decorated one wall; next to it dangled a group photo of black-masked men with bare bronze torsos and legs cocooned with rattles. I recognized the figures as *pascolas*, ritual clowns who dance and joke at fiestas—and dream visions in sacred service to the supernatural.

The Yaqui are from northwest Mexico. With the Mayo, Tarahumara, Papago, Seri, Pima, Cora, Huichol, and Tepehuan, they share the heritage of native Americans in Arizona and New Mexico. Scholars designate this territory, which cuts across the United States-Mexican border, a "culture area." Customs, ceremonies, and indigenous languages know no national boundaries. The Mexican portion is even called "The Other Southwest," a land stretching east of the Gulf of California, across the desert, and up into the rugged Sierra Madre. This was the territory through which the legendary Chichimecs wandered on their way south to establish Aztec dominance in Mexico's other culture area, the land anthropologists call Mesoamerica.

Mesoamerica was dominated before the Spanish Conquest by

Streamers festoon the mask of a Lenten celebrant. Northwest Mexico's Mayo Indians fashion goatskin hoods to represent Judas—evil betrayer of Christ. Their cult combines Christianity with indigenous religion in a weeks-long passion play ending on Easter Sunday.

urbanized people. The land still bears their artifacts, and their descendants remain scattered across central Mexico in a potpourri of cultures—Nahua, Mixtec, Tarascan, Otomí, Huave, Tlapanec, Amuzgo, Trique. Though separated by custom, language, and geography, they are united by similar beliefs and subsistence habits.

Each community, each family, each individual is a unique blend of history: the grandeur and struggles of pre-Hispanic cultures; the heritage of the Spanish colonial system which struck its cultural blows with an uneven hand; the mix of Catholicism with ancient religions; and the interpretations of drama, dance, and art which can resist new styles stubbornly, adopt outside influences enthusiastically, or combine all into creative new forms of ritual and belief. This combining of old and new—syncretism to the anthropologist—was

In an Easter week procession (above), the image of the Virgin is led through the streets of a Mayo pueblo near Los Mochis, in Sinaloa State. As worshipers pray at the Stations of the Cross, masked Judases wearing leggings of moth cocoon rattles disrupt and mock the ceremony.

Representing chaos battling against order, they parody Mayo culture and mime sickness, sex, and body functions. A child kneels (opposite) during a symbolic funeral for Christ, in which the forces of mischief will try to steal ceremonial candles and flowers.

Rejoicing Judases run from church after the Gospel recounts the death of Christ. They topple crosses in temporary triumph. But when bells signal the resurrection, they return to be baptized, symbolizing the salvation of the wicked. Pascolas, who myth says were present at the birth of Christ, announce the good news (above). A Mayo deer dancer (right) joins the pascolas miming a deer hunt that shows their respect for the forces of nature and their love for God. "Those who sing deer" accompany the performers, playing a water drum and rasps and chanting sacred lyrics.

perfectly illustrated by the view from Potam's quiet town office. Beyond an empty expanse of plaza sat a boxy brick church. Surrounded by a cemetery bristling with shiny blue and white crosses, the church seemed an oasis of religion surrounded by the dead.

Startlingly, about 40 men marched single file across the square. They wore leather hoods molded into human caricature with pointed wooden noses, bugged eyes, and pouty lips. Enormous artificial ears were painted with colorful flowers of the *tlaloache,* a hallucinogenic plant. Black capes and garishly painted wooden swords completed the costumes. Sandaled feet churned up a billowing cloud of dry dirt so the figures seemed to float—an ethereal crowd suspended in the pink and gold light of late afternoon.

"Those are the *Chapayeka,*" said Pablo, the village secretary. "They represent the evil forces of Judas which take over our Yaqui town during Lent. They will be destroyed with the ascendance of the good forces of Jesus on Easter Sunday." On that holy day these same masks, which stared at me so unblinkingly, would be blown up by firecrackers, reduced to ash within four minutes. The characters are players in a passion play: a depiction of Christ's life, death, and resurrection given a Yaqui setting and a Yaqui interpretation. Neighboring Mayo practice a

With traditional colors and patterns of Tarahumara sashes, Indian artists using local dyes emblazoned the walls of their Catholic church in Cusarare, Chihuahua State (above). Pine torches blaze in a nighttime game of Tarahumara kickball (right). Known for their endurance as runners, the speedy athletes kick a wooden ball along marked courses through isolated mountain country. Competing pueblos wager beads, cloth, blankets, and animals. Women run similar races, propelling a wooden hoop with a stick.

similar reenactment, but with a more carnival-like atmosphere.

Pablo took me to the *capitán* of the Chapayeka. I wanted permission to photograph their ceremonies. After a long discussion in Yaqui, the captain said "No"—politely but firmly. "To protect our children, we do not want our most sacred rites reduced to images of curiosity. But come, participate with us. See, taste, hear, and feel what it is like."

With their help, I took part: I marched in the processions, wailed over Christ's death, danced in the streets with his resurrection, and ate the beef-and-bean soup served with thick wheat tortillas. Throughout the ceremonies, I listened to the steady rhythms of the tambour drums, the buzz of the rasps, the shrill tunes of the hand-carved harps and violins which all combine into Yaqui music.

Viviano, the pascola shaman who could "understand all things," tried to teach me to dance. He lent me a mask carved and painted with a large pink tongue, a cross on the forehead, and lizards crawling up the cheekbones. "All Yaqui are warriors," this man of visions and ironic humor said to me. "We have defeated all who have tried to conquer us. We have our own government, our own rules."

Not all cultures of Mexico have such strong identities. Some Indians feel defeated by mestizo Mexico, the combination of Indian and Spanish races which comprises the bulk of the population. Others thirst for modernization. They see it as an escape from poverty and prejudice. Roads and radios reach out to touch people in different ways. A truckload of pink plastic bowls can change the aesthetics, culinary habits, and economics of an entire region.

Several years ago, I lived among the Tlapanec Indians of the State of Guerrero. The same bureaucracy which governs the seaside resort of Acapulco also rules my subsistence-level former neighbors. The Tlapanec, however, by centuries of defeat and disruptive revolutions, had been pushed out of their lands and scattered over the all but impenetrable southern Sierra Madre mountain range.

They lead isolated lives, delicately balanced on the success or failure of crops. Women bear children and bury too many of them. Those who survive the tough first five years leave their mountain homes to attend school and "learn the Spanish language, the ways of Mexico." Sparks of joy came when we bathed communally in the streams and the women tried—unsuccessfully—to teach me to pound my clothes into cleanliness upon river stones.

The ancient remained. A mountain cave ceremony demanded animal sacrifices to a rain god whose bloody offerings were eerily illuminated by torchlight. A night-long wedding *(Continued on page 159)*

Tight coils of torote branches form a Seri basket (opposite). Small bands of Seri Indians used baskets to transport food gathered in the Sonoran Desert, until they settled in permanent villages less than 50 years ago. Designs on the baskets are related to those of ceremonial face-paintings—a custom now practiced only on special occasions, like the capture of a leatherneck turtle (left). Signs of good luck, the turtles are ritually painted and kept in a sanctuary, then released in the Gulf of California after a week-long fiesta.

Bright-colored yarn pressed into wax-faced wooden panels creates a Huichol yarn painting (left). Craftsman (right) uses centuries-old symbols taken from the complex Huichol religion to give meaning to the storytelling tableaux, whose brilliant outlined shapes mimic images seen by eaters of peyote, a hallucinogenic cactus. The Huichol, like the Tepehuan (below), walk far into the desert to gather the plant, which they say are the tracks of the sacred deer. Properly collected, it too is sacred, and essential in some religious rites. It is as deeply revered as corn itself.

A Tarascan fisherman (opposite) casting his net in Lake Pátzcuaro follows an old tradition. Even the name of his state, Michoacan, comes from an Aztec term meaning "the land of the fishers." Minnows (left) eye an uncertain future as the mile-and-a-half-high lake, suffering from pollution, yields dwindling supplies of its famous white fish and trout. Chinchoros—long collective nets—allow cooperative fishing (above) from canoes hollowed with ax and adz out of tree trunks. The new nets replace picturesque but inefficient one-man throw nets.

ceremony was directed by shamans who could have guided Aztec nobility through the same rites. Stone idols maintained their place in ritual. The old grimy ones were traded regularly for new shiny models—tourist copies put to sacred use. Yet the people want progress. They waited patiently for a road which finally came, inching its way over rockslides. They fought real and legal battles over the ownership of a few rows of corn and beans on communal lands. They learned to coexist with neighbors who speak Nahuatl and Mixtec. They embraced a Catholic mission and an Indian Institute coordinating center.

Recent Mexican government programs respect the variety of customs and ways of life of indigenous peoples. Health and family planning programs, for instance, incorporate traditional healers. Schools teach in native languages. Nationally sponsored agencies encourage and help market folk arts and crafts.

Indifferent to changes, gentle rhythms and symphonic smells provide the framework for daily Indian life all over Mexico. Men go to their fields, slashing and burning the old vegetation to provide nutrients for the new. Women tend the cooking fires. Balanced sturdily over the flames—on three rough stones—are the *comales*, the round clay griddles for toasting the pancake-like corn   *(Continued on page 166)*

Skilled coppersmiths long before the arrival of the Spanish, the people of Michoacan carry on a Tarascan art. At outdoor forges (left), often using scrap metal, craftsmen at the town of Santa Clara del Cobre make beautiful objects of hand-hammered copper.

TOTONACS

Raising a roof in time-honored fashion, Totonac Indians of Veracruz State gather materials from widely scattered locations. Except for a machete, they will use no modern tools. Vines (above) cut only during certain phases of the moon—for religious and practical reasons—will bind walls and timbers together. A durable red grass (right) will serve as roofing—and may last 30 years. Bamboolike tarro (opposite) will be split to build the house walls.

Up goes the framing (opposite), each component chosen for certain qualities. The corner posts—chihol logs that when dry can shatter a machete—may last a thousand years and are often handed down through generations. Softer, pliant woods serve as rafters and framing, and tabaquilla poles will form a rigid support for the thatching.

Workers use a machete (left) to notch a framing timber, a rock-weighted cord (above, left) as a plumb line, and special clay (above, right) from a nearby hill that, when mixed with chopped thatching, provides a durable adobe plaster.

To build such a house often takes more than a year, with the real building coming in occasional, nearly explosive cooperative endeavors. But this house, constructed especially for this book, took only four months of collecting and a few weeks to assemble.

House completed, a workman trims the thatch (above) and a Totonac family moves in. Benches, stools, a table, and a clay hearth for indoor cooking constitute the furnishings. Floor mats of palm provide sleeping accommodations.

Ancestors of these Indians greeted Hernán Cortés when he arrived in Mexico in 1519. As staunch allies in his campaign against the Aztecs, they escaped much of the violence that decimated other Indians. Recent archaeological evidence indicates that wandering peoples flourished in Veracruz as long as 80 centuries ago.

tortillas. Corn and chilies are ground into all-purpose meals and pastes, hypnotically pushed by the *mano,* or stone rolling pin, down the slightly angled rock *metate* on its prehistoric three-legged base. "Ay, señorita," a Nahua woman once said. "We make babies, we make blouses, and we make tortillas. We do not have time to figure out why we do these things and who we are."

And who are they? The answers emerge in the innumerable ways in which they express their customs and beliefs. The weaving of indigenous cloth, for instance, is an exploration into the consciousness of centuries. The skilled weaver deftly interlaces the precisely spun yarns, manipulating the warps and wefts, the shuttles and picks. Ancient designs become one with the cloth—diaphanous or thick depending on its eventual use. Artisans draw their colors from plants, or sea snails, or cactus mites, or even from the bright synthetics which many women now find as appealing as their ancestors found indigo. They re-create a fabric whose meanings may have been forgotten, but whose sense of "rightness" remains.

Each region produces its own distinctive pottery. A pot rises as a union of the clay and of the hands that shape or coil it. An indigenous pot curves upward into a lip whose shape has been perfect for countless generations for carrying water or boiling beans. The thickness of the porous unglazed clay keeps liquids cool or foods unscorched. The designs—with all their local expressions—flow. They tell stories, provide protection from evil, depict realistic scenes or confounding abstractions. A Huastec pot has symbols of birth, death, and afterlife. Zapotec blackware gets its color from a pre-Columbian firing technique. A Tlapanec bean pot seems only the most functional shape except for the handles carefully formed as stylized animals.

Cultural surprises pop up anywhere. I have driven down isolated mountain highways and through broiling towns—to all appearances barren. And as if from nowhere appeared piles of costumes, palm mats, pots, and the noise of intricate negotiations: an Indian market.

The rhythm of a week is punctuated by a parade of people and goods. Markets are the core of Indian economics. They are also a time for people to get together—to gossip, to exchange prized items, to learn about the world beyond their isolated settlements. Oaxaca City, Toluca, and Huauchinango are among the famous large markets in Mexico. But even small towns have their special plaza days.

During fiestas, markets overflow with festive foods. Wraps of warm tortillas guard gastronomic delights ranging from steamed squash blossoms—"a banquet in a taco"—to meats *(Continued on page 172)*

Feather-tipped tinsel and paper crests, imitating that of the sacred quetzal, sway atop dancers' heads in the Nahua town of Cuetzalan, Puebla. Natives believe both bird and dance originated there, the meaning of the dance possibly rooted in religion and astronomy.

168

To the haunting sounds of a three-note reed flute and a tiny, double-headed drum (above), Totonac voladores, or fliers, perform their rituals 100 feet above the ground. Hired performers, they prepare for a flight atop a pole erected at Veracruz's ancient site of El Tajín (right). First their leader dances and plays to the four cardinal compass points in an orientation reminiscent of Aztec rituals. Then, in elegant spirals, the fliers swoop downward on unwinding ropes, each completing 13 revolutions for a total of 52—the number of years in the Aztec "century."

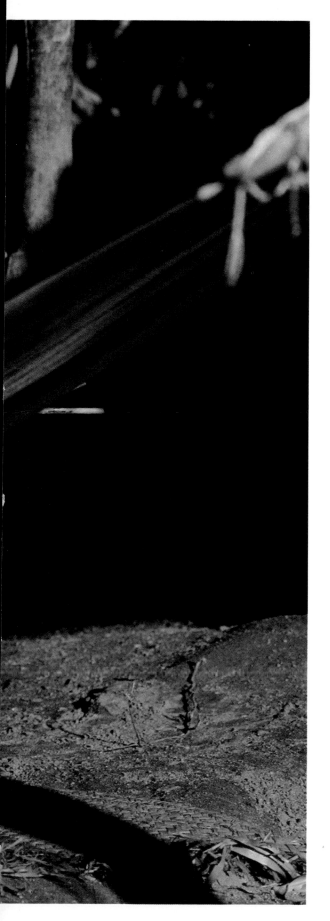

Sea snails (left) pried off the rocks of Oaxaca's Pacific coast secrete a rare purple dye woven into this Mixtec woman's skirt. Amuzgo and Tequistlatec Chontal Indians scour the beach for Murex purpura; they tease its clear juices onto hand-spun cotton thread. Exposed to the sun, the dye evolves into yellow, chartreuse, and finally the famous Tyrian purple. Cloth using this dye is woven on backstrap looms kept taut by body pressure. The murex-dyed piece becomes an heirloom, its permanent fishy smell a hallmark of authenticity.

rendered electric by accompanying hot peppers. In addition to staples of corn, beans, squashes, chilies, and turkeys which the Spanish found when they arrived, there are a range of regional delights for the discriminating: amaranth cakes, corn fungus, algae, waterfly-egg patties prepared with a nopal cactus relish, fat live ants, toasted grasshoppers, armadillo prepared in a spicy *mole* sauce of chili and chocolate by coastal Mixtec matrons, tamales wrapped in banana leaves by Zapotec women, and sweet Lake Pátzcuaro white fish fried crisp and served with a spicy soup named for the Tarascans who fish the lake.

Herbalists sell cures for whatever ails the body. A red flower shaped like a hand is said to cure pains of the heart. Another dried plant controlled fertility before any birth control pills. And *curanderos* practice time-honored methods for relieving sicknesses caused by "soul loss" or an "imbalance of hot and cold" in the blood.

Another aid to the infirm is a pilgrimage. A church, cave, or sacred tree can pound with the sudden fervor of dances or flagellations—or vibrate with awe and reverence. Most shrines were also sacred sites for gods of pre-Hispanic religions. The site of Mexico City's Basilica of Guadalupe, for instance, was the home of Tonantzin, an Aztec earth goddess. Every December 12, the day of the miracle of Guadalupe, thousands make the pilgrimage, some on their knees as a special penance. Penitents line up to view the cape of Juan Diego, the Nahua youth visited in 1531 by the Virgin, who left her image on the garment.

Chalma, a town west of Mexico City, was the ancient abode of cave gods. Every Sunday it also is the destination of pilgrims, those who revere "the black Christ who makes so many miracles." The sick dig pebbles from the cave walls and press them against their breasts to prevent heart attacks. Others bathe in the streams. Penitents celebrate the fulfillment of their promises by drinking *pulque,* the fermented juice of the maguey plant that was the Aztecs' drink of the gods.

A more general celebration is death. Throughout Mexico, Indians celebrate the Day of the Dead, November 2. The living hold graveyard picnics for their "little dead ones." It is not a tribute to the macabre, but an exaltation of life. Death is seen as that which defines vitality. Mexico City candymakers manufacture sugar skulls inscribed with the names of loved ones. Rural people line paths with flower petals to guide departed ancestors to their specially prepared altars. Favorite foods are placed on grave sites along with marigolds so that those who return can savor the essence of former earthly delights. This is an old custom, perhaps rooted in pre-Hispanic human sacrifice. That grisly ritual was essential to the Aztecs because it appeased the gods and brought life to the crops. Now the ancient customs combine with the Catholic All Saints' Day—another example of syncretism.

I am reminded again of the depth of traditions in this fascinating country. The indigenous cultures are not remnants of dead and dying civilizations. They are examples of living social systems, kept vital by faith in their heritages and a dynamic ability to adapt and change. Nothing in Mexico ever dies forever. It returns to bring new life.

CARIBBEAN

The Caribbean has long been a cultural crossroads of the New World—a million-square-mile area bounded by Central America and northern South America and hemmed in by an arc of hundreds of tropical islands. Here, wave after wave of settlers have met and mingled—and often warred. Here, too, is the meeting place of continents, linked by a narrow land bridge. Along this corridor came Ice Age hunters and, later, ancient traders from the north seeking gold, blue-green jade, and other treasures. Theirs were relatively sophisticated societies—growers of corn who lived in densely populated communities and traded extensively, bringing their gods, their calendar, their art styles.

But natives of the Caribbean were, by and large, of South American cultural ancestry. Most of them lived in small- to medium-size villages located near the water. They fished, planted root and tuber crops and some grains, built canoes, and slept in hammocks. Arawak-speaking people lived on the larger Caribbean islands, Carib speakers on the smaller isles. Both inhabited the northern coast of South America.

At the end of the 15th century, when the world of the Caribbean Indian was to become the New World of the European, the islands and the mainland rim around this sea were inhabited by a great diversity of people—Indians who maintained cultural levels ranging from nomadic hunter and gatherer to sophisticated urbanite. The Tairona of northern Colombia, for example, grew high-yield crops to support a network of politically independent towns. Tales of Tairona graves brimming with gold attracted the attention of Spanish treasure seekers.

The first confrontations between western Europeans and native Americans took place on the islands of the Caribbean—with disastrous consequences for the Indians. By 1548, less than 60 years after Columbus's arrival, scarcely 500 Arawak could be counted on Hispaniola. One chronicler estimated that more than three million Indians had died there between 1494 and 1508—victims of disease, forced labor, and armed aggression. The Indians of coastal South and Central America fared somewhat better, chiefly because the terrain made them more difficult to reach. So it was that the Caribbean, heart of Spain's New World empire, became once again a crossroads of cultural upheaval.

Above: Taino wooden figure with shell inlay, Jamaica, A.D. 1500. Opposite: Cuna *mola* (layered cloth panel), Panama.

CROSSROADS CULTURES

Bernard Nietschmann

Scowl of gold glimmers through the ages on a four-inch Tairona pendant—perhaps a warrior or deity. "When they went to war," wrote a 16th-century Spanish chronicler, "they wore crowns, patens on their chests, and beautiful feathers and many other jewels."

From far out over the Atlantic come the winds—the northeast trades—sweeping across the long chain of islands of the Caribbean. Brisk, warm, laden with moisture, the winds blow across the Bahamas and San Salvador, where Columbus first landed and where the Lucayo Indians once lived. Deflected over island barriers, the winds release their moisture on the windward slopes, then pass on to leeward, and across the open sea toward the distant shores of South and Central America.

Windward and leeward: These are the dominant directions of the Caribbean; the Indians who lived here knew it and, as farmers and fishermen, they adapted their livelihoods to it.

Long before Columbus, Indians from South America—and perhaps North and Central America—colonized the islands, as well as the isthmus that links the two continents. These earliest people, in places known as the Ciboney, may have reached Hispaniola and Cuba as early as 3000 B.C. They lived close to water; spent their days fishing, hunting, and gathering; and used tools made of stone, bone, wood, and shell.

A second wave of migrants, Arawak-speaking Indians from South America, began island-hopping along the Caribbean chain around the time of Christ. By Columbus's day they had reached as far north as the Bahamas and occupied much of the Greater Antilles, displacing most of the primitive hunter-gatherers who had preceded them. These Island Arawak, called "Indians" by Columbus, were skilled farmers, sailors, and potters. They were a generally peaceful people with a highly developed social structure. A *cacique*, or hereditary chief, ruled each province. Beneath him were regional subchiefs, village headmen, nobles, commoners, and slaves—mostly prisoners taken in raids.

The Island Arawak lived in scattered villages that numbered several hundred inhabitants. Their houses, made of wood and thatched with palm and straw, had hard-packed dirt floors. Upper classes lived in rectangular dwellings, the lower classes in round ones. Furniture included wooden stools and *hamaca*—hammocks made of woven cotton.

Many villages had ball courts lined with stones in which two teams of up to 30 players sought to keep a rubberlike ball in the air without using

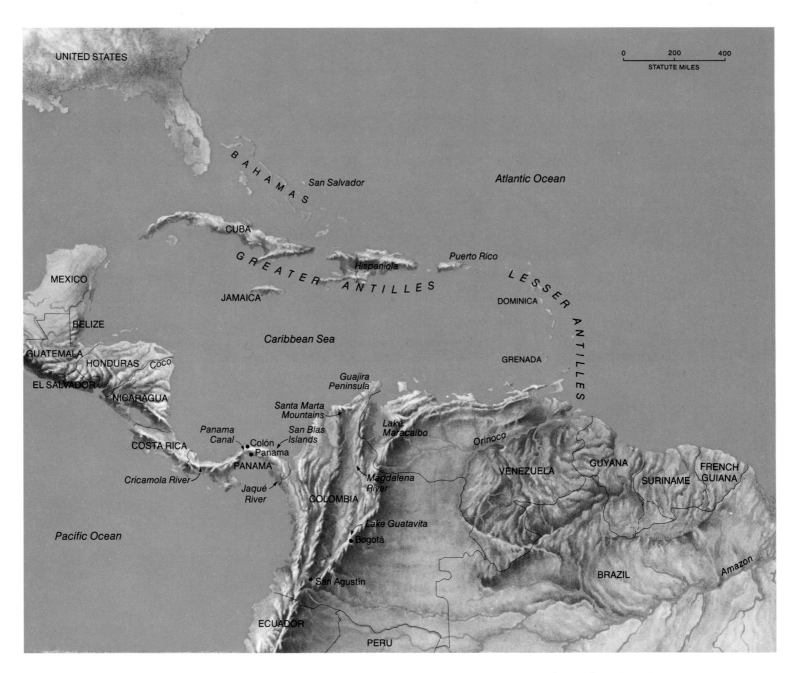

UNITED STATES

0   200   400
STATUTE MILES

B A H A M A S

San Salvador

Atlantic Ocean

CUBA

G R E A T E R   A N T I L L E S

Hispaniola

Puerto Rico

L E S S E R   A N T I L L E S

MEXICO

JAMAICA

DOMINICA

BELIZE

Caribbean Sea

GUATEMALA

HONDURAS   Coco

GRENADA

EL SALVADOR

Guajira
Peninsula

NICARAGUA

Santa Marta
Mountains

Lake
Maracaibo

Panama
Canal

San Blas
Islands

Orinoco

COSTA RICA

Colón
Panama

GUYANA

PANAMA

VENEZUELA

SURINAME

FRENCH
GUIANA

Cricamola River

Jaqué
River

Magdalena
River

COLOMBIA

Pacific Ocean

Lake Guatavita

Bogotá

BRAZIL

Amazon

San Agustín

ECUADOR

PERU

The great bowl of the Caribbean,
clamped vise-like between the jaws of
two continents, covers an area of more
than a million square miles. Most of it is
tropical, with dense rain forests and up
to 350 inches of rain a year on the island
of Dominica. Other parts are nearly
desert dry—less than 30 inches of rain
on the Guajira Peninsula north of Lake
Maracaibo. The terrain is equally
varied, ranging from a few feet above
sea level to nearly 19,000 feet in the
mountains of Santa Marta along the
coast of northern Colombia.

hands or feet. A grounded ball scored a point for the opposing side.

Supernatural forces were propitiated through anthropomorphic idols, called *zemis,* carved from wood, rock, and other materials. The zemis, regarded as intermediaries with the supernatural world, were believed to exercise power and influence over people.

The Island Arawak were exceedingly sophisticated farmers. Many of their crops were grown on fields heaped with little mounds—which reduced erosion and retained moisture. The mounds were fertilized with wood ash, urine, and plant wastes, and in dry areas extensive canal systems brought water to the fields. A 16th-century Spanish chronicler noted admiringly that the Indians of one particularly arid province "made many and fine irrigation ditches that were needed to water their conucos or properties in all the surroundings of their city, which lies in a great plain." The Arawak grew manioc as their dietary staple, sweet potatoes, arrowroot, peanuts, many root and tuber crops, and small quantities of corn, beans, and squash. They also cultivated cotton, which was used for cordage and cloth; tobacco, from which they made cigars and snuff; calabashes, which provided containers; peppers for seasoning; and, on Puerto Rico, pineapples, which were used as trade goods with other islands.

The sea provided the Arawak with protein, although they also hunted rodents, lizards, and birds. Fish were caught with nets, hooks and lines, spears, and traps. Sea turtles and manatees were harpooned. Along the south coast of Cuba the Arawak used suckerfish tied to thin lines to locate submerged turtles. They also drove fish into seaside enclosures and kept them penned until needed. The Arawak made seagoing dugouts from cedar and cottonwood trees. Some were very large and were propelled by as many as 50 paddlers.

Soon after his arrival in the New World, Columbus began to hear reports of yet another group of natives—the ferocious Carib, reputedly eaters of human flesh from whose name derives "cannibal." The aggressive Carib had begun invading the islands only a few centuries earlier, but already they had conquered most of the Lesser Antilles from the Island Arawak, killing the men and carrying off the women.

Island Carib, unlike the Arawak, maintained an essentially classless society. They had no strong regional chiefs. War chiefs led raids, but when the fighting was over, their power to lead ended.

Carib villages were small and usually located near a stream. After the Europeans arrived, most settlements were relocated to the windward sides of the islands, near steep slopes and rough waters that offered protection from surprise attacks. A Dominican friar who lived among

Vibrant hues of the tropics reflect in a parrot's plumage and (overleaf) in a sunrise along the windward shores of Dominica. Indians of the Caribbean often kept the birds as pets and embellished themselves with feathers during dances and ceremonies.

182

the Carib during the 1600s provided the best early description of their life: "They are divided into families, and these families are composed of several households that live together and form sorts of hamlets under the head of the family."

Their houses, he wrote, were round, thatched with palm fronds, very dark inside, with but a small fire or small doorway for light. In the center of the village stood the men's house, an oval structure 60 to 90 feet long and with room for about 120 men. The women lived apart in huts surrounding the men's house and were responsible for cooking, planting and cultivating, and making cotton cordage and pottery.

Island Carib practiced slash-and-burn agriculture. The men carved out clearings in the forest and set fire to them; women and children planted the cleared plots with manioc, sweet potatoes, corn, beans, pineapples, and peppers. Tobacco was grown to smoke, and the Carib also brewed a potent alcoholic beverage—a mash made from fermented manioc, sweet potatoes, and pineapples.

The Carib spiced their dishes with a hot-pepper sauce made from fish bones, red peppers, manioc juice, and crab chunks. Crabs were a favorite food and were often taken at night by torchlight. Spiny lobsters were caught by divers weighted with rocks, and fish were landed with hooks, arrows, spears, and poisons. Turtles were hunted at sea.

The Carib were expert seafarers and canoe builders. They constructed 20-foot fishing craft and 35- to 40-foot seagoing dugouts that were better designed and more seaworthy than those built by the Arawak. Planks fitted and lashed to the hollowed-log hull gave it additional freeboard in heavy weather. Finely shaped paddles sanded smooth with sharkskin and coral propelled the craft.

But neither peaceable Arawak nor fighting Carib were long able to withstand the onslaughts of European colonization. Columbus himself set the pattern for their exploitation—and eventual extermination—when he contemptuously described the Arawak as "without arms, all naked, and without skill at arms and great cowards." Thus, he reported, "they are good to be ordered about, to be made to work, plant, and do whatever is wanted, to build towns and be taught to go clothed."

Spanish treatment of the Island Arawak was harsh. Forced to become slave laborers, they died off rapidly. Introduced livestock soon overran Arawak fields. Diseases relatively harmless to the white man became mass killers of indigenous people. Hispaniola, which had more than a million Indians when Columbus arrived, had only 60,000 left less than two decades later. By 1513 there were no more Lucayo Indians in the Bahamas—they had been seized and removed en masse to work for the

Riddle of a lost tribe: Fangs bared, a demonic jaguar-man devours a victim—presumably a human. More than 300 of these and similar monuments have been found in the hills of Colombia's San Agustín district. Little is known about the Indians who carved these effigies—not even their tribal name. The oldest figures date back some 1,500 years and, although discovered by the Spanish in the 1750s, have been systematically studied only recently.

The family (opposite) represents an 18th-century artist's view of the Carib.

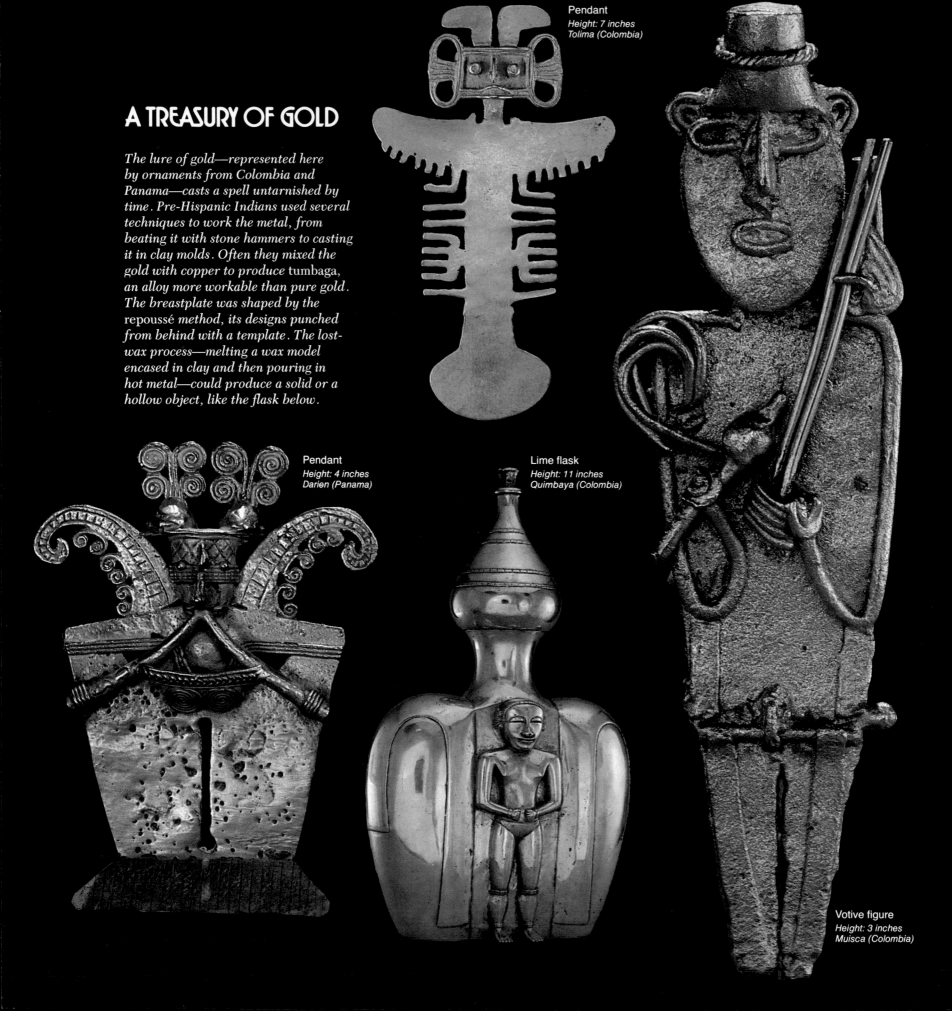

A TREASURY OF GOLD

The lure of gold—represented here by ornaments from Colombia and Panama—casts a spell untarnished by time. Pre-Hispanic Indians used several techniques to work the metal, from beating it with stone hammers to casting it in clay molds. Often they mixed the gold with copper to produce tumbaga, *an alloy more workable than pure gold. The breastplate was shaped by the repoussé method, its designs punched from behind with a template. The lost-wax process—melting a wax model encased in clay and then pouring in hot metal—could produce a solid or a hollow object, like the flask below.*

Pendant
Height: 7 inches
Tolima (Colombia)

Pendant
Height: 4 inches
Darien (Panama)

Lime flask
Height: 11 inches
Quimbaya (Colombia)

Votive figure
Height: 3 inches
Muisca (Colombia)

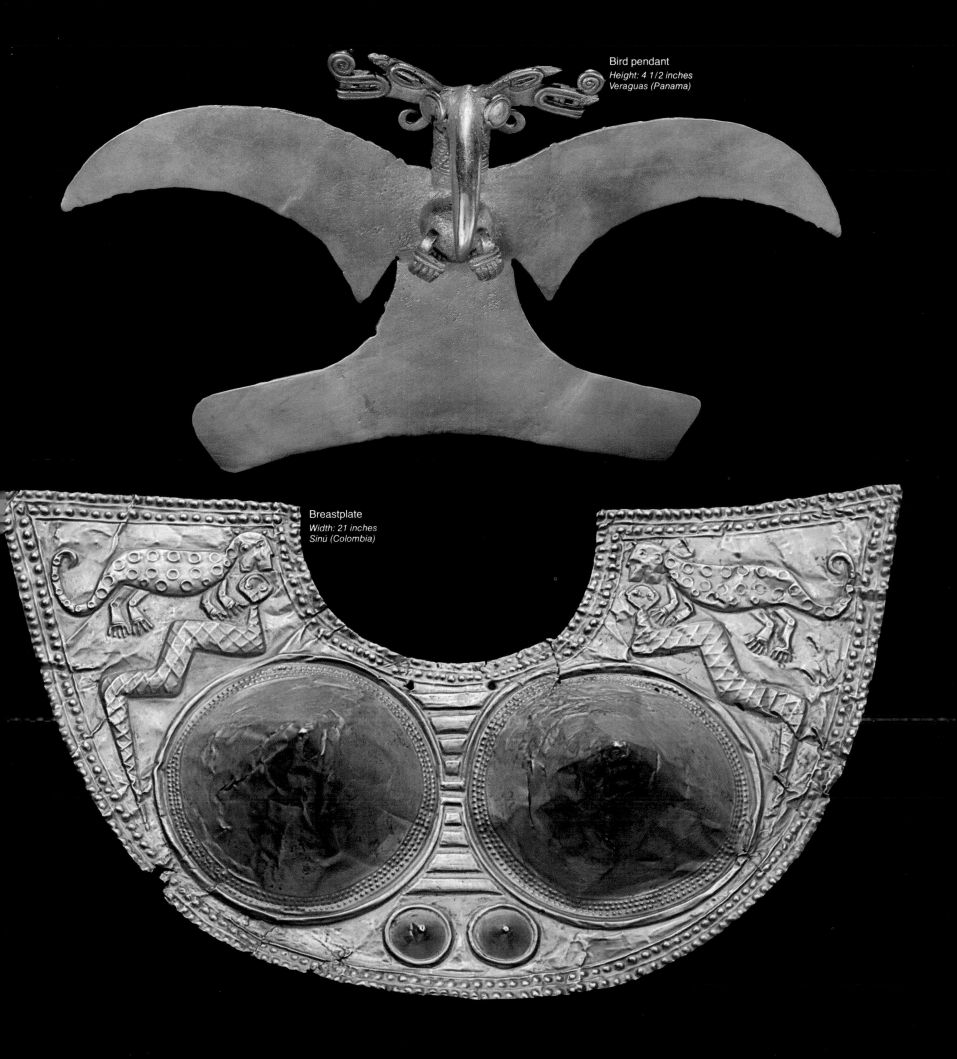

Bird pendant
Height: 4 1/2 inches
Veraguas (Panama)

Breastplate
Width: 21 inches
Sinú (Colombia)

Spanish hacienda owners as gold miners and plantation hands.

The Island Carib, although they stiffly resisted English, French, and Dutch settlement of the Lesser Antilles during the 17th century, fared little better. As one French traveler put it in 1700, "there are no people in the world so jealous of their liberty, or who resent more the smallest check to their freedom." And on Grenada in 1650, the last of that island's Carib hurled themselves into the sea from a cliff rather than endure capture by pursuing French soldiers.

Today only remnants of these Indians linger in the eastern Caribbean—a few thousand Cubans of Arawak descent, about 2,500 Carib on a reservation in Dominica, and about 90,000 Black Carib scattered along the coast from Belize to Nicaragua. All have intermarried with other races or ethnic groups, although some of them retain vestiges of the life-styles followed by their Indian ancestors.

But not all Indians of the Caribbean region suffered irreparably from contact with Europeans. Some actually prospered. Most of the Central American coastline had little to attract the Spanish newcomers, who concentrated instead on the Panama area for slaves and gold. Heavy rains, coastal swamps, poor harbors, and rough, reef-filled offshore waters discouraged settlement. *(Continued on page 192)*

Source of the legends of El Dorado— The Golden Man—Lake Guatavita shimmers beneath a lowering sky near Bogotá, Colombia. Into these waters, it was said, Muisca Indians threw heaps of gold and emeralds to celebrate the coronation of each new ruler. Rumors of these fabulous events began to circulate in the 1540s, soon after the conquistadores overran the area. The king himself, clad only in fine gold dust (above), took part in the ceremonies. Attempts to drain the lake produced the notch in its lip—and not much else.

Gold-adorned Tairona Indians of Colombia's Santa Marta Mountains welcome traders from the coast in this idealized re-creation of a little-known culture. With the more simply dressed coastal people, the Tairona bartered gilded copper jewelry, cotton blankets, and parrot feathers for salt and fish. In exchange for emeralds mined by Chibchan tribes to the south, they gave highly polished beads of carnelian, agate, and quartz.

Clever engineers as well as merchants, the Tairona mastered their jungle environment and its long rainy season by constructing circular terraces of stone with intricate drainage systems. On the terraces they built houses similar to those of the Kogi, a modern Santa Marta tribe, and planted crops that included corn, manioc, and potatoes.

Priests, warriors, and artisans mingled in a tight network of towns linked by stone stairways, roads, and bridges, and inhabited by nearly 300,000 people. Though socially cohesive, the towns maintained political autonomy, an independence that retarded Spanish incursions until the early 1600s, when the last Tairona chiefs were captured and their cities burned.

With spirited play, Taino Indians of
Puerto Rico strive to keep a rubber ball
in the air without using hands or feet.
Men and women, boys and girls take
part in this Caribbean version of pelota,
a ball game known from South America
to the southwestern United States.
Although the ball may strike the ground,
it must be kept in motion within the
rectangular batey, or ball court, here
bordered by stone slabs. Spectators
cheer their favorites during the festive
event. Onlookers often wagered prized
possessions on the play of the ball, and
important decisions sometimes hinged
on the outcome of the game. Players
went naked, except for married women,
who wore short skirts. Some painted
their bodies or decorated themselves
with stamped designs. One man,
perhaps a principal player, uses a
wooden hip ring to help carom the
heavy ball into the air.

The Miskito Indians of eastern Nicaragua and Honduras flourished partly because of their alliance with English, French, and Dutch pirates. The pirates taught the Indians how to use firearms and, in return, the Miskito provisioned their ships and provided pilots and recruits for raids against the Spanish.

John Esquemeling, a 17th-century surgeon-pirate who sailed with British buccaneer Henry Morgan, wrote of the Miskito: "Through frequent converse of these Indians with the pirates, they sometimes go to sea with them, and remain with them whole years, without returning home; so that many of them can speak English and French, and some of the pirates their Indian language. Being very dexterous at their javelins, they are useful to the pirates in victualling their ships. . . . For one of these Indians is alone able to victual a vessel of one hundred men." Another freebooter, Raveneau de Lussan, observed of their seafaring skills: "These men are the boldest in the world in braving the perils of the sea . . . in small boats that the average sailor would scorn; in these they remain three or four days at a stretch, as unconcerned, despite the weather, as if they were part of the boat."

Today's Miskito, numbering about 70,000 people, inhabit a 400-mile stretch of the coast and another 300 miles up the Coco River. The coastal Miskito of Nicaragua obtain much of their food from the water. Fish are taken with hook and line, spear and harpoon; green turtles are harpooned and netted at sea; and manatees are hunted in the lagoons. Canoes carry hunters along creeks into the forest in search of land animals such as white-tailed deer and peccary. Crops are grown in small fields near waterways where canoes can be used for transport.

To grow their crops, the Miskito clear land in the forest. The cut vegetation is allowed to dry for several weeks before burning. Crops are then planted in the ash-fertilized fields. Like most tropical farmers, the Indians plant throughout the year, leaving their food undisturbed in the ground or on trees until it is needed. Manioc, bananas, plantains, and coconuts make up the bulk of their crops, and can be harvested all year round. Rice, the only seasonal crop of the coastal Miskito, is sold for cash and is also a major staple, as are beans.

Manioc and the meat of the green sea turtle are among the staples of coastal Miskito diet. Manioc roots, taken fresh from the fields, are peeled and boiled. The turtle meat is cut into cubes and cooked in its own fat and coconut oil. Coconuts provide the Miskito living along the coast with valuable products. Husks are dried and used as fuel. Young, green "jelly" coconuts yield a refreshing beverage and a delicious soft meat. Mature nuts have a thick *(Continued on page 200)*

Flippers thrashing, a captured sea turtle is hauled aboard a Miskito boat off the coast of Nicaragua. A good haul will yield three or four turtles before the end of the day—meat enough to last the village several days. A Guaymí child (opposite) peers from the doorway of his *thatched house near the Cricamola River in Panama. Elevated dwellings like these, made accessible by log ladders, are often built in marshy areas. Seldom repaired, such a house may last five years before the family moves out and rebuilds.*

ISLAND CUNA

Marks of beauty—a nose ring and stripe drawn with dye made from the jagua plant—adorn the face of a Cuna maiden. Headscarf and close-cropped hair proclaim her passage from girlhood to womanhood after arduous ceremonies that include four days of cold baths and, in former times, burial up to the shoulders in the ground. The Cuna reckon descent from the mother, reserving such rites for girls only. Marriages are arranged by the parents. At the proper moment (in one version), the groom is seized and dumped into the bride's hammock. If he stays, the wedding is on; if not, he flees.

Encrusted with Cuna dwellings, Big Orange Island rises from the reefs of Mandinga Bay. Some 900 people live here—using every inch of space.

Scenes of Cuna life: Constraints of
fashion—beaded arm and leg
wrappings—occupy two belles seated
before a bamboo house on Korbiski
Island. Arranging the beads into precise
geometric patterns, an exacting task,
may take them most of the morning.

Flanked by two elders, a village chief
on Mulatupu Island conducts a town
meeting. Such sessions take place daily
on many islands, and usually include
women and children. A council headed
by a chief presides over each Cuna
island or village. Sessions often begin
with a chanted recitation of tribal lore

and history. A "singing chief,"
sometimes assisted by subchiefs,
performs the office. The remainder of
the meeting is concerned with more
mundane pursuits—perhaps settling a
quarrel between families, discussing
how to improve mail service, or
planning a forthcoming ceremony.

Illness among the Cuna is treated by a
shaman, a healer trained in herbal
medicine who, according to Cuna belief,
has the ability to communicate with the
spirit world. He may use the wooden
figures called uchus (left) to summon a
healing spirit to his patient.

Clad in molas and wrap skirts, Cuna
women engage in dockside barter with
an itinerant Colombian trader. Vessels
such as this form a linchpin of Cuna
economy, bringing supplies and cash to
exchange for coconuts—and providing
contact with the outside world.

The multilayered mola, here deftly cut
and stitched into a sun pattern, may
require hundreds of hours of work.
Girls—and some albino boys—learn the
art as young children. The cloth panels,
a colorful outgrowth of body painting
and tattooing, have also become an
important cash source in recent years.

200

meat from which is extracted coconut milk and cream. The Miskito also process oil from coconuts. "Drop nuts" rich in oil are preferred, but coconuts are also picked from the tree by a climber with a bark rope looped around his ankles. With three well-placed slashes, a machete-wielding Miskito can husk a coconut in less than 10 seconds. The husks are stacked to dry and the nuts are carried to the village—often a hike of five or six miles with a 70-pound load.

Women of the village extract the oil—a laborious process that requires eight to ten hours of work per gallon. The hard coconut shell is chipped off and pieces of meat are shredded on a grater made from a large tin can with nail holes punched in it. The meat is then mixed with water, squeezed, and filtered through burlap into a large metal drum. The first filtering produces coconut cream; the second yields coconut

milk, some of which is saved for cooking. The meat left over, called trash, is fed to the village pigs and chickens.

Meanwhile, a coconut-husk fire glows under the drum. As the mixture inside the drum heats, oil rises to the surface and is ladled off—often into large plastic bleach bottles washed up on the shore.

The Miskito are renowned builders of dugout canoes. Those who live inland build a special craft called a *pitpan* that is extremely maneuverable in river shoals and rapids. Coastal Indians build a seagoing dugout called a *dori*. By far the most graceful and painstakingly built canoes are those used for hunting sea turtles. About 20 feet long, a turtle dori carries two men—"captain" and "striker"—far to sea in all kinds of weather. The best canoes are made from mahogany logs, but other kinds of wood are also acceptable. A suitable tree close to the water is felled. The log is cut roughly to size and burned and dug out with ax, hatchet, and adz. The rough-cut canoe is then floated to the village where it will be worked on for about three months.

The hull is carefully shaped with hatchet and adz. Holes bored into the hull to gauge thicknesses are plugged with cedar. To improve stability and handling, the hull is flared by filling it with water and wedging the sides apart with wooden sticks pounded down every day for a week or so. Mangrove-root ribs are fitted, the sides are built up with hand-hewn cedar planks sawn so finely they need no caulking, and stem and keel pieces are attached. Masts, booms, seats, and other fixtures are added and, finally, nail holes are filled with a putty made by mixing paint with the ash from burned termite nests. Six-foot paddles shaped from mahogany planks serve to steer the boat when under sail and are also used to propel it through the surf.

Most sailing canoes have a dozen different woods, each selected for certain characteristics. Such craft can carry heavy loads and are virtually unsinkable. If they swamp or capsize, all that has to be done is to bail them out. If an oversize turtle is caught, the canoe is submerged beneath it and bailed until it comes up with the turtle inside.

No one is more adept at catching sea turtles than the coastal Miskito. These large marine herbivores, weighing up to 400 pounds, graze on the sea grasses that grow in the shallow waters off eastern Nicaragua. But their movements from one pasture to another depend on a host of variables such as wind and current, condition of the pastures, time of day and night, seasonal weather shifts, and migration routes to a distant nesting beach in Costa Rica. Generations of hunting experience and acute observation equip the Miskito to determine where they will be momentarily plentiful—most of the time.

Cuna women from a mainland settlement ply the Mandinga River, hoping to sell or trade their wares to island-dwellers at the river's mouth.

Scooping corn from a canoe, a Chocó girl from the forests of Panama relies on the wind to help winnow kernels from *debris. A necklace made from coins, and designs drawn with dye adorn her upper body and arms. Today about 5,000 Chocó live in Panama, several hundred of them along the Jaqué River in Darién Province. They are known for their baskets and carved animal figurines.*

Goats of the Guajiro tribe of northern Colombia drink their fill at an oasis scooped by government bulldozers. The Guajiro, a seminomadic tribe numbering some 50,000 people, inhabit an arid peninsula that juts into the Caribbean. Chiefly herders of goats, they move from water hole to water hole, living in cactus-roofed houses with few walls. Men wear pants and shirts; women don a long-sleeved gown called a manta and sometimes paint exposed skin to ward off the sun. Emerging from a goat corral, the woman (far right) will close off its entry with sticks.

The Miskito catch turtles either with nets or by harpooning them. Set over coral reefs where the reptiles retire for the night, the anchored nets entangle them when they come up to breathe. Harpooning the turtles requires considerably more skill. Captain and striker furl the sail and unstep the mast as they approach a likely turtling ground. Catching sight of their prey, a turtle that has risen to breathe, they paddle quickly toward it. Now the striker rises and, with canoe bobbing up to a hundred feet away, hurls his harpoon in a high, arcing trajectory. If his aim is true, the harpoon will fall almost vertically, piercing the edge of the shell. Thrown too flat, it would glance harmlessly off the shell; too hard, it would penetrate too deeply. Thrown to hit the middle of the shell, it might kill the animal. The object, of course, is to capture the turtle with minimum damage so that it can be kept alive until needed.

Several turtle-processing plants operated for about a decade in eastern Nicaragua, buying all the green turtles the Miskito could supply. But commercial exploitation soon brought about a rapid decline in the turtle population and, in 1977, forced a halt to such activities. Today the Miskito continue to plant and fish and hunt in the forests and at sea, but the shortage of money—and soaring prices for imported goods—makes them feel poor in what is, essentially, an environment rich in natural resources.

The Caribbean area of Central America is home to many other Indians, including the Paya of Honduras, the Sumo and Rama of Nicaragua, the Bribri and Térraba of Costa Rica, and the Guaymí, Chocó, and Cuna of Panama. Of these and other people, the San Blas Cuna are perhaps the most remarkable for their cultural persistence.

Today's San Blas, one of four Cuna groups, are descendants of Indians known collectively to Spanish conquerors as Darién Indians. Like other indigenous people, they were killed and enslaved by the thousands during the 16th century. But the forebears of the Cuna survived by retreating ever deeper into the rain forests of what is today Panama and, like the Miskito, by forming alliances with pirates and buccaneers. One of the earliest descriptions of the Cuna comes from Lionel Wafer, a pirate forced to recuperate among them after a gunpowder accident burned his leg. "The *Indians* undertook to cure me," he wrote, "and apply'd to my Knee some Herbs, which they first chew'd in their Mouths to the consistency of a Paste. . . . This proved so effectual, that in about 20 Days . . . I was perfectly cured."

According to Wafer, the Cuna had chiefs, a stratified society, and lived in villages with thatched houses. The men wore a gold plate in their nose, the women a gold ring. Both sexes wore a long cotton garment on ceremonial occasions. They planted bananas, plantains, and corn, and they hunted. When Wafer rejoined his crew after several months, his friends at first did not recognize him: naked, painted with plant juices, and wearing a large gold plate in his nose.

Trade with Europeans, beginning as early as 1600, gradually attracted a growing number of Cuna to the San Blas coast. Gold miners, pirates, and colonists from short-lived French and Scottish settlements all traded with them. Indians moving to the coast located their villages on rivers near the sea. Later, British and American traders began to exchange manufactured goods for coconuts and turtle shell. The Cuna planted coconut trees along the mainland shores and on some of the outlying islands. By 1850 they began to move onto the islands, leaving the swampy, mosquito-ridden mainland.

Although the Indians maintained trade, they strictly limited outside contact and foreign influence. The intrusion into their area of Afro-American creoles and Panamanian police early this century led to uprisings and bloodshed—until laws passed in the 1930s guaranteed the Cuna their traditional local autonomy.

Today the San Blas area encompasses more than 375 low-lying coral islands within sight of mainland mountains that rise abruptly from a narrow coastal plain. Pinched between a coral barrier reef and the cordillera, the San Blas Cuna have spread east and west to occupy some 50 islands and eight mainland settlements from the Panama Canal to the border with Colombia.

Their population numbers more than 25,000 people. The islands are so small and so densely inhabited that the villages literally cover nearly every inch of available land. On some of the islands living space has been increased by piling lumps of coral and other landfill into the sea. Soil brought from the mainland by dugout canoe enables dooryard gardens to flourish on the otherwise nutrient-poor islands. Small but carefully tended, these miniature gardens bloom with medicinal and ornamental flowers and shrubs, spice plants—even fruit trees. Cuna villages are tidy and well maintained. The ground around each house is swept daily to keep it free of grass, weeds, and litter of any kind. Individual houses, communal areas, and the islands themselves are neatly groomed and cared for.

The Cuna live in rectangular, one-room houses measuring about 20 by 40 feet. The houses have dirt floors and thatched roofs. Their walls are made of split bamboo or cane lashed with vines. Inside, the houses are dim, cool, and airy. Hammocks, baskets of clothing, and other articles hang from beams and rafters. Drinking water is kept in clay

Scarred by deep ravines, the Santa Marta Mountains of northern Colombia serve as home to the little-known Ica Indians. Fewer than three thousand live in the area, tending gardens on the lower slopes and herding livestock on the rock-strewn pastures seen here.

Ica Indians gather near the gateway to one of their villages to celebrate the feast day of Saint John (June 24). Efforts to Christianize the tribe have largely failed, although baptism and other rites may have been adapted to Indian ceremonies. Women (right) harvest coca leaves from bushes planted and tended by men. Tribal custom permits only the men to chew the mildly narcotic leaves, a practice they indulge in daily. A grooming session occupies an Ica group, including a mamo, or shaman (second from right), seen here with his bag of toasted coca leaves.

vessels half buried in the earthen floor. Stools, a table, and a small wooden trunk complete the furnishings. Food is cooked in a small shed adjacent to the house, where a fire is kept alive until needed.

The Indians depend on the mainland for most of their food, water, and firewood. Women and girls make daily trips from the islands in small dugouts called *cayucas* to draw water from the rivers and to transport firewood. Most of the food crops and half of the coconuts are grown on the mainland—on plots carved out of the forest. Such gardens produce corn, bananas, plantains, limes, avocados, and other crops. Men armed with shotguns hunt peccaries and other animals. They catch sea turtles with nets, and fish with nets, spears, and baited hooks.

To earn cash, the Cuna sell coconuts—mostly to Colombian buyers. Some of the men hire out as laborers and service workers in Panama City and other towns, returning to the islands with their savings. For years the handling of money, as well as trade with the outside world, was considered the province of the men. But more recently the women have found a ready market for the sale of their *molas*—intricately appliquéd blouses and cloth panels—and so have begun to contribute substantially to household income. The molas, perhaps more than any other product, have brought international recognition to the Cuna.

A mola consists of several layers of brightly colored cloth with designs cut out to reveal contrasting colors beneath. Often the designs are inspired by modern themes—pictures from magazines and catalogs, advertisements, and product labels.

To see a Cuna woman in everyday dress is to behold a blaze of color. Molas, bright skirts, red bandannas, gold nose rings and earrings, and limbs adorned with silver and gold present a kaleidoscope of hues and patterns. Much of a family's wealth may be displayed in the gold and silver coins and jewelry obtained by the men in Colón and worn by the women on the islands. The men, by contrast, are less colorfully dressed—regular shirts, pants, and a felt hat or baseball cap.

The Cuna even now isolate themselves from the outside world. Marriage with outsiders is discouraged. Visitors must obtain permission to visit some islands. Each island is presided over by a chief and most laws adhere to Cuna custom. Cuna history is recited at nightly meetings by storytellers trained to memorize the old traditions.

The Cuna also have the highest incidence of albinism in the world and, in the past, such "moon children" were thought to have special powers. Today, shamans who use medicinal plants and carved wooden figures to cure, as well as mystics, oracles, and chiefs, all strive to reinforce traditional Cuna customs and beliefs.

The mola is a fitting symbol of Cuna adaptation to the world beyond their islands. What once were body designs have been translated into textiles and integrated into Cuna life. The mola is a product of acculturation—but it is also unquestionably Cuna.

Whether the Cuna are known to outsiders because of their molas, or because of albinism, or because they are among the world's shortest people, they also should be known for something else: They persist.

D own the Pacific side of South America runs the continent's craggy backbone—the Andes Mountains. River gorges slice between 20,000-foot massifs towering above coastal desert to the west and tropical jungle to the east. On lofty plateaus only two seasons are felt year round: summer during the day and winter at night. Climate varies dramatically with altitude—in some places tropical plants flourish within a few miles of perpetual snow.

Here, over the millennia, the Indians have adapted to the high, thin air. They have relatively larger chests, and extra rich blood helps them live at heights up to 17,000 feet, though most settle between 8,000 and 13,000 feet. And yet, from their windswept aeries, Andean peoples even before the time of Christ were in touch with the world below. Cotton traded from coastal or eastern valleys has been found in cloth unearthed in the highlands, and wool from highland alpacas and other camelids appears in early coastal fabrics.

The most complex civilizations of aboriginal South America arose in the Andes. The last and most advanced of these cultures was that of the Incas. When the Spaniards arrived, the Inca realm stretched some 2,500 miles from Colombia to Chile. Upon almost a hundred disparate nations, the Incas had imposed a common language, a state religion, a universal system of law. The Inca overlords called their sprawling empire Tahuantinsuyu—the Four Quarters of the World. It is specifically the Indians now living in what was once Tahuantinsuyu whom we call "Andean" in this book.

The strong unifying influence of the Incas is still apparent. Today most Andean Indians speak Quechua, the lingua franca of the Incas. But though the Spaniards continued the process of homogenization begun by the Incas, many Andean peoples retain a semblance of their local identity. The Quechua-speaking Otavalo of Ecuador were skilled weavers in Inca times; since then they have expanded their artistry into a lucrative worldwide business. Rebellious of first Inca and then Spanish rule, Indians of the treeless altiplano and the shores of Lake Titicaca were allowed to keep their Aymara language and much of their culture. The Chipaya also kept their Uru tongue. They still live on the desolate salt plains of southwestern Bolivia—an area so wretched that the Incas decided it was not even worth adding to their realm.

Above: Late Chavín ceramic bottle, Peru, 900-700 B.C. Opposite: Feather poncho, Peru.

SOLDIERS OF THE SUN

Loren McIntyre

With haughty mien an Inca nobleman gazes down the centuries. Fleshed in silver, adorned with shell inlay, this head from a figurine less than eight inches high portrays an orejón, or big-eared man, at nobility's loftiest level. Only one of such rank could wear huge plugs and braided headbands and hold high office in the realm of the Incas.

The Incas. Even now their very name conjures visions of imperial grandeur, of mountain strongholds and hidden citadels, of untold treasure in silver and gold, of alien invaders and slashing swords. The Incas dwelt in one of the last great secret wonderlands on earth; only among the stars may humankind again happen upon an unexpected continent and an empire unknown.

The empire ranged 2,500 miles along the western edge of South America, reaching across parched sands, over lofty snowpeaks, and into jungle without horizons. Royal roads threaded the land; heart-stopping suspension bridges spanned dark gorges.

Its emperor, the Lord Inca, believed the sun had founded his dynasty. "O Sun, my Father," he would pray, "let thy sons the Incas be conquerors and despoilers of all mankind," and he commanded subject peoples to honor the sun—servant of Viracocha, the creator—above all local gods. When he journeyed through his mountain realm, carried in a curtained litter by blue-liveried bearers and flanked by warriors with maces and slings, his people called down blessings from the slopes: "Ancha hatun apu, intipchuri—Great and powerful lord, son of the sun." "Little short of adoring him as God," a chronicler wrote.

His queen was his sister, and his harem of 600 included the fairest maidens from a hundred conquered nations. He lived in sumptuous palaces and wore robes of bat fur and hummingbird feathers, discarded after one wearing. He ruled a welfare state where everyone was looked after in return for unceasing toil; the punishment for brazen laziness was death. He called his empire Tahuantinsuyu, the Four Quarters of the World. Now we call all its inhabitants Incas; then the title Inca applied only to the numerous royal family. Its men wore huge plugs in earlobes that might touch their shoulders.

At the spiritual center of the Inca Empire the sun's golden disk was housed in the Coricancha, a stone temple with slabs of gold on its outer walls and golden straws woven into its thatched roof. An inner courtyard was adorned with golden fountains; a garden was planted with golden corn; and golden hummingbirds drank droplets of gold from the throats of gilded flowers. In one dark chamber old women wearing

214

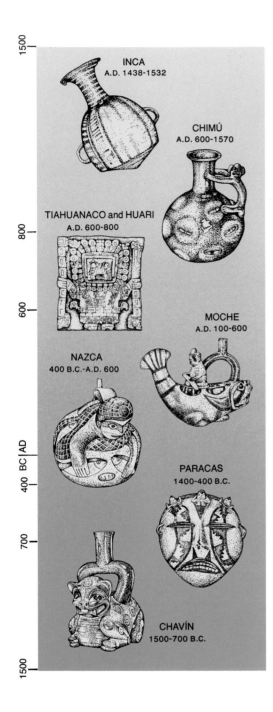

INCA
A.D. 1438-1532

CHIMÚ
A.D. 600-1570

TIAHUANACO and HUARI
A.D. 600-800

MOCHE
A.D. 100-600

NAZCA
400 B.C.-A.D. 600

PARACAS
1400-400 B.C.

CHAVÍN
1500-700 B.C.

1500

800

600

400 BC|AD

700

1500

Fashions in clay and stone rose and fell like the cultures they now chronicle. Art and statecraft do not always march in step; though the Chimú kingdom toppled about 1466, its artistic influence endured. Here Andean cultures are dated on a calendar of art styles.

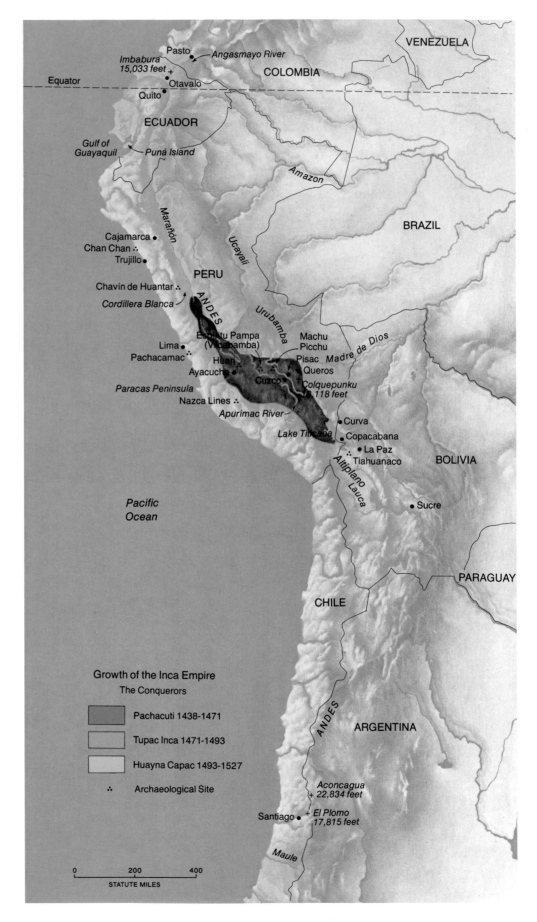

VENEZUELA

Pasto *Angasmayo River*

Imbabura 15,033 feet

COLOMBIA

Equator

Otavalo

Quito

ECUADOR

Gulf of Guayaquil — *Puná Island*

Amazon

BRAZIL

Marañón

Cajamarca

Chan Chan

Trujillo

PERU

Ucayali

Chavín de Huantar

ANDES

Cordillera Blanca

Urubamba

Espíritu Pampa (Vilcabamba)

Machu Picchu

Lima

Pisac *Madre de Dios*

Pachacamac

Huari Queros

Ayacucho

Cuzco

Paracas Peninsula

Colquepunku 18,118 feet

Nazca Lines

Apurímac River

Curva

Lake Titicaca

Copacabana

La Paz

Tiahuanaco

BOLIVIA

Pacific Ocean

Altiplano

Lauca

Sucre

PARAGUAY

CHILE

Growth of the Inca Empire
The Conquerors

Pachacuti 1438-1471

Tupac Inca 1471-1493

Huayna Capac 1493-1527

⊹ Archaeological Site

ANDES

ARGENTINA

Aconcagua + 22,834 feet

Santiago *+ El Plomo 17,815 feet*

Maule

0   200   400
STATUTE MILES

masks of gold fanned flies from golden mummies of earlier kings.

South America, the unexpected continent, had obstructed Christopher Columbus's attempt to reach Cathay. Spaniards were still beating along its northern coast in 1502 when Francisco Pizarro arrived. In 1513 he shared Vasco Núñez de Balboa's discovery of the Pacific, and in 1524 he began voyaging south, pursuing rumors of treasures like those Hernán Cortés had just seized in Mexico. By 1529 the aging adventurer, then in his late 50s, had earned from his king the title Governor and Captain General of Peru—a bit presumptuous, since Peru belonged to the Inca, an absolute monarch neither King Charles I of Spain nor Pizarro yet knew about. Nor did they know the Inca Empire was twice the size of Spain.

The land of the Incas stretched along the spine of the continent; all but a bit of it lay below the Equator. Its capital, Cuzco, was centered in the Andes, longest and second highest mountain range in the world, at a place that should have been quite beyond Pizarro's power to penetrate with his daring band of 168 Spaniards. But the empire—numbering perhaps six million Indians after a century of astonishing growth—was sorely beset by plague, possibly smallpox imported by Spaniards. And while Pizarro probed south, from 1524 to 1532, the Inca died of the disease and the empire was wrenched by a catastrophic civil war between two Inca heirs.

The prevailing Inca, amidst his army and his delusions of invincibility, was off guard 600 miles north of the capital when men on horseback rode up from the coast. In one of the most dramatic confrontations in history, Pizarro captured the Inca, his land, his people, and his treasure during a single twilight hour.

How long had this empire of the Incas—who thought they ruled all the known world—awaited discovery by aliens beyond their ken?

The Inca creation myth said the Supreme Being modeled men and women of clay, gave them language and song, and sent them underground. In time they emerged in caves, lakes, hills, and valleys. The myth wears well, for the first Andean settlements did pop up in all sorts of far-flung places, each with its own tongue.

About 45 rivers—more in the past—flow westward from the Peruvian Andes alone. Some early hunters followed the ribbons of green down to the desert coast and stayed to fish, piling seashells into great mounds still perceivable today. Their coastal hamlets were separated by 8 to 80 miles of intervening sands, where in some places dormant seeds spring to life only once every 20 or 30 years. At first, game was plentiful in the nearly treeless grasslands of the *(Continued on page 218)*

OVERLEAF: *Stark altiplano—the high plain—sprawls below Bolivian peaks. Ancient seas receded, leaving Lake Titicaca to the north, salt flats to the south—and between, a flatland where only irrigation and ingenuity could make crops and civilizations flourish.*

215

Along a continent's rampart (opposite) marched Incas questing for empire. Pachacuti began with conquests around Cuzco. Tupac Inca led troops from Chile to Ecuador; Huayna Capac thrust into Colombia—to win a world the Spaniards would turn upside down.

Migrants from the mountains, Andean condors perch on a Pacific crag (right). Spaniards slew the great vultures as symbols of Indian paganism. But today, in one Andean festival, villagers tie condors briefly to the backs of bulls as symbols of the Indian triumphant.

218

high Andes—mastodons, gigantic sloths, and four humpless cousins of the camel: the vicuña, alpaca, guanaco, and llama. After the mastodons and sloths died out and man settled down to farm, he became dependent upon the llama, and the llama on man: a truly symbiotic relationship. The only large American beast of burden, the llama was a producer of dung for fuel and fertilizer, and also a source of wool and some companionship. After its death—often by ritual sacrifice—the llama provided a hide and good-tasting meat.

Agriculture brought population growth—most of it natural, for there was little further migration from the north. Arrivals from overseas there may have been, as suggested by 5,000-year-old Japanese-like relics found on the coast of Ecuador, and by the long un-Indian beards on effigies from the Peruvian coast. But Indians throughout South America spring from the people who came by land from Asia millennia ago. Pure-blooded ones are easily recognizable, even today, as Indians, with nothing approaching the variety of appearance and customs of the races spreading over Europe, Asia, and Africa at the same time.

More than a thousand years before Christ, urban settlers on both coast and highlands began producing pottery in prodigious quantities. So industrious were the potters that more than a million examples of their art survive intact. On some fields, usually near cemeteries, one walks not upon the ground but upon acres of potsherds.

Recurrent themes of horror, death, and sacrifice—like fiends with a human head in one hand, a knife in the other—appear on pottery, in gigantic statues, and in textiles. The finest cloth was found in the Paracas Necropolis, on the southern Peruvian coast: garments and tapestries in striking colors and designs, and weaving as fine as 250

From a town of tombs—the ancient necropolis unearthed in 1925 on the Paracas Peninsula—came wondrous finds out of Peru's storied past. Many of the site's hundreds of burials were wrapped in superb embroideries. In this one (right) a demon leaps from the mists of mythology with a head taken as a trophy slung under one curving arm. Some of the Paracas textiles contain stitches in the millions and may have taken years of a life that predated Christ's. Staring out of an even longer past, a stone head (left) adorns a 3,000-year-old Chavín temple in central Peru.

threads to the inch. Royal mummies wore eight wrappings of more than 3,000 square feet—enough to shroud a modest American home.

Garments of ancient Andean nobles were set off by ornaments of gold and silver, shell and jade. Enormous plugs elongated their earlobes. In Colombia, noses were fitted with ornaments up to a foot wide. Head deformation was much in the mode for centuries. By binding the skull of a child it could be shaped like a football poised for kickoff.

From central Peru sprang the Chavín jaguar cult in stone. The big-cat motif spread throughout the central Peruvian highlands and even along the coast, beginning about 1500 B.C. Then it suddenly disappeared. This portent of empire was the first culture to spread far beyond its valley of origin, but it was probably a holy empire, not a military one.

Between 400 B.C. and A.D. 600 a number of regional states appeared. The Lima culture built hundreds of adobe pyramids; most have been bulldozed, but some still occupy several city blocks. Tiahuanaco, a huge ceremonial center of stone and statuary, stands near the south end of Lake Titicaca. Some of the polished and precisely squared stone blocks weigh more than 100 tons and were held together by copper clamps.

Still another culture is Nazca, famed for polychrome pottery, near the south central coast of Peru. Themes include birds, killer whales, and turbaned warriors carrying trophy heads. Musicians are recurring subjects, and many museum collections have an example of the Nazca one-man band: a seated musician playing a panpipe with his mouth, a trumpet with his ear, a gourd rattle with his trumpet hand, and a drum beneath his knees which he beats with his private parts.

The most revealing relics of the A.D. 100 to 600 period are Moche ceramics from the north coast of Peru. Almost every aspect of Moche life is sculpted on water jars: princes and priests, prisoners and jailers, weavers and beggars, musicians and surgeons, the old and diseased. Moche fishermen go to sea in little reed boats identical to those used today, and warriors bring home naked prisoners with ropes around their necks and their noses cut off.

The recurrent theme of warfare was prophetic, for the first wave of imperial conquest soon swept over most of the central highlands and coast of Peru. Warriors from Huari, a stone city near Ayacucho, won and lost an empire between A.D. 600 and 800. Although the Spanish chroniclers mentioned Huari, the site of the ruins was lost until 1895 and its story was not resurrected until the 1960s. Nearly 100 Huari-built or Huari-dominated sites have now been identified.

Huari engineers may have paved the way for the Incas. The famed "highways of the sun" possibly followed in parts the routes of highways

Like snapshots in clay, Moche pots mirror their makers in countless candids—some nearly 2,000 years old. A life begins as two midwives aid a mother in labor. Another ends in a sigh of agony as a naked prisoner sags against his bonds while a bird pecks out an eye.

A couple share an intimate moment with potter and posterity. Sleep drugs the child at their side, but it is coca that glazes the gaze of a man dipping lime—a catalytic agent—from a gourd. In elegant portraits like the one at far left we glimpse forgotten notables.

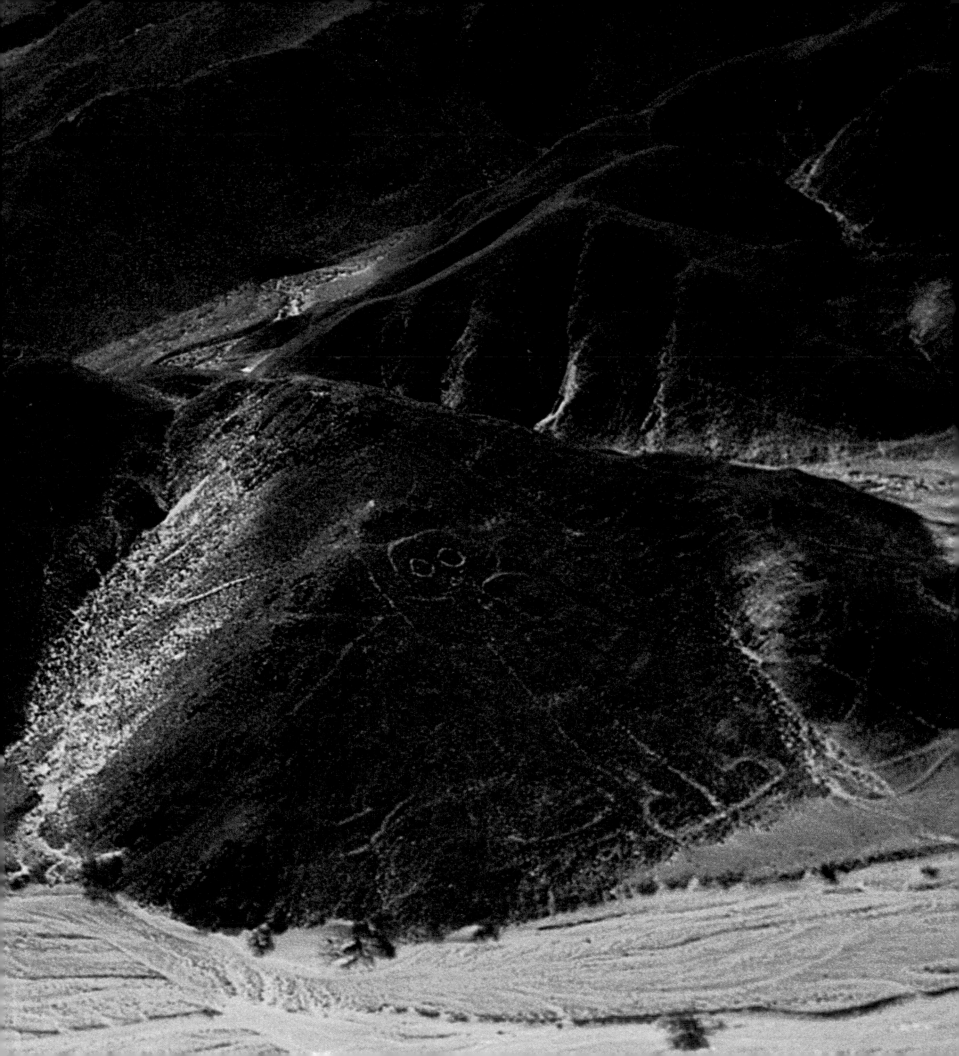

begun by the Huari in order to consolidate their conquests.

One survivor of Huari hegemony was Pachacamac, the most famous shrine on the Pacific coast. From earliest Huari times, Pachacamac's oracle had attracted pilgrims and dignitaries bearing gifts, who prepared themselves by fasting. When they approached the oracle— walking backwards—prophecies in a horrifying hiss came out of mouths of idols or recesses in adobe walls.

After A.D. 1200 or so, history was remembered and reported to Spaniards who came with notebooks and questioned aged Indians about their origins. Chroniclers learned about pre-Inca federations and kingdoms that flourished while Europe was in its medieval era.

Most powerful was the moon-worshiping kingdom of Chimor, an immensely wealthy dynasty of nine successive monarchs who eventually controlled some 600 miles of coastline from their capital at Chan Chan. Its vast adobe ruins still sprawl over nine square miles of desert near Trujillo. Chan Chan was the largest city of pre-Columbian South America, with about 50,000 people. They lived on corn, squash, lima beans, sweet potatoes, chili peppers, and lots of fish caught by both hook and net. The Chimú monarchs loved gold. Although Inca conquerors later carried most of their splendid artifacts to Cuzco, so

Artists unable to admire their own masterworks etched a stiff-winged hummingbird (below) and an enigmatic "owl man" (opposite) into an arid plateau in southern Peru. Not until airplanes of the 1920s bore men aloft did human eyes fully view the famed Nazca Lines, a tangle of ruler-straight lines and runway-like swaths amid a bestiary of outsize creatures: whales and birds, a monkey and a spider. Crews 12 to 20 centuries ago hefted millions of rocks to expose the soft, lighter-colored subsoil and thus "draw" each figure. For the eyes of gods? No one can say.

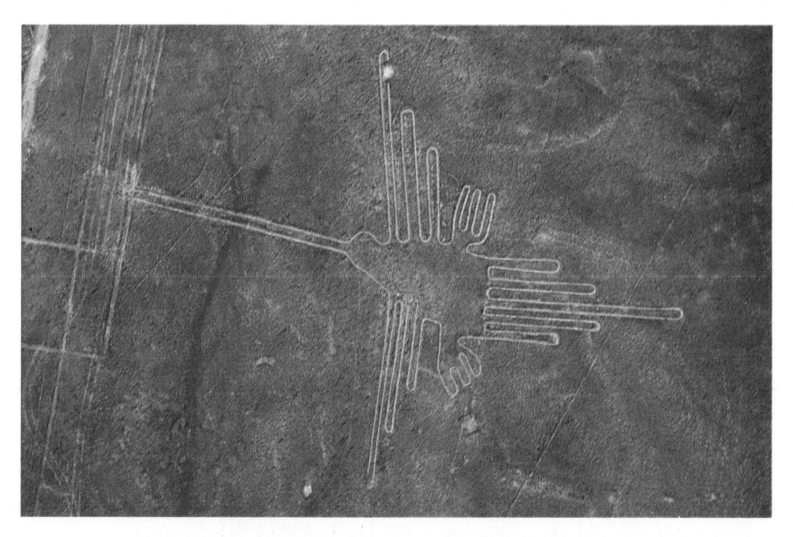

much was buried in graves that Chan Chan has literally been a gold mine ever since the Spaniards first probed the sand with their swords.

About A.D. 1400, several fierce tribes of the old Huari heartland formed the Chanca Confederation. The Chanca believed themselves to be descended from the puma and wore feline heads on top of their own. About 1438 the Chanca marched on their traditional enemy, the kingdom of Cuzco, whose ruler called himself Viracocha Inca.

Viracocha was the eighth in a dynasty of kings who claimed their founding father and his sister-wife came from the Island of the Sun in Lake Titicaca. The couple and their kin had wrested the narrow valley of Cuzco from its aboriginal inhabitants and built there a temple to the sun, which later Incas rebuilt in polished stone and called Coricancha.

Much of that marvelous temple still exists. Beneath its foundation lie crude stone walls built by the previous inhabitants, and above rises the Spanish Church of Santo Domingo—a splendid if tragic example of archaeological stratification opened up for every tourist to see.

The first eight Incas of the dynasty controlled an agricultural state so small they could virtually see from one side to the other. Early Inca armies raided, but did not conquer, their neighbors. Then the eighth Inca saw Viracocha—the lord creator—in a dream, and presumptuously took the name Viracocha. He began to take over towns around Cuzco and liquidate their chieftains; with neighboring nations he worked out alliances. When the puma-cult Chanca armies climbed up the mountainsides toward Cuzco, Viracocha—now old and enfeebled—fled with his women to a fortified country estate. A Chanca general called on Cuzco to capitulate lest he dye his lance in Inca blood.

But one of Viracocha's sons, Prince Inca Yupanqui, chose to stand fast. In the free-for-all, the prince and his generals hewed straight for the feline idol the Chanca carried into battle. When they captured it, hordes of onlookers poured from the hills and mobbed the demoralized Chanca, stripping wounded and dead of weapons and ornaments.

"Even the rocks turned to warriors," declared Inca Yupanqui. From then on, Inca armies bore sacred stones into battle. But they won more territory by diplomacy than by war, since many nations gave up rather than fight invisible warriors symbolized by the magical rocks.

The lords of Cuzco quickly bestowed the red-tasseled forehead fringe of highest office on the new hero, Inca Yupanqui. He named himself Pachacuti—"cataclysm," or "he who overturns the earth." He was the ninth Inca and would become the first of the emperors, though his kingdom then measured less than 40 by 80 miles of rugged highlands. Pachacuti lived up to his name, storming repeatedly out of Cuzco and

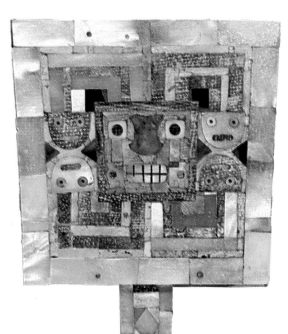

Golden gloves of a Chimú mummy reach for a ritual knife. Chimú goldsmiths knew skills the Incas perfected—and Spaniards ignored as they melted booty into ingots. Huari artists, early contemporaries of the Chimú, crafted this shell-and-turquoise mirror (left).

breaking Indian nations to his will. Historians recognize him as a remarkable innovator and organizer, possibly the greatest genius of the American Indian race. The social and political changes he made still touch people's lives throughout the Andes.

The most revolutionary change was to make Quechua a common language—not easy in a continent of babel, of more than a thousand tongues. Few communities spoke Quechua in 1438 when Pachacuti took the royal fringe. Ninety years later, at the zenith of the empire, perhaps six million Indians had learned it, through a policy of population exchange between Cuzco and distant provinces. Today about ten million people speak Quechua.

Those who gave in without a fight found the Incas to be benign and able administrators who regulated every detail of their subjects' lives from womb to tomb: whom to marry, which crop to grow, and of course taxes. Since money was unknown, taxes were paid in forced labor—the *mita*, Quechua for "a turn." Subjects "took turns" at mining and public works such as shaping steep mountainsides into stone-walled terraces for agriculture. Sowing and reaping used up only two months each year; there was lots of time left over for waging war, feasting, and "taking turns" to avoid idleness and unrest. The mita netted the Inca more than a billion work hours a year to invest in imperial grandeur.

Early in his reign, Pachacuti evacuated Cuzco and used mita labor to rebuild it in stone as a holy place. Working from clay models, stonemasons split rock by drilling small holes, wedging it apart, and polishing it with sand and water. They used stone hammers and axes, and bronze chisels. So well did they build that many walls in Cuzco and its outskirts have withstood 500 years of earthquake, war, and urban

Chan Chan sprawls in empty splendor over nine square miles of Peruvian desert. Nine compounds served monarchs as palaces, then tombs, in a city larger than the conquering Incas' own Cuzco. A courtyard's stylized animals still flick their tails (above).

ruin and renewal. Many carefully shaped and fitted stones were simply too big and heavy—up to 150 tons—to have been incorporated into Spanish churches and buildings.

As befitted the divine son of the sun, Pachacuti poured booty into Coricancha—Golden Enclosure, the religious hub of the Inca universe. Polished stone walls, one straight, one a grand parabola, surrounded massive stone temples housing Inca gods. Inti, the sun, ranked first among sky gods that served the creator Viracocha. His idols were a golden sun disk embossed with a human face, and Punchao (sunrise)—a hollow golden sun-child that held the mummified hearts of Inca kings.

After the sun ranked Ilyapa, Thunder, god of weather. His sister kept a jug of water drawn from a heavenly river, the Milky Way. Thunder was the crack of Ilyapa's sling when he hurled a stone, breaking the jug to make the rain fall. With the Conquest, *ilyapa* also came to be the Quechua word for "gun."

Many other Inca citadels had sun shrines with priests and sorcerers, while *huacas*—holy places and things—were everywhere, in thousands: tombs and temples, mountains and meadows, springs and stones. Boundary markers were huaca, and so were *apachitas*, piles of stones marking mountain passes or landmarks on the trail, where a traveler should add another rock, a quid of coca, or a worn-out sandal. Venus was huaca, twins were huaca, and so was an unusual stone, a double ear of corn, or a person born feet first. These and other unusual things, including enemy idols, were regarded with awe. Each Inca emperor had a personal, portable huaca which he called "brother"; it protected and advised him. Pachacuti's was an image of the thunder god.

In time, Pachacuti grew so godlike that subjects—even nobles— entered his presence barefoot, eyes downcast, bearing token burdens on their backs. He ran the empire from Cuzco, while a favorite son, Tupac Inca, conquered territories as far reaching as ancient Rome's.

With an army chroniclers estimated at 200,000 men, Tupac Inca thrust north into Chinchaysuyu, the northwestern quarter of the empire. In Ecuador his sister-wife bore him a son who would become eleventh Inca. Tupac Inca vowed not to stop until he reached the uttermost sea. A Spanish chronicler reported that he built a fleet of log rafts and ventured into the Pacific Ocean with 20,000 men. The tale helped inspire a modern explorer, Thor Heyerdahl, to test the legend by sailing from Peru to Polynesia in a raft called *Kon-Tiki*—one of the names of Viracocha, the creator god.

Tupac Inca then marched down the coast to conquer the kingdom of Chimor. He adopted Chimú ceremonies, sent to Cuzco goldsmiths and

Giant steps climb sunward at Pisac, a ceremonial center built in the 1400s near Cuzco. On a high saddle sat homes, shrines, and tombs. From curved terraces, watered by canals and hemmed by stone walls 15 feet high, sprouted corn to feed the Inca Empire.

silversmiths from Chan Chan, and drove south to absorb into the Inca pantheon the shrine and oracle of Pachacamac. Then from his beloved highlands he thrust down the steep river valleys and besieged the seaside chieftains one by one. His staging areas can still be seen toward the lower ends of the turbulent rivers.

Captured chiefs and their holiest huacas were displayed in Cuzco. The emperor's high priest trod symbolically upon prostrate prisoners before sending them home. Lesser captains were committed to a dungeon full of toads and serpents, or fed alive to jaguars. Such cruelties warned other nations to submit without a fight.

Tupac Inca fought deep into the rain forests of the Antisuyu, the empire's northeastern quarter. He was better prepared than Pachacuti, having learned that padded armor got soggy with sweat in the jungle, that there was no elbow room among the trees and vines to twirl a sling, and that good slingstones could not be picked up off the forest floor as they could in the treeless altiplano. Despite unaccustomed heat and humidity, strange diseases, monstrous snakes, and enemy blowgun darts that flitted unseen between the trees, the highland armies reached the jungle flatlands, brought back ornately painted bowmen, and paraded them, naked and shivering, in Cuzco.

Ranging from wetlands to desert, Tupac Inca pressed nearly 2,000 miles into the Condesuyu, the southwest quarter of the empire, and conquered a region in Chile and Argentina bigger than Spain. On volcano rims as high as 22,057 feet, climbers have recently found Inca shrines, llama droppings, and even the frozen bodies of youths buried alive in sacrifice to the dynasty's sun. Thrusting to the same latitude as the tip of Africa, 35° South, Tupac (Continued on page 239)

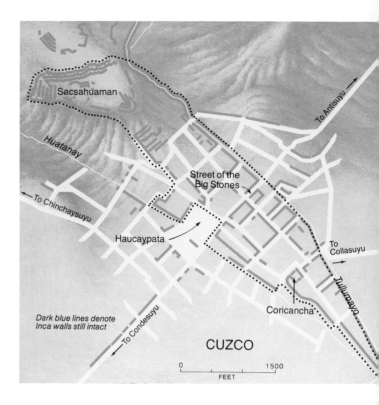

Saw-toothed walls of stone defend Sacsahuaman, Inca fortress (opposite) above Cuzco. In the ancient capital's Street of the Big Stones, mortarless joints seem to echo the city's geometric plan. Cuzco is laid out in the shape of a puma (above); its head is Sacsahuaman.

THE INCAS

232

A nobleman's life hangs in the balance as an Inca surgeon performs a delicate trepanation. The doctor makes a square incision into the skull with an obsidian knife. An assistant prepares to stanch the bleeding with a cotton bandage, while another holds the drugged patient by his legs. With such surgery, common in pre-Conquest Peru, doctors may have treated headaches, seizures, or battle injuries, or ventilated evil spirits. Ancient graves have yielded hundreds of skulls with healed or partly healed trepanations, proof that patients survived the drastic procedure, some even to endure it more than once.

Pages 234-235: From the Four Quarters of the Inca world, rich tribute flows into the imperial city of Cuzco. For weeks prior to Inti Raymi, the Festival of the Sun, llama trains laden with textiles, grains, gems, and precious metals bring the annual payments to royal and religious storehouses. At left, a packtrain from Antisuyu, its lead llama decorated with ear tassels and bells, enters the city from the east. Beyond the llama, three Colla men, watched by an awed housemaid, present bags of gold objects to a quipu camayoc, an official tallier of the emperor's treasure. At center, bare-chested Anti carry their tribute of colorful macaws. From the right another caravan joins the street leading to the Haucaypata, Cuzco's main plaza. There, at winter solstice, the emperor poured libations from his elaborate dais. For eight days the Incas honored the sun with prayers, animal sacrifices, and dances.

blackened by soot; there were no windows or chimney. Food was stored in attics, in large jars, and in pits dug in the floor. A three-legged clay stove had holes for pots on top and a stoking hole in front.

To blow life into its embers the women rose earliest. With heavy rocker stones they milled corn or *quinoa*—a high-altitude grain—and boiled a thick soup for breakfast. It took awhile; in the high, thin air, boiling water is hardly hot enough to scald.

Outside the house, llamas and alpacas huddled like so many bushes of fleece. By sunup the farmers were carrying their foot plows to fields still tinged with frost—unless it was midyear, the time between planting and harvest, when the Inca was likely to call men up for military service. On active duty a puric could not work his land, so neighbors stood in for him with no compensation except meals.

The farmer ate once more, in the afternoon, from dishes laid out by the women on the bare ground or on a cloth.

By nightfall the farm family was once again secluded in its sturdy hut, with a drape drawn across the doorway and secured with a stone. The men hunkered against the walls with their tunics pulled down over their knees. All slept in their clothes. The silence was broken by the chirps of guinea pigs as they scavenged scraps in the darkness, fattening themselves for the cookpot. Only if it had been a day of festival and ritual drunkenness might there be much rumpus after dark.

Tupac Inca died about 1493, the year that Columbus returned to Europe with ten Indians in tow and reported a short route to the Indies where "most of the rivers yield gold" and women went scantily clothed. The docks soon swarmed with men lusting to embark for the Indies.

Meanwhile, in Cuzco, the dead emperor's favorite women and servants were being strangled so they could join him in the hereafter, and the council of long-eared Incas named one of Tupac Inca's 62 sons to be eleventh Inca. Huayna Capac, Young King, celebrated his coronation by marrying his sister—as only a ruling Inca could—and witnessing sacrificial rites in Cuzco's great square, Haucaypata, which over the years had been drenched with the blood of guinea pigs, llamas, captive chieftains, insubordinate members of the royal family, and even children.

Soon Huayna Capac set forth with his generals on a grand tour of all Four Quarters of the Tahuantinsuyu. Blue-clad sweepers and bearers cleared the way and carried him in splendor all the years of his journey. Worshiped almost as a god and behaving like one, he received gifts of beautiful concubines and bestowed fine cloth, featherwork, and tax-free captaincies on regional leaders. He dispensed Inca justice, quelled

Hunger, thirst, fatigue: Relief was in the bag for the owner of this modern-day coca-leaf pouch, adorned with tassels and embroidery befitting use on Sundays and special occasions. Sucked with lime made from shells, bones, limestone, and quinoa stalks, the leaves release cocaine.

Inca was finally stopped by Araucanian archers at the edge of a cold rain forest of conifers. He drove his golden boundary stakes into the banks of the Maule River, some 2,400 miles south of the warm soil he had earlier claimed along the Equator.

However vast these distances, Inca outposts kept in touch with Cuzco through swift-footed messengers called *chasquis*, who moved information about 150 miles a day along the royal roads of the sun. Each chasqui, dwelling awhile in a conical mud hut alongside the road, knew a two-mile stretch of imperial highway well enough to run it barefoot on a starless night. Armed with a sling—the badge of Andean man, wrapped around his head—and sometimes a star-headed mace, he carried a coded message on a *quipu*.

Quipus were series of colored and knotted strings used to tabulate statistics: corn production, llamas, weapons, enemy fallen. Not having written words or numerals, but employing a decimal system like ours, the Incas used quipus to keep track of their empire. *Quipu camayocs*, keepers of the quipu, coded and decoded the information. They knew whether a yellow string signified gold or corn, and whether knots counted farm boys recruited for war or minor gods.

After subduing a province, the Incas sent administrators, including a quipu camayoc and an inspector—a *tucuyricoc*, "he who sees all." The inspector, who returned every five years, divided everybody into 12 age groups, from infants to ancients. The quipu camayoc recorded the census, making note of specialists such as soldiers, soothsayers, and stonecutters, and listing livestock, land, and water. The takeover team distributed food and garments to the needy, aged, and infirm; taught Inca religion; and organized work on roads and warehouses. All land, and all llamas in excess of ten per family, belonged to the state, while houses and belongings remained personal property.

Quipus and clay models of the newly conquered terrain were sent to Cuzco. Chosen sons and the holiest huacas were held hostage in Cuzco so that the sacred city would become the center of the new subjects' universe. Select tribal groups sent to Cuzco settled on the outskirts; Cuzco itself was a compound inhabited by Inca nobles, their retinues, and such members of the inner sanctum as the "chosen women"— virgins who lived in convents and made clothing. All men had to wear regional headdress such as woolen caps with earflaps and nets with dangling cords.

Pachacuti decreed that all farmland be divided three ways. The best land was tilled by communal action; its harvest fed the clergy and was burned to placate the gods. The community cultivated the next portion for government, to feed officialdom and to fill vast warehouses with rations for use in time of famine or war. The third share of land yielded just enough to feed the *puric*, the common man.

The puric was a farmer, and his wife and children were farmers, like nearly everyone in the highlands, where there was little forest but cactus, and large birds to hunt were few. The family dwelt in a one-room hut of sod or stone—sometimes adobe—with a thatch roof

On precipitous mountainsides at Machu Picchu, Inca ingenuity meets the challenge of an inhospitable topography. Stone terraces hold back the precious soil, providing level spaces for planting, preventing erosion, and facilitating irrigation. Men break the sod with foot plows and move backwards, while women follow, bending to turn the clods with their hands. Farmers built terraces in every available space, even near the top of Huayna Picchu, the rocky peak behind the 8,000-foot-high city. At right, a laborer rests from his thirsty work and drinks a cup of chicha, *a beerlike beverage, as two women—one of them carrying a baby on her back and spinning alpaca wool—exchange greetings and news. Soldiers man the watchtower at upper right. Within the citadel people crisscross the plaza to the left of which, atop a terraced prominence, stands the* inti huatana, *or sundial stone, just visible to the left of two small buildings. According to tradition, the inti huatana—"place to which the sun is tied"—prevented the sun from disappearing over the northern horizon during the winter. Possibly the stone's changing shadow served astronomer-priests as a measure of the sun's position in the sky and helped them follow the rhythm of the seasons and determine the proper times for planting and festivals. The role of Machu Picchu in the world of the Incas remains enigmatic, a mystery further deepened by the discovery that most of the skeletons found in the city's burial places were those of women—perhaps maidens dedicated to the service of the sun and other sky gods.*

rebellions, built citadels and palaces, and moved populations thousands of miles from their homes.

Around 1515, Huayna Capac marched beyond the Equator, little knowing that when he returned to Cuzco some 13 years later it would be as a litter-borne mummy with plaques of gold covering his empty eye sockets. Farmer-warriors marched with him, 200,000 strong, gathering strength from the populace along the way. Since they had to cross narrow suspension bridges and thread through tunnels, since they had to wait for trains of llamas which foraged on the march, and since dignity required the emperor to travel at leisure, the columns of troops must have measured 60 miles from the vanguard to the last camp follower and must have taken perhaps ten days to pass a point en route.

Huayna Capac took along 2,000 women and a favorite son, Atahuallpa. At his birthplace in Ecuador the emperor paused to build a pleasure palace inlaid with mother-of-pearl. Farther north he founded the empire's northern bastion at Quito.

Huayna Capac's sojourn in balmy Ecuador was ridden with bad times. His thrust into the goldsmithing cultures of Colombia was blunted by savage Pasto Indians. While he pounded golden stakes into the bank of the Angasmayo River to mark the northern boundary of the empire, Ecuadoreans in his wake revolted. When he annexed the Ecuadorean coast, treacherous cannibals in the Gulf of Guayaquil slipped the lashings of log rafts and drowned many of his nobles; the highlanders could not swim. Troops mutinied and tried to go home to Cuzco, which had become a mere compound of priests, bureaucrats, quipu camayocs, and warehousemen.

While Huayna Capac lingered in the north, and Atahuallpa campaigned, chasquis came running with many a dire message. Three halos ringed the moon. A sick eagle fell from the sky. The earth quaked and mountains collapsed. A comet appeared and it was green. At the great Apurímac River suspension bridge near Cuzco, the oracle—a hag of royal blood—said bearded beings would subvert the empire. In 1527 frightened messengers from the coast reported that such creatures, wearing silver jackets and bearing sticks that spoke thunder, appeared in floating houses, then sailed away.

Inca folklore tells of the coming of the pestilence. In Quito a black-cloaked chasqui delivered a small casket, telling Huayna Capac to open it himself by command of the Creator. Moths and butterflies flew out, spreading a plague that took perhaps a quarter of a million lives. The emperor himself was stricken. Twice he named an heir and twice the auguries foretold disastrous reigns. Then Huayna Capac died, the

"A plant that the Devil invented for the total destruction of the natives," growled a 16th-century Spanish cleric as Indians took to using coca leaves once reserved for the elite. They still do, sorting the leaves (lower) and chewing them by the cheekful (upper).

242

Kin to camels that roamed ancient North America, the camelids loom large in Indian lore. Today two kinds run wild: the guanaco (left background)—once counted in millions but now in tens of thousands, mainly in southern South America—and the vicuña (left foreground), hunted for its prized wool until laws saved it from extinction. Domesticated by pre-Inca herdsmen, the alpaca (right foreground) and llama (right background) probably descend from the guanaco. Neither has the strength for draft duties—llamas will carry packs but not humans.

last of three emperors—father, son, and grandson—who had ruled their unique universal state from 1438 to 1527. His mummy was carried back to Cuzco dressed and armed as if alive. Indians watching from the mountainsides plucked eyebrow hairs—forlorn votive offerings—and blew them into the wind.

In Cuzco the high priest conferred the fringe on the twelfth Inca, Huascar, a son of Huayna Capac and his sister-wife. Atahuallpa avoided the ceremony, staying in Quito with his battle-hardened army. Summoned to Cuzco, he sent envoys instead. Huascar cut off their noses and sent them back with an insulting gift of women's clothing for Atahuallpa—who then proclaimed himself king of Quito, a nation apart.

Huascar sent a raw army against his insurgent half-brother; Atahuallpa's brilliant generals crushed it. That encouraged them to strike south. Huascar recruited army after army of farmer-soldiers from Peru, Bolivia, Chile, Argentina, the Amazon jungle. They died in battle; it was said the pestilence was not as cruel as Atahuallpa.

Chroniclers told that more than 150,000 Indians died in the final conflict of the War Between the Brothers, near Cuzco. A crafty Quito general ambushed Huascar, tumbling him from his golden litter. Cuzco's defenders fled in terror: The son of the sun had fallen.

Along the roads of empire trudge today's descendants of yesterday's warriors and the beasts that served them both. Without draft animals or even the wheel, Inca road builders challenged "mountains so steep and frightening, that in some places . . . the bottom couldn't be seen," a Spanish soldier noted, "and . . . it was necessary to dig out the slopes from live rock, in order to make the road wide and flat; all of which was done with fire and picks . . . and wherever there were mountains of trees and grasses, they made it flat, and paved with stone."

244

Northern generals dressed Huascar in women's clothes and forced him to eat excrement in public and witness the mutilation and death of his multitudinous harem and courtiers. The northerners sacked the city, desecrating Tupac Inca's mummy, for his descendants had sided with Huascar. They tried to erase the past by burning quipus and killing quipu camayocs, the rememberers.

Atahuallpa had traveled halfway from Ecuador to Cuzco when chasquis brought word that silver-shirted aliens came riding into the mountains on giant beasts. Curious, he paused at Cajamarca, in northern Peru. He sent gifts and invited the bearded strangers to come. He felt secure with his army of 30,000 to 80,000 men, although his veteran troops were pillaging Cuzco. He was incredibly naive, whereas experience on three continents was Pizarro's secret weapon. Even so, Pizarro had colossal nerve to invade a mysterious empire with a mere 62 mounted men and 106 foot soldiers armed with swords, crossbows, a few ineffectual guns, and a prayer book. But with his priceless horses—the keys to mobility and Spanish power in the Conquest, far more than firearms—he would probably have gone ahead even had he known the empire numbered six million.

Pizarro was the archetypal conquistador, ruthless and self-confident. He carried along his title of Governor and Captain General of Peru; his coat of arms displayed a llama. And he hewed to Cortés's example in Mexico of recruiting Indian renegades; many accompanied him.

Nearing Cajamarca, they passed smoldering towns and corpses swinging from trees, testimonials of Atahuallpa's wrath in the War Between the Brothers. They found Cajamarca deserted, evacuated overnight by order of the Inca. The *(Continued on page 248)*

On a cat's cradle of gossamer, Andean villagers teeter across the roiling Apurímac River on a bridge first built by Inca engineers and renewed by their descendants ever since. An Indian artist named Guamán Poma, his hand bound by Spanish style, made such a bridge look tame (right). A chronicler, noting that the Incas built their bridges "where the rivers are narrowest and most terrifying," sketched one better in words: "And so it lies suspended in mid-air, far above the water. . . . It trembles very much; all of which goes to the head of someone unaccustomed to it."

He is but a villager, yet he raises a chalice to the sun (above) as did Inca emperors long ago. For this is Inti Raymi; in the ruin of Sacsahuaman (left) Indians keep alive the ancient ritual celebrating the Andean winter solstice in June. Down an altar that is not stone but painted cloth on wood (right), past a llama that in ancient times would soon be sacrificed, men in priestly garb bear a symbolic mummy; thus did emperors attend such ceremonies even in death. Corn festoons the altar's rim, symbol of the harvest—then and now the focus of this timeless rite.

tents of Atahuallpa's army now spangled the far mountainsides.

Pizarro's brilliant cavalry captain, Hernando de Soto, was the first Spaniard ever to meet a Lord Inca. Leaving 20 riders near the Inca encampment, de Soto rode alone through a corridor of halberdiers, an Indian interpreter behind him on his horse.

Atahuallpa sat unmoved on a royal stool. De Soto declined to dismount. Atahuallpa accepted an invitation to dine with the Spaniards next day. Before departing, de Soto showed off his steed, wheeling and rearing. Some of the Inca's bodyguard flinched.

That night Atahuallpa executed the cowards. He prepared a march on the town, and sent troops to cut off the Spaniards' escape. He planned to castrate some as harem guards and sacrifice others to the sun.

In town, the Spaniards whetted their swords, heard Mass, and prayed for salvation from this impasse far from the sea. They set a trap Atahuallpa had unwittingly provided. They would hide in vacant buildings with doorways high enough for horse and rider that opened on a great walled plaza. With the example of Cortés and Moctezuma in mind, Pizarro hoped to entice the Inca inside and capture him.

The next day, Saturday, November 16, 1532, marked a change in Andean culture and history so violent that its repercussions still resound. Atahuallpa unnerved the Spaniards by starting his procession toward Cajamarca and then stopping while the fields filled with soldiers: The Spaniards feared night attack. The Inca finally got under way as the setting sun struck the gold and silver medallions of his retinue—richly dressed nobles in litters and hammocks preceded by dancers and singers whose triumphant cries "sounded like songs of hell." With 80 lords carrying his litter, Atahuallpa rode toward town thinking that horses were useless after dark and that the aliens were hiding in fear. Indeed, "many Spaniards wet their pants from terror without noticing it," an eyewitness recorded.

The cortege entered the empty plaza and five or six thousand soldiers squeezed inside the walls. Atahuallpa called to the Spaniards. A Dominican friar came out, clutching cross and breviary, and read Atahuallpa his rights—the *requerimiento* that Spaniards had to make known to natives before drawing their swords. This extraordinary document—which came from church and crown—began with a history of the world and described the Christian faith and the pope's award of the Indies to Spain. The listener was advised to accept church, pope, and king, lest conflict and death be "your fault."

The priest handed the prayer book to the Inca. Atahuallpa saw it as a small huaca, a minor god of thin squared leaves. He threw it down on

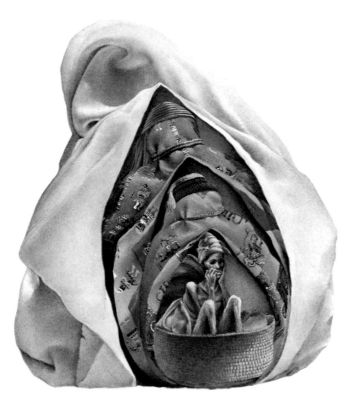

A youngster still huddles against the mountaintop cold that killed him in sacrifice to the sun 500 years ago. Perhaps numbed by coca for his ordeal of honor, he bore a bag of coca, images of silver and gold, even his baby teeth and nail parings, lest he search the afterworld for his body parts. Nobles at Paracas exited in greater splendor, basketed with tools and trinkets (left) and wrapped in as many as 150 cloths, many richly worked and many never worn in life. Bundles within bundles were topped with turbaned "heads."

the pavement. The priest scuttled away, calling on God.

Bugle blasts startled the Indians. Guns thundered. Hoarse voices raised the war cry, "*Santiago! Y a ellos!*—Saint James! And at them!"

Four-footed monsters charged out of dark doorways, hooves clanging on flagstones, breastplate bells jangling. Their lances spitted bodies. Swords spattered Indian blood. Screams rent the twilight air.

Preternatural dread seized the Indians. They panicked, breaching the plaza wall, trampling one another into piles of crushed bodies in their frenzy to escape. But the litter bearers held firm, and reserves replaced those fallen. Not until nearly all their hands were chopped off did Atahuallpa's golden platform tip over. Pizarro personally plucked the Inca, unhurt, from the melee.

Panic spread to the thousands on the plain. Hooves thudded on fallen bodies as lancers rode down fleeing Indians. Seven thousand were massacred, according to an Inca body count.

Atahuallpa ruled eight months from prison in Cajamarca, wearing the imperial fringe, his authority unquestioned. He had his brother Huascar executed. Chasquis sped his orders throughout the realm to collect ransom for his release.

The Inca agreed to fill a 17-by-22-foot room once with gold and twice with silver. Llama trainloads of idols, fountains, chalices, and jewels began to travel the royal roads to Cajamarca, although—for hatred of Atahuallpa—many a temple custodian in the south resisted the levy. It took half a year to fill and refill the room with treasure.

The value of the original artifacts would be enormous today, but all were melted down. Even magnificent pieces that Pizarro spared and sent to Spain as part of the "royal fifth" (the king's share) were quickly converted to coin. Each soldier's share was 45 pounds of gold and 90 of silver. Riders received two shares each, de Soto four, and Pizarro thirteen. The crown got some 2,600 pounds of gold and 5,200 of silver, enough to initiate a new cycle of warfare and inflation in Europe.

At Easter time in 1533, Spanish reinforcements arrived from Panama. Denied equal shares of the ransom, they clamored to get rid of Atahuallpa and plunder Cuzco, a thousand land miles to the south.

In July the Inca emperor was sentenced to death for murdering Huascar and for treason against the strangers within his own realm. To avoid the Spanish punishment for heresy—burning at the stake, with loss of mummification and afterlife—Atahuallpa accepted baptism and took the name of his captor, Francisco.

Then the Spaniards twisted a cord around the neck of Francisco Atahuallpa, strangling the thirteenth Inca in the dynasty of the sun.

Mists of mystery becloud Machu Picchu, a stone aerie that eluded soldier and baptizer but fell instead to the siege of years. Vacant chambers gape toward the sun, once a god and giver of corn to fuel the fires of conquest, now a mute witness to glories long eclipsed.

BELIEVERS IN THE MOUNTAIN GODS

Loren McIntyre

Veiled in jewels, a crimson-plumed coraza—sponsor—assumes the guise of an Inca king. He pays homage to past and present in the fiesta of San Luis Obispo, patron saint of Ecuador's Otavalo Indians. Another pageant, the fiesta of Saint John, coincides with Inti Raymi, Inca observance of the winter solstice. Celebrants don cardboard masks and down bowls of fermented chicha, a corn-brewed beer.

It took the Spaniards 40 years to dispossess the royal family and stamp out Inca rule. But the Europeans never did vanquish the gods that live in the stones and springs and distant snows of the Andes Mountains. They could hardly overthrow an *apu*, a mountain god, such as the one that towers 18,118 feet in a lonely land too high to till, about 50 miles east of Cuzco. Its name is Colquepunku, this god-mountain, and to this great giver of health many Indians of southeastern Peru try to journey at least once in a lifetime. Thousands go in June, just after the annual disappearance from the night sky of that most revered of star clusters, the Pleiades. This pilgrimage of penance and regeneration is called Qoyllur Rit'i, Star of the Snow.

I went along in 1981, trekking by night. A full moon lit the trail but shed no warmth against bitter cold on glaciers 16,000 feet above sea level. Climbing almost to the summit, devotees stood shivering in the snow until moonset, then put candles into icy hollows.

When the first ray of daybreak glinted on the peak of Colquepunku, we all knelt in the snow. I felt like an outsider, since the seven-starred Pleiades do not speak to me and I cannot sense the earth "coming alive"—as my Indian friends can at this signal of the time to sow.

Below the snow line, hundreds of young women had built little corrals and farmhouses of stones, stocking them with white pebbles for the sheep and llamas they hoped to own someday. One shyly assured me that some peaks conceal palaces and haciendas full of livestock.

Only young men, masquerading as bears, make the midnight climb to the Colquepunku glaciers. That first burst of sunlight they await is called *punchao*—the same name the Incas gave their sun-child, a treasured gold image which the Spaniards finally captured four decades after they strangled Inca emperor Atahuallpa. By that time, 1572, the Andean Indians—beset by wars, epidemics, and cultural shock—had plummeted from about six million to one-fourth as many. Dismal servitude in the mines crippled their will to live. Thousands died on jungle expeditions led by Spaniards seeking cities of gold. Newcomers slaughtered the great llama herds. Iron-shod hooves battered the royal roads. Bridges and irrigation systems *(Continued on page 258)*

Performers in a timeless tableau, Otavalan washers rinse wool in an Andean pool, sudsing with juice from the cabuya plant. All family members work. Children and old people ball wool and pick it clean of burs. Women card and spin, each producing about a pound of yarn daily. A man's work includes setting up looms and weaving. He dips the yarn in synthetic dyes for bright colors (crushed walnut husks yield brown hues) and hangs the skeins out to dry. Woman plying yarn (opposite) wears embroidered homespun with coils of gilded and coral beads.

Designed for tourists, many Otavalan textiles reflect modern motifs: a smoker lighting a cigarette; interlocking birds; a crocodile head. Saturday mornings the market of Otavalo, nestled in northern Ecuadorian highlands, bustles with buyers and sellers. Dealers snap up ponchos, shawls, homespun copies of English tweeds. Indians purchase factory goods, kerosene, dyes sold by the pinch. Within a matter of hours the market empties. Then taverns fill as craftsmen slake thirsts with fiery aguardiente—sugarcane rum. The family workshop (above) vies with factories to produce textiles for export. Increasingly, weavers turn to synthetic fibers and power looms, relying less on old-fashioned upright rigs and native yarns. Vanishing too are primitive backstrap looms that helped make Otavalan ponchos world famous.

went to ruin. Bereft of the Incas' totalitarian supervision and demoralized by the colonists' civil wars, Indians fell under the abusive control of resurgent local chieftains. Though free under Spanish law, few Indians knew how to claim their rights.

For closer control and religious conversion, authorities tried to sweep Indians into artificial towns. But it was mostly the new mixed-blood population that adjusted to urban life; full-blooded Indians chose to live nearer their ancestral lakes and stones.

Yet the church made progress, for Christianity held much in common with the Inca religion: nuns and convents; confession; registry of births, marriages, and deaths. Roman Catholic ceremony blended into Indian ritual in a thousand ways. The movable holiday of Corpus Christi, for example, fitted the time of the Snow Star pilgrimage. At the sanctuary of Qoyllur Rit'i, I found a shrine to the 20th-century Virgin of Fátima.

About 60 trail miles north of Apu Colquepunku lies Queros, a remote enclave of Inca tradition. I once hiked there with Hilarion, a taciturn Indian guide who spoke little Spanish. Though scarcely five feet tall, he was as nimble as a llama and carried a heavier load. He shouldered my backpack while I carried only a camera, yet I could not keep up. I would worry about losing my way in the treeless heights—but then I would come upon him sitting at a fork in the old Inca trail, peeling a lapful of small boiled potatoes from the hundred or so he toted in a folded cloth. Wordlessly he would offer me a double handful and then upend his *chuspa*—a small, woven shoulder pouch like those found in ancient graves—and pour out a sprinkling of toasted corn. I munched the kernels and lagged behind again.

From a summit we came down into cloud and entered Queros without seeing it. Stone huts occupy a ledge on the mountainside, facing east. Most Queros days last only five or six hours: Morning sun warms the village, clouds envelop it by noon, then the sun goes behind the mountain. Few of Queros's 40 or so families were at home. Most of them spend days and nights at mountaintop or valley farms. Far above Queros lie steep fields where about a hundred varieties of potatoes grow, and higher still hang grazing lands. Far below are cornfields, but I never saw them; I gave up all notion of descending the trail when I learned that a llama with a load of corn had just fallen over a cliff.

Instead, I climbed the heights with a Queros headman called the Inca Kepac. His short-sleeved tunic resembled the ancient Inca garment, but his hair was shorter than in the old days because the *mistis* (mestizos and whites) ridiculed his braids on a trip to Cuzco years ago.

One night the Inca Kepac and I shared (Continued on page 267)

Brightly dressed Salasaca dancers of central Ecuador celebrate Corpus Christi, a Roman Catholic feast that coincides with a harvest festival rooted in Ecuador's pagan past. The Indians descended from mitimaes *removed from Bolivia and resettled by the Incas.*

SNOW STAR PILGRIMAGE

Pageantry paints a rainbow of costumes on a slope bright with sunrise and snow. It is June in the Peruvian Andes, and thousands of celebrants from highland villages and towns gather to observe Qoyllur Rit'i—in Quechua, the Star of the Snow—an annual festival rooted deep in their Inca heritage. Wending their way with song and dance to this remote shrine some three miles above the sea, pilgrims traverse gorge and mountain by moonlight—for in ancient legend the naupa runa, *the old ones, lived by moonlight before the sun was born. The first sunrise turned these savages to rocks; then civilized humans were created. Now participants celebrate new life as the procession winds downslope in the rising sun.*

Candleglow and glacier ice silhouette the ukukus, the "bear-men" in shaggy robes of llama wool. One or two from each village—usually youths ready for manhood—rise around midnight and trudge from the Qoyllur Rit'i shrine to a glacier at 16,200 feet. There they plant a cross and set up candles. Then they heft chunks of ice, later to be melted into healing water. Some pilgrims brave the biting cold in sandals, for pain and penance are part of their role. Assembled at the cross (opposite) they carried up the mountain, they welcome the dawn of a new life.

Beaded headdress of glass, metal, and plastic on his back, a celebrant (above) awaits the serpentine procession that crowns the Qoyllur Rit'i fete. Another festoons its wearer's brow (far right) as the celebration begins. Crowns of macaw feathers adorn the chuncho dancers, evoking dark jungles far below that shielded a few of the "old ones" from the newly created sun. Next year a village may send new pilgrims, but they will wear the old costumes their forefathers wore as they enact anew the timeless drama of the pilgrimage to the Star of the Snow.

a small stone hut with Hilacucha Quispe, a girl of 12 who said her parents were harvesting potatoes on a distant mountainside. I asked whether she were frightened at being left alone.

"Only of pumas," she replied. "One comes at midnight to steal sheep. When I scream and throw stones, it runs away."

Thick smoke from a cookfire in the middle of the hut reddened my eyes and worsened the discomfort of breathing and sleeping at high altitude. Guinea pigs scampered over my sleeping bag in the dark and I swore—to Hilacucha's mirth—that I preferred them dead to alive. About 4 a.m. she blew on the coals, scattering soot and smoke, and soon served scraps of guinea pig meat, which I relish, and soup of *chuño*—dehydrated potato—which I tasted and set aside. Chuño nourished Inca armies and is still a staple of the Andean diet.

Chuño is prepared in June, when Andean days are sunny and the nights are frosty. The coldest night is supposed to be the eve of the feast of Saint John the Baptist, the 24th of June, when lambs are due to be born and festivals mark the time to wean llamas and to reap potatoes and barley. Widely celebrated as the Day of the Indian, the 24th is when the Inti Raymi (Sun Festival) is enacted at the massive Inca fortress of Sacsahuaman above Cuzco. Inti Raymi is now a pageant drawing thousands of tourists each year. I first saw it 30 years ago when Indians knelt in the frosty Cuzco night before the house of the man who yearly played the role of Inca. When he appeared on the balcony they wailed, as if he were the Inca incarnate.

On Saint John's Eve, burning bunchgrass blackens mountainsides almost to the snow line. A Peruvian Indian told me that setting such fires is called *konuy;* the purpose is to fight frost. "But it is perilous; the frost may get angry and cast spells on the crops."

From Bolivia to Ecuador, youngsters show off on Saint John's Eve by jumping over higher and higher bonfires. On a street corner in Otavalo, a town hard by the Pan American Highway in northern Ecuador, I saw an Indian girl stumble into the flames. Her white taffeta party dress caught fire and she called for help in Spanish. Bystanders rescued her.

In their Ecuadorean eyes the girl was probably not Indian, since in these highlands not bloodlines but dress, language, and residence determines whether a person is considered Indian, mestizo, or white. Indians are those who speak Quechua, live in the countryside, and wear traditional clothing and long, braided hair. While all three groups worship the Christian God, many Indians also believe in the mountain gods—and demons, even the rainbow. In almost all South American cultures, the rainbow is bad; in Ecuador it *(Continued on page 272)*

Garbed in Sunday-best hats and shawls, highland Indians crowd a cobblestoned plaza in Pisac, near Cuzco, to display textiles, ceramics, and produce. Linked by the Quechua language instead of blood ties, the highland Indians stem from nations conquered by the Incas.

A geyser of chaff erupts as highland Indians flail grain in the Sacred Valley of the Incas. The May harvest in the Cuzco region begins before dawn with prayers to earth and sky; then farmers, singing as they work, glean terraced fields built by their Inca forefathers.

OVERLEAF: *Model for Thor Heyerdahl's Ra, totora-reed boats transport Indians on Lake Titicaca. Grouped with Aymara-speaking Peruvians, some lake dwellers trace their past to the ancient Uru people, their bowlers presumably to British railway builders.*

Man-made island built of matted totora reeds undulates like a mattress under villagers' tread. Dense brakes of the air-filled reeds fringe Lake Titicaca, its more than 3,000 square miles fed by snowmelt from Andean peaks. Fabled as the abode of the Inca sun god, it won new fame as a home for record-size trout, introduced in 1939. Indians dip cone nets for smaller fry, native catfish called suche *and South American relatives of carp and perch. These they split and set out on reed mats to dry (above). The sun-dried fish are cooked (left) by smoking them over a fire.*

272

violates virgins. "Prudent Otavalan Indian girls avoid sunlit waterfalls where the naughty colors play . . . or at least they did in my day," said Julian Muinala, 68-year-old Indian headman of Peguche hamlet.

We were sitting near the Peguche waterfall that cascades down the slopes of Imbabura, Otavalo's 15,033-foot sacred volcano. Don Julian wore Otavalan clothing—white culottes, blue poncho, felt hat, rope-soled slippers—and he slapped one palm with an ear of fresh-picked corn, the most venerable of Indian crops since pre-Inca times. I knew him to be a sophisticated world traveler, so I asked whether he still felt a sort of empathy with Pacha Mama—Earth Mother.

"Well, all Otavalan are rooted in the soil of this valley. I came home from Puerto Rico last week to harvest this corn with my own hands, and when it is done I am going on a business trip to Frankfurt, Germany."

Don Julian is an elder of the Muinala Lema family, master weavers, reputed to be descended from tribal chieftains who resisted the Incas, then Spaniards, while clinging with fierce independence to tilted farmland high on Imbabura volcano. Even in distant times almost every Otavalan cottage had a Spanish wooden loom on its veranda. By mid-20th century, Otavalan weavers had won fame as the finest in the land. Julian and others got into marketing abroad. Now Otavalan men and women in native dress peddle piles of ponchos and shawls on street corners from New York to Buenos Aires, and even sell woolens to denizens of the sweltering Amazon. One of Julian's sons is a weaver in Barcelona, Spain, and two others live in Los Angeles, California.

"How many Otavalan live abroad?" I asked.

"Thousands. The Muinala Lema family alone operates looms all over Colombia. Also in Caracas, the Canary Islands, and Bahia in Brazil. If everyone came home at once, they'd have to sleep in the streets."

The men weave, the whole family sells, and the women pocket the money. I wondered, "How do you invest the profits, Don Julian?"

"We used to buy up farmland. Now there's none left in the valley. So we're going into retail trade. Clothing stores. My son Alonso and his wife María Elena own a record shop in town and another up north."

Not all Otavalan are affluent, and one sees Indians given to ritual intoxication and public collapse on feast days—though perhaps no more so than in Inca times. But as often, one sees Indians, smartly dressed in traditional costume, riding taxis driven by whites. They enjoy a growing demand for their rare, handwoven textiles in a market depressed by the ordinariness of mass production.

On the other hand, popularity of mass-produced plastic trinkets has stifled Andean Indians' craftsmanship in jewelry for their own use. And

Braiding hair into thin plaits, Chipaya women perpetuate a hairstyle found on skulls in chullpas, *ancient burial towers that rise from southern Bolivia's arid high plain. Chipaya claim the tomb builders as ancestors, a people they believe to be older than the sun.*

mass production of modern miracle drugs has sorely hurt the Callawaya, a community of Bolivian Indian healers who were once the consummate Andean travelers. The Callawaya dwell in a snow-peaked fastness northeast of Lake Titicaca.

Traditionally, a Callawaya man left home shortly after marriage to roam the Andes, departing on foot. He returned three to ten years later, astride a mule. He wore an ornate silver cross on his chest and carried a sack of talismans and herbs on his back—a kit of such powerful magic that no one would dare to open it even though its owner lay sprawled in a drunken stupor at the side of the road. So great was his reputation for healing mind and body that the Callawaya traveler found free food and shelter wherever nightfall might overtake him, be the household Indian, mestizo, or white. While away, he never communicated with home, and the years did not matter. To him—as with many Indian peoples—time was of little concern.

The Callawaya were medicine men to the Incas and still speak a secret language—perhaps the same one that the royal family kept to itself according to chroniclers of the Conquest. Callawaya men now speak four languages: the secret one (which is kept even from their women), Spanish, Quechua, and Aymara—the tongue spoken by most

Tangled stalks of quinoa, once a food for Inca armies, burdens a Chipaya gathering in the harvest. Hardy above timberline, tolerant of drought and frost, the plant yields milletlike seeds used as a cereal for making flour and thickening soups. Threshed with clubs, the high-protein grain is winnowed by a Chipaya mother outside her sod-walled home (below) on the Bolivian altiplano. Threshing of the pigweedlike plant takes place in circular sod enclosures that deflect gales blowing across the treeless plain. Dust storms howl most afternoons for half the year.

Indians who dwell around the shores of 120-mile-long Lake Titicaca.

In the 1960s Callawaya medicine was overtaken by antibiotics, with which any upstart druggist might effect dramatic cures. What saved the culture and livelihood of the Callawaya was their adding antibiotics to their herbal remedies. That, and their skill at psychic treatment: When an Indian needs a glimpse of the future, or a cure for impotence or fright or unrequited love, few modern doctors can match a Callawaya. In fact, I found no university-trained doctors whatsoever in Callawaya country the last time I was there.

One day, after an exhausting climb, I arrived very much under the weather at Curva, a mountaintop Callawaya town concealed in the mist and slashing rain of the Apolobamba range. I sought out headman Octavio Magnani for treatment of my altitude sickness and abdominal distress. He prepared a teaspoonful of melted frost to diminish my shortness of breath. But I simply could not swallow the little black pills Octavio prescribed to dispel my belly cramps when he allowed they were toasted pellets of llama dung. Some items he let me see in his kit were less exotic: kaolin to calm bowels, quinine for fevers, spiderwebs to stop bleeding, and bee venom for arthritis.

Many of Octavio's remedies were psychosomatic and invoked the local gods. Good fights evil and gods battle demons in eternal struggles between being and nonbeing, well and sick, day and night, dry and wet, solid and liquid. Avoid water, advised Octavio; a bath can kill. He healed with opposites, some obvious, such as applying heat to remedy chills. He was appalled when I said I liked hot coffee with ice cream to end a meal. "It might well spell the end of you," he warned, "to ingest such conflicting forces." Octavio had adopted his fine Italian surname,

Casting sacrificial llama blood into the Lauca River, a poncho-clad Chipaya pays homage to pagan gods (right). Chief among them is Pacha Mama, Earth Mother, honored with gifts of coca, chicha, and decorated bits of lard. Supplicants recite prayers for bountiful harvests and kiss the earth in adoration. Pagan rites mingle with the celebration of Christian feast days, as the Indians splatter the blood of animals on their houses in hopes of gaining wealth. A ram slaughtered for food receives ceremonial blessings on an altar cradling the head (left).

Magnani, on a trip "across the great pond" to Rome. He was born Mamani (Hawk, in Aymara), one of the most common names in Bolivia. My guide whispered to me that Octavio has been "struck three times by lightning," which has assured his seniority over lesser seers who have been "struck only once or twice."

"Today we send our sons to universities in Argentina, Chile, and Peru . . . to places we traveled in our youth," Octavio told me. "Some abandon nomadic ways and become doctors in the cities." Octavio hinted that Callawaya doctors keep amulets in their black bags. "They still know how to breed alpacas and how to cure melancholy and wind."

Wind, *el aire*, causes much fatal illness, according to Andean lore. When I once fell sick in Cuzco from viral hepatitis, a leading local medical doctor diagnosed my collapse as due to *un aire*. Although he prescribed coca leaf tea, I lay bedridden in Lima, feeling more dead than alive, for five months. As both Callawaya and our own ancestors believed, cold drafts bring sniffles, rheumatism, and earache. The Callawaya caution not to urinate against the wind; it causes venereal disease. A windstorm embodies the devil, and cold is his weapon.

Within their universe of opposites, the Callawaya believe they lead a dual existence in a real world and in a dream world. A soothsayer's main task is to interpret and ameliorate the dream world.

Music heals. Not Western music, but vigorous rhythms blown from powerful lungs into enormous pentatonic flutes and wooden panpipes, punctuated by deafening drumbeats, like a fast march in a minor key.

In all the years of my travels among the Indians of South America, I have watched for signs of a pan-Indian conscience, of a yearning—political or even spiritual—for union and common cause among the communities and tribes and fragments of nations which still endure yet seldom seem aware of another's existence. I detect none. Each community seems to consider itself self-sufficient and destined for survival, although the doom of American Indians and their ways has been predicted ever since the Conquest.

Around 1700, Guamán Poma—Hawk Puma—penned 1,179 illustrated pages of protest against abuse of Indians in Peru. To this Indian artist it was so bad that "to write it is to cry." He worried that "Indians will be wiped out" or will end up as mestizos. But Indian ways have weathered nearly 500 years of Western civilization, although their culture may yet be squeezed out by the sheer weight of schools, telecommunications, and tourists. Andean Indians now number many millions, and recent reforms have brought them social and political recognition unknown since Inca times.

At the Snow Star pilgrimage, I watched Indian men carry chunks of glacial ice down from Apu Colquepunku. The women melted it and thickened it with barley to make a rejuvenating beverage. I sipped some, scalding hot, in readiness for the long trek homeward. While I did not personally experience any tremors of rebirth, I do remain convinced that these believers in the mountain gods will persevere into the next century and the next.

A M A Z O N I A

It is born high in the Peruvian Andes, a trickle no wider than a man's hand. Northerly it tumbles, rampaging down the canyons as the Apurímac; later it meanders as the Ucayali. The mountains fall behind and the jungle closes in. Now it joins the Marañón, turns east, and flows across the top of Brazil, taking the name it will bear until it ends its 4,000-mile journey to the Atlantic: the Amazon River.

The mighty sum of more than a thousand tributaries, the Amazon drains one-fifth of all the world's river water from a basin three-fourths the size of the contiguous United States. Here, rain falls at least 130 days a year for an annual accumulation of 60 to 180 inches.

For the white man much of the basin remains unexplored, mysterious, even forbidding—a land where marauding army ants or schools of piranhas can strip a crippled animal to the bone. Not so for the Indian tribes who have made this dark jungle their home for millennia. Their peril lies in the clash of cultures. Caught between the Stone Age and the Space Age, they respond in varying degrees to the pull of each. Some find jobs in the occasional mines, mills, and farms along the rivers or back roads. Others plant, hunt, fish, and forage as their forebears did; a steel ax may be an Indian's only nod to the distant world of metal and machine.

That ax will see much use, for land must be cleared often if crops are to be grown. Incredibly, most of the land is not as rich as the lush vegetation would suggest; over the millennia its soil has been leached of most nutrients, leaving plants to cling to topsoil only a few inches deep. Aborigines learned to clear a plot, grow two or three crops until the yields declined, then abandoned the garden to clear and plant anew. With limitless stretches of territory, groups could keep at arm's length, avoiding subjugation and consolidation. To this day the basin remains a domain of small tribes.

The Amazon basin is the heart of Amazonia, a term that may have different limits for different people—the geographer, archaeologist, ecologist, ethnologist. Thus this section of the book includes neighboring areas, from the Guiana highlands in the north and the Brazilian highlands in the east to the Gran Chaco in the south, where a lowland plain broken by scrub forest is home to a few hardy Chaco tribes.

Above: Galibi painted wooden stool, Suriname. Opposite: Palm roof thatch of a Tukano house, Colombia.

DWELLERS OF THE RAIN FOREST

Robert L. Carneiro

Elaborate feathered diadem and other finery mark this Bororo, a man of distinction. Amazonia's warm climate requires few or no clothes; Indians embellish the body itself. Men, with more free time for beautification and ceremony, preempt the fine feathers. Women wear simpler adornments.

In April 1500, the Portuguese navigator Pedro Álvares Cabral, blown off course as he sailed from Lisbon to India, caught sight of a promontory on the coast of Brazil. This landfall, at about 15° South, was one of the first known sightings by Europeans of the great tropical region now known as Amazonia.

On shore near this spot there happened to be a group of Tupinambá Indians. Curious about these unknown people, Cabral dispatched a boat to make contact with them. Vaz de Caminha, chronicler of the voyage, in a letter to the king of Portugal, reported of the Indian men: "They were dark and entirely naked, with nothing to cover their private parts, and carried bows and arrows in their hands."

The expedition soon continued on to India, and so brief had been their encounter with the Tupinambá that Cabral and his men seem to have gotten no hint that these Indians were cannibals.

Not until 42 years later did prolonged contact with Amazonian Indians take place. In 1542 Francisco de Orellana led a Spanish expedition of 57 men down the Amazon. They had come overland from the Andes to the Napo River, a tributary of the Amazon, where they built boats. In these craft they eventually sailed 3,000 miles, all the way to the Atlantic, encountering many Indians along the way. Sometimes these encounters were friendly, but often they were hostile, and more than once the Spaniards had to fight for their lives.

Gaspar de Carvajal, Orellana's chronicler, noted that when they tried to land at a certain point on the lower part of the river, they were attacked by fierce Indians led by warrior women. "We ourselves saw these women, who were there fighting in front of all the Indian men as women captains, and these latter fought so courageously that the Indian men did not dare to turn their backs, and anyone who did turn his back they killed with clubs right there before us. . . ."

These female warriors, the Spaniards were told, came from a distant village where they lived by themselves, associating with men only for the purpose of having children. Boys born from these unions were killed, and only the girls were raised.

This story reminded the Spaniards of the warrior women of Greek

Caribbean Sea

Atlantic Ocean

Island Carib

Orinoco

VENEZUELA

GUYANA

GUIANA

Galibi

COLOMBIA

HIGHLANDS

SURINAME

FRENCH
GUIANA

Yanomamö

Tumucumaque
National Park

Vaupés

Equator

Tukano

AMAZON

Negro

Amazon

ECUADOR

Manaus

Jívaro
(Shuara)

Witoto

Bora

Xingu

Tocantins

Tupinambá
(extinct)

Yagua

Iquitos

Tikuna

Jurúa

Purus

Madeira

Tapajós

Krahó

Marañón

PERU

BASIN

Northern
Kayapó

B R A Z I L I A N

Shipibo

Mekranoti

São Francisco

Conibo

Ucayali River

BRAZIL

Xingu
National Park

Araguaia

Karajá

Campa

Amahuaca

Aripuanã
National Park

Txukahamaí

Araguaia
National Park

H I G H L A N D S

Tupinambá
(extinct)

Piro

Kamayurá

Lima

Apurímac
River

Waurá

Kuikuru

São Marcos

Shavante

A N D E S

BOLIVIA

Bororo

Brasília

G R A N

Paraguay

Pacific Ocean

CHILE

Tupinambá
(extinct)

Mataco

PARAGUAY

São Paulo

Rio de Janeiro

Toba

Asunción

C H A C O

ARGENTINA

Paraná

0   200   400

STATUTE MILES

legend, the Amazons. As the story spread among Europeans in America, the great river, then called the Marañón, gradually became known as the Amazon.

(Despite the wide currency that this legend proved to have among Amazonian Indians, no village entirely of women has ever been found.)

In the middle 1500s perhaps five million Indians lived in the Amazon basin. The rain forest provided a rich variety of plants and animals which they could exploit for food, shelter, tools, weapons, utensils, and other necessities. We do not know just when the first Indians entered the basin, although by 5000 B.C. a thin population of Paleo-Indians, as archaeologists call them, probably covered much of the region. These Paleo-Indians lived by hunting, fishing, and gathering, possibly relying on spears to kill game. They lacked canoes, so at first the large rivers were barriers to travel instead of avenues of communication.

Adaptation to the rain forest probably proceeded slowly until the adoption of agriculture around 2000 B.C. By permitting Indian settlements to become larger, more permanent, and more secure, agriculture gave a big impetus to Amazonian cultural development.

Superior hunting weapons made their appearance. The bow and arrow probably diffused into Amazonia from the north, but the blowgun may well have been invented in the region. The stone ax came in with agriculture as an implement for clearing the forest for planting. And eventually the canoe was invented, or perhaps brought down from the north, giving the Indians a new means for spreading throughout the river basin. By the time Orellana and other European explorers penetrated Amazonia, a highly adapted Indian culture occupied much of the basin, where in many isolated pockets it remains to this day.

In the course of my fieldwork as an anthropologist, I have lived with and studied two representative tribes of Amazonian Indians, the Kuikuru of central Brazil and the Amahuaca of eastern Peru. These two societies, similar in many respects but markedly different in others, have taught me something of the wide range of adaptations that Indian cultures have made to a rain forest environment.

Many species of monkeys live in the trees, along with sloths and many kinds of game birds. On the ground, Indians hunted both savanna deer and the smaller forest deer, tapirs, peccaries (both collared and white-lipped), and various large rodents, such as capybaras, pacas, and agoutis. Although today almost all Indians in Amazonia live by farming, none has entirely given up hunting, fishing, or gathering.

The amount of food obtained by hunting varies from tribe to tribe. Among the Amahuaca it provides some 40 percent of the diet; among

OVERLEAF: *Rain forest flanks a maze of meandering tributaries. Amazingly varied, with thousands of plant species, the forests—of limited value as timber— long oozed rubber around the world. Soils are poor; the living forest recycles nutrients for a rich flora and fauna.*

285

Pulsing aorta of a continent, the Amazon courses 4,000 miles from the Andes to the Atlantic carrying more water than any other river in the world. It rivals even the Nile in length. The river's realm, 2.5 million square miles, once was home to five million Indians.

A big mouth and colorful plumage make the toucan conspicuous to the eye and ear throughout the river jungle. Native people call it "crazy bird"—for its raucous cry and treetop antics—and shoot it for food and feathers. The enormous beak is light for its size.

the Kuikuru, less than one percent. Most tribes use hunting bows six feet in length and drawing 60 pounds or more. Arrows are about as long as bows. Centuries before the principle of rifling was hit upon by European gunsmiths, Amazonian Indians used it on their arrows. They attached the feathering in spiral fashion, which made the missiles rotate in flight and thus fly truer to their mark.

Forest Indians prefer to hunt singly or in pairs, since they usually stalk lone animals. The Amazonian Indian can read signs of the forest as we might read a book. Thomas Whiffen, an English army officer and sportsman who traveled among the Bora and Witoto in 1908, wrote:

"I have known an Indian [to] stop and tell me that when the sun was in a certain position, that is to say half an hour previously, seven Indians passed that way carrying a tapir, which had been killed when the sun was there—indicating another position. It was killed a long distance away, and the bag must have been a tapir on account of the evident weight. He took up a leaf on which was a spot of blood, coagulated. He pointed to tracks on the ground, to prove the question of numbers and distance. The men who passed were weary, he knew it by the way their toes had dropped on the ground."

I can verify the Indians' remarkable ability to recognize animal tracks. During one hunting trip I took with two Amahuaca, they pointed out to me the tracks of armadillo, raccoon, deer, agouti, collared peccary, paca, giant armadillo, otter, tapir, caiman, and oriole. Moreover, to attract game within shooting range, Indian hunters often imitate the cries of their quarry. Once I casually asked an Amahuaca hunter to imitate a few animals for me. One after another, he proceeded to imitate the cries of no fewer than 35 different animals.

In northern and western Amazonia, hunters use blowguns, mostly against arboreal game, especially monkeys. The dart is so light that purely as a missile it is worthless, but tipped with *curare*, the famous poison, it becomes deadly. Curare blocks nervous impulses to the muscles, so they become flaccid. A monkey wounded with a curare-tipped dart will not cling to a branch as one shot with an arrow often does. Instead, it slumps to the ground, easy to retrieve. The curare formula may contain 30 ingredients—including stinging ants and powdered snake fangs—most of them for magical effect. The active ingredient comes from sap of the vine *Strychnos toxifera*.

The rain forest of Amazonia contains more species of plants than any area of comparable size in the world. The Amahuaca say that if their crops failed, they could survive on wild tubers, fruits, and nuts. The greatest delicacy found in the forest, though, is honey. I know of no

Huts rim a spoked-wheel Krahó village in eastern Brazil (top). Residents beat paths to the plaza where meetings convene, and around the periphery in log-carrying relay races. Teams of men thus develop speed and endurance for hunting treks. The doughnut-shaped shabono of the Yanomamö of Venezuela (bottom) houses several families. Each man may build his own curved lean-to. Any spaces between are filled in with boughs, vines, and leaves, completing the oval co-op. Addition of an outer palisade of logs helps ward off raiders.

tribe that does not crave it. Several species of honey-making bees live in the forest, and they have a wide variety of rare nectars to choose from. Their honeys delight the palate with a spectrum of tastes, some subtle and delicate, others so pungent they leave the throat burning.

Edible insects—grasshoppers, ants, larvae of bees and wasps—add tang to the native diet. Some Indians prize a large fat grub that lives in the trunks of rotting palms. The Yanomamö of southern Venezuela find the grub by putting an ear to a dead palm trunk and listening for the sound of the grub crunching its way through the pith.

Among my indelible memories of Indian life are the fishing trips I took with an old Kuikuru named Faifuá. Time and again I watched intently as Faifuá, standing poised in the canoe, drew his bow, waiting to loose an arrow at a fish I could barely see. Often I was ready to wager he would miss. He had to allow for the movement of the fish, the movement of the canoe, and the refraction of light in water. But then the bowstring would twang, the shaft would fly, and the next thing I knew a fish was thrashing in the water, transfixed by Faifuá's arrow. He hit with better than 50 percent of his shots.

The most productive fishing method of all uses poisonous forest vines to stupefy fish. Sections of vine are put in the crotch of a forked stick

A man's hearth marks his place in a shabono. Here wives and offspring rest in hammocks or decorate baskets. For privacy couples go outside into the bush. Against insect invaders like roaches the fence is no defense. Pests may get so bad in a year or so that the only cure is to burn the house and rebuild.

289

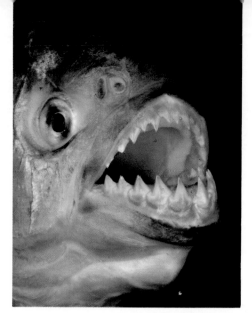

A Kamayurá archer stalks fish from a dugout canoe, which has superseded the bark canoe in the Upper Xingu region. Bait may be dropped on the water to lure fish into range. Amazonia's multitude of fishes includes Serrasalmus nattereri, *most savage of a score of* piranha species. Its razor-sharp teeth can be utilized as saws, yarn snips, or scissors for cutting hair. Despite the piranhas' presence, Indians freely enter most moving waters. A Witoto of eastern Peru (above) wades in to attend to a plaited fiber fish trap.

driven into the river bottom. Then the fisherman crushes the vines with a club. As the sap disperses through the water, it paralyzes the fishes' breathing apparatus but leaves the flesh edible. Fish poisoning is practiced during the dry season when water is low and the current slow so the poison lingers long enough to take effect. In the Upper Xingu region a village fish-poisoning expedition may yield half a ton of fish.

Though hunting, gathering, and fishing enhance the quality and variety of the Indian diet, for almost all tribes the single most important subsistence activity is agriculture. For some tribes, such as those of the Upper Xingu, gardening may provide 80 to 85 percent of the food.

By all odds the most important crop raised in Amazonia is manioc (*Manihot esculenta*), or cassava, a shrub with starchy tuberous roots. Even with indifferent cultivation, it will yield four or five tons of tubers per acre. Indians use flour made from the root to make gruel or to bake into cakes. Tribes of northern South America bake thin, crisp cassava cakes; in the Upper Xingu, cakes are thicker and softer and are often spread with fish paste to make an open sandwich.

Besides manioc, Amazonian Indians plant corn, sweet potatoes, yams, squash, taro, arrowroot, beans, and peanuts. Some tribes, including the Amahuaca and Yanomamö, now rely heavily on bananas and plantains, both of Old World origin.

Amazonian gardeners practice shifting cultivation, known also as slash-and-burn. Toward the end of the rainy season, a man fells an acre or two of trees and leaves them to dry. Just before the next rainy season begins he sets them afire. The ashes add mineral nutrients to the soil. Stumps and charred tree trunks lie strewn through the plot. Crops are planted in the spaces between. Men do the clearing and in some tribes the planting as well. Generally, in a tribe where men spend much time in hunting or warfare, the women plant. A digging stick or a hoe is used to loosen the earth for planting.

Planting is time-consuming, tedious work, and somewhat dangerous, for gardens attract snakes and stinging insects. One day while I was living with the Amahuaca, two men were removing some piled-up fence posts from a corner of my house. Curled up at the bottom of the pile was a boa constrictor. As news of the discovery flashed through the village, women came running from every direction, every one of them highly excited. The men had uncoiled the snake and stretched it to its full length, about eight feet. As each woman reached the snake, she went to the tail end and carefully picked at certain colored scales. I watched, utterly baffled. What on earth was going on?

Afterward, I found out. The Amahuaca believe that picking at the

A soft tread and silent but lethal weapon aids a jungle food quest (opposite). The blowgun of Amazonia may be two to three times as long as the hunter who uses it. The Yagua marksman carries a ball of kapok fluff and a quiver full of poison-tipped darts across his chest. The fluff is wrapped around the butt end of a dart before it is inserted in the blowgun. A huff of breath expels the missile. Another Yagua, armed with a single-barrel shotgun, brings home the day's catch, which includes a large male howler monkey and a toucan.

scales of a boa's tail markings protects a woman against the painful sting of the *isula*, an inch-long, glossy-black ant that infests the gardens.

As long as gardens keep producing well, they are replanted. But generally, after two or three years, fertility declines, and weeds take over, so it is easier to abandon the plot and clear a new one elsewhere.

Amazonian villages are occupied considerably longer than gardens, sometimes 10 or 20 years. The more settled the village, as a rule, the more elaborate the dwelling. Thus the Amahuaca, who occupy a house no more than a year or two, take few pains with its construction. A man and wife can put up a house in three days: The first day they cut the materials, the second day they erect the framework, and the third day they thatch the roof. On the other hand, tribes that expect to occupy a village for a generation or so apply all their skill to house construction.

The most impressive houses are probably those on the upper Rio Negro and in the Upper Xingu. The Tukano of the Rio Negro build houses about 90 feet long, 60 feet wide, and 25 feet high. Slabs of bark, often painted with colorful designs, form the walls, and the roof is thatched with palm leaves. Such a *maloca*, or large communal dwelling, may house an entire village of 100 persons or more.

The Kuikuru, like the other tribes of the Upper Xingu, live in houses with a sturdy pole framework carefully covered with grass thatch. An Upper Xingu house, which may be 70 feet long, looks like a giant, oval haystack, since roof and wall form a continuous curve from the top of the house down to the ground. Such houses often have only tiny doorways, and it takes a visitor's eyes a while to get accustomed to the gloom. What he is likely to see then is a varied assortment of furniture, tools, utensils, ornaments, and weapons, strewn casually about.

For a non-Indian, living in an Indian house takes getting used to. Besides the perpetually dim light, you have to cook your food on the ground, over a fire whose acrid smoke seems always to pursue you, no matter where you move, making your eyes smart painfully.

Then there are the insects. The Kuikuru house I lived in for a time was populated by an enormous species of cockroach called an *útusi*. Next to the 3½-inch útusi our city-bred cockroaches seem as dainty as ladybugs. An old Indian house is a veritable insectarium. Many a night, when the last Indian has drifted off to sleep, the visitor may be kept awake by the bugs chomping their way through the thatch above.

Each family in a house has its own hearth for cooking. Close by, hammocks are strung, usually radiating out from the center posts to smaller posts along the wall. The hammock is an Amazonian Indian invention; it keeps the sleeper safely above the concourse of vermin on

Hanging upside down by the rigid hooks on its paws, the three-toed sloth sleeps by day, moves by night, foraging leaves and buds. Some tribes eat sloth meat; others avoid it. The flesh of the anteater (top) is generally regarded as unpalatable. With curved claws it tears into an ant or termite nest, inserts its long tongue, and licks up the insects. A more widespread game, the capybara (bottom) tastes like fish. The world's largest rodent, the riverine mammal may reach four feet in length and weigh more than 150 pounds.

296

Leaning towers of tortoises proclaim the success of an overland hunting trip. The reptiles, taken alive, will be roasted for a feast climaxing a round of ceremonies that may have lasted many months. In 1542 Spaniards descending the Amazon visited Indian villages where hundreds of turtles "large as leather shields" were penned in ponds until needed as food. Turtle eggs were gathered for food and oil. Once nomadic, the Mekranotí (right) still go trekking in the forest. All the villagers, carrying garden produce as trail fare, may be away for weeks. Some treks serve a ceremonial purpose, others are for gathering supplies, and some may simply satisfy the urge to trek.

the ground. A Kuikuru man slings his hammock above his wife's, and it is her responsibility to get up in the chill of the night and tend the fire.

Other than hammocks, there is little furniture. Men usually sit on wooden stools, often carved in the form of a bird or a mammal, while women sit on palm leaf mats laid on the ground.

Utensils may include baskets; gourd ladles, spoons, and bowls; calabash water bottles; fire fans, graters, griddles, mortars, pestles, and, of course, pots. Pottery is almost universal in Amazonia, ranging in quality from the thick, coarse pots of the Yanomamö to the skillfully made and beautifully decorated vessels of the Shipibo and Conibo.

Indian houses need no clothes closets. It is common for one or both sexes to go naked. A number of tribes, though, wear some form of pubic covering, often a penis sheath for a man and a G-string for a woman.

The tribes of western Amazonia employ a backstrap or belt loom to weave skirts and other garments from cotton grown in the fields. Among the Shipibo, Conibo, Campa, and Piro of the Montaña, men wear a long, nightshirt-like garment called a *cushma*, while the women wear a wraparound skirt and sometimes a blouse.

In Amazonia women give birth with little formality. Often a woman's mother or other female relative assists at the delivery, and a woman with skill as a midwife may also be present. Infants are raised with indulgence and receive great warmth and affection from both parents. A child is almost never struck. The Kuikuru were appalled to learn that American parents sometimes spank their children!

The life of an Indian boy is pretty nearly idyllic. Armed with a toy bow and arrow made for him by his father, he shoots at grasshoppers, lizards, and birds. Seldom is he required to do serious work. A girl, however, while still very young, may have to help with the household chores. I knew an eight-year-old Kuikuru girl named Tukuti who, in the skill and care with which she spun cotton or prepared manioc, was as mature and responsible as a woman twenty years her senior.

But also in the village was a six-year-old girl named Aitá, who was delightfully irresponsible. One day Aitá broke the meterstick I was using to measure an archaeological test pit I was digging and, fearing the consequences, ran away. When she showed up the next day she waited with her head lowered until I had finished scolding. Then, her face brightening, she asked, "Now that it's broken, can I have it?"

At puberty Indian youngsters leave childhood behind and become, in the eyes of their society, full-fledged adults. Most tribes have some kind of formal puberty observance. Boys are often subjected to some ordeal to prove their manhood. In the Guianas, the most dramatic such trial is

Bitter manioc, the Indians' staff of life, must be freed of poisonous prussic acid. Peeled tubers are grated into pulp (top) using a rasp made of palm root. Then the moist pulp is placed on a flexible strip of plaited fiber (bottom), which is then twisted to force out the juice.

Implements vary from tribe to tribe. The woman (opposite) uses the more efficient tipití, a basketwork tube. A tipití is squeezed by pressing on the pole. The processed pulp is baked into pancakes. After hours of boiling, the milky juice becomes a palatable drink.

the ant ordeal. A straw plaque into which dozens of stinging ants have been "woven" is pressed against a boy's chest. Although the ants sting unmercifully, the boy is supposed to show no sign of pain.

A pubescent Kuikuru boy wrestles with an anaconda. By pitting himself against it, the boy hopes to acquire some of its strength. After wrestling the nonpoisonous snake, the boy lets it bite him. Then he kills it, slices it open with a knife, and smears its fat on his body.

Girls' puberty rituals also may be quite severe. A Tikuna girl has every strand of hair plucked from her head, then undergoes a simulated attack by "evil spirits," men dressed in grotesque masks of bark cloth. More typically, a Kuikuru girl may spend a year or two in puberty seclusion, sitting by herself in a partitioned area of her house. During this time she lets her hair grow long, and when she finally emerges her bangs may cover her face. If the girl marries immediately thereafter, the groom cuts her bangs as part of the ceremony.

Once their puberty rituals are over, boys and girls—now men and women—are free to mate and marry. Many tribes permit marriage between persons of the same village, but a few require that one find a spouse in another village. In the latter case, the couple lives either in the village of the groom's parents (patrilocal residence) or in that of the bride's parents (matrilocal residence). In matrilocal societies the groom often must perform bride service, usually helping his father-in-law clear a patch of forest for a new garden.

While weddings receive slight social recognition, death is an occasion for great concern among Amazonian Indians. People fear that the soul of the deceased will remain behind as a ghost and annoy or endanger the survivors. One purpose of a funeral, therefore, is to compel the soul to leave the area and proceed to the afterworld.

Most commonly the corpse is buried in the ground wrapped only in a hammock or covered with mats. Or it may be buried in an urn. Usually, urn burial is a "secondary burial," with only the bones of the deceased being placed in the vessel.

The Bororo of south central Brazil practice elaborate burials. They first bury the body in a shallow grave, watering it daily to hasten the decomposition of the flesh. For a month the whole village joins in one ritual after another, almost every day. The rituals include a jaguar hunt and an inspection of the grave by two mythical beasts. After the month has elapsed, the corpse is disinterred and the bones are cleaned of flesh, washed, painted, and feathered. The decorated bones, in a specially made basket, are then given final burial in a swamp.

What kind of afterlife can a person look forward to? Conceptions vary,

Metal tools unknown a few decades ago ease the toil of land-clearing for the Txukahamai. Their new garden plot and village site lie within Xingu National Park, established to shield Indians from outsiders and reduce intertribal war. These two wear the traditional lip disk.

302   but usually the soul of the deceased goes to a village in the sky, not unlike the one in which he lived. Amazonian Indians have little notion of a rewarding heaven or a punishing hell, and people generally go to the same afterworld, a pleasant if not idyllic place. A Kuikuru soul, arriving in the village of the dead, can look forward to meeting Isagifeñú, the aunt of the sun. She squeezes milk from her one large breast and serves it to the soul. Day after day the milk nourishes the soul so that it returns to the size and vigor it knew in life.

Living Amazonian tribes have a relatively simple social structure. There are no social classes and the only division of labor is that based on age and sex. Villages are politically independent of one another. Most have a headman or chief, but he persuades rather than commands. And at that, not always successfully. As anthropologist John M. Cooper once put it, "One word from the chief and everyone does as he pleases."

But villages have informal ways of getting things done, often based on the obligations of kinship. All village life revolves around the nuclear family: a man, his wife, and their children. Several nuclear families may in turn be aggregated into an extended family. Among some societies, like the Yanomamö, individuals may be further aggregated into lineages, and in a few societies, such as the Tikuna, lineages have expanded and crystalized into clans.

Gê-speaking groups of central Brazil, such as the Shavante and the Northern Kayapó, have a more elaborate social organization than their non-Gê neighbors. A village is divided into two halves, called *moieties*. Moiety membership is sometimes based on descent, but it can rest on such distinctions as whether a person was born during the dry season or the rainy season. Gê moieties sometimes   *(Continued on page 310)*

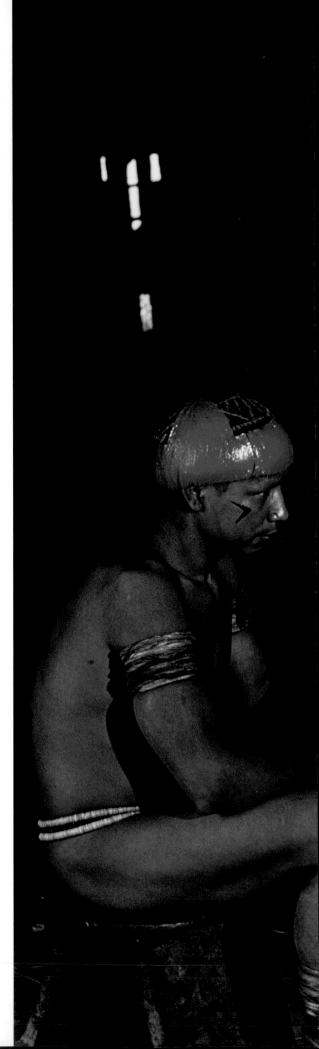

Scarlet seeds of urucú, *a cultivated shrub, color ceremonial and everyday activities. Urucú provides dye, insect repellent, and greasepaint to decorate human bodies. The Indians boil the pasty covering from the seeds, releasing a red pigment. Then they mix the pigment with oil and shape the congealed mixture into a ball ready for use.*

Gathered in the men's house, social center of their village, Waurá tribesmen of the Upper Xingu ready themselves for the afternoon events (right). Urucú plasters their hair into a helmet; oil sheens their muscular bodies; urucú and genipa, a black vegetable dye, add finishing touches of geometric pattern. For dances and war games, men lavishly embellish their bodies; women may make up with only a red line across the brow. Most Indians pluck all facial and body hair. Wrestlers believe their arm bands increase their strength.

RITUAL AND PAGEANTRY

Festivities reign in the dry season, May to September. At the peak of the manioc harvest, women toil dawn to dusk, but men's work is soon done and a daily round of dance, athletic contests, and practice for the annual mock war begins. Waurá warriors hone their spear-throwing skills using a straw man as stand-in opponent (left). Cane spears heaved at visiting tribesmen during the war games have blunt wooden or wax tips. Costumed even for rehearsal, men paint themselves as forest creatures, influenced by the rich world of myth where humans and animals, nature and supernature freely mingle.

A gourd rattles, a bamboo tube thumps the ground, and palm skirts shake rhythmically as befeathered Waurá dancers keep time—and the beat of the fishnet dance goes on. Hunters supply macaw and toucan feathers. Most villages of the Upper Xingu region keep a caged harpy eagle "mascot," periodically cutting its feathers. Rites perhaps spiritual in origin now survive in a playful atmosphere. Following a group fishing trip, for instance, men dressed as spirits pester the women, demanding food. A successful pair emerge from a thatched house, loot in hand.

308

In a dimly lit sanctum, the men's house,
a Waurá trio play the sacred flutes.
Called jakuí, the four-foot flutes
personify the potent spirit that dwells
under rivers and lagoons. Tribesmen of
the Upper Xingu play and dance to the
jakuí to commune with the spirit. The
instruments are kept hidden in the men's
house, a clubhouse and afternoon
gathering place, central to the village
but off limits to women. When the flutes
are played outside, women must seclude
themselves in their own houses. Should
a tribeswoman—either by design or
accident—ever look upon the jakuí, the
prescribed penalty is gang rape.

compete against each other in sporting events. Moieties also carry out a number of reciprocal functions, such as burying each other's dead.

While much of life in an Amazon village is easy and casual, it has its formal side too. Indeed, ceremonies form a central part of life. Although they are often religious, they are sometimes purely social and secular. Thus, while the Kuikuru name most of their ceremonies after spirits, they perform them in order to sing and dance, to eat and drink.

The women, who prepare the brew for feasts, start the fermentation by chewing some corn or manioc mash, and spitting it into a bowl. The bowl is then covered and kept in a dark corner. In about three days a mildly alcoholic beverage results. Mild it may be, but drunk in huge quantities, it can produce a grand intoxication. To get drunk faster, some tribes induce vomiting when they feel their stomachs getting full, and then drink some more.

Drinking bouts at ceremonies may lead to pleasant diversions, such as the consummation of a love affair. But as inhibitions dissolve, grudges sometimes surface and quarrels break out. When violence threatens, the women, who tend to drink less, often hide the weapons.

A Conibo man will take the opportunity of a drinking bout to accuse another of adultery with his wife, and a club fight may ensue. Since both men are royally drunk by then, the fight often appears to be in slow motion. But when he finally has his adversary down, the cuckold whips out a special adultery knife (formerly made from a toucan's beak) and cuts the back of his rival's head from ear to ear. An Amahuaca I knew, who had lived for a time with the Conibo, bore scars of at least four such cuts. A man regards these scars much as Don Juan regarded his saber cuts—as evidence of success as a lover.

Use of psychoactive drugs intensifies certain Indian rituals and ceremonies. The Amazon basin produces many narcotic plants, some of which profoundly alter consciousness. Of these, the most widely used is *ayahuasca*, or *yagé*. A potion made by boiling this forest vine produces vivid and colorful hallucinations which the Indians interpret as experiences of the soul or as visitations from the spirits. Indeed, ayahuasca is often drunk in order to see spirits, since they are thought

Txukahamai men master a monster, a water-dwelling anaconda. The constrictor may reach 30 feet in length. Nonpoisonous, it lives mainly on river animals and is of little menace to man. Amazonia also teems with huge insects and spiders such as the tarantula (left).

to be very knowledgeable and ready to impart valuable information.

Another well-known drug is coca, whose leaves are chewed with lime by several tribes in western Amazonia. Chewing coca stills hunger pangs by preventing the rhythmic contractions of the stomach walls and is also thought to increase one's endurance.

The most important narcotic plant of all is tobacco. From its first domestication, probably somewhere in Amazonia, tobacco has spread to every corner of the world, and is smoked recreationally as far away as the highlands of New Guinea. In Amazonia, though, tobacco is smoked primarily as an accompaniment to shamanistic practice. The Indian shaman, like shamans the world over, seeks the aid of spirits in diagnosing and curing illness. To get in touch with spirits, he inhales tobacco smoke deeply, or swallows it, and goes into a nicotine-induced trance. In curing, a shaman often blows smoke on the affected part of a patient's body, and then draws from it a magical dart or other foreign object which he tells the patient has caused his illness.

Another common cause of illness is soul loss. Perhaps one's soul left his body during sleep and failed to return, or perhaps it has been stolen by an evil spirit. In any case, it must be recovered or the patient will die. Soul recoveries are often the shamans' most dramatic performances.

Hallucinogenic drugs form an integral part of the life of some tribes. Yanomamö men contact their spirit world by inhaling ebene snuff. The powerful drug is made from tree bark. Men pair off and blow the powder through tubes into each other's nostrils.

To recapture a soul, a Kuikuru shaman first makes a *kefegé*, or straw doll. He blows tobacco smoke on the doll to bring it to life, and then uses it as a "magnet" to draw the missing soul away from the evil spirit.

During one soul recovery I witnessed, Agaku, the Kuikuru shaman, had himself paddled to the middle of the lake. Reaching a spot directly above where the evil spirit was supposed to live, he dived to the bottom, clutching the kefegé to his chest. A minute later, he broke the surface of the water, screaming in the most unearthly manner, and was hauled into the canoe. After more wild screaming, Agaku suddenly "died." All the while, he clutched the kefegé tightly, and when he came to, he told those around him that, with the help of the doll, he had succeeded in wrenching the missing soul away from its spirit captor.

A shaman conducts his practice for the benefit of the society. A witch or sorcerer uses his power to injure or kill people. Any misfortune, from toothache to death, may be attributed to sorcery. And if the misfortune is serious enough, a shaman may be called in to verify the diagnosis and to identify and punish the sorcerer.

There are two common ways to practice sorcery. One is to shoot a magical dart or some similar object into the body of the victim. The other, called *exuvial magic,* is done by getting hold of something belonging to the victim—a strand of hair, nail parings, some saliva, an item of clothing—and working witchcraft on it. Whatever is done to the exuviae is then supposed to happen to the victim. There is little evidence that anyone actually practices sorcery, but the *belief* that they do is one of the most disruptive elements in Indian life. In 1975, when I returned to the Kuikuru village after an absence of 21 years, I found that some 40 Kuikuru had left the village and moved in with another tribe because of accusations or suspicions of witchcraft.

All Amazonian tribes believe in spirits. Most spirits are associated with particular animals or plants, but they are thought of as having human form. The supernatural beings in which the Indians believe are usually not powerful or exalted enough to be called gods. The Kuikuru do sometimes refer to the sun, whom they call Giti, by the Portuguese word Deus, or God. During mythological times Giti played an important role as an innovator and organizer, but it seems more accurate to call him a "culture hero" than a god. If a god at all, he is an "otiose" god, one who accomplished his mission on earth in the dim past, and now stands back and allows things to run by themselves.

The mythological beliefs of Amazonia are exceedingly rich. Many of the myth motifs, such as the great flood, the theft of fire, and the sky ladder, have counterparts elsewhere in the world, but others are

Prescription for a mysterious ailment: a supernatural bedside manner. These Yanomamö shamans surround a malaria patient, trying to cure by magic. They chant to the demons believed to cause illness, massage the patient, and attempt to draw the evil spirit out of his body.

A tsantsa, or shrunken human head (right), attests to the force of the Indians' belief in spirits. When a Jívaro killed an enemy, he shrank the victim's head to fist size, a process meant to drive away the dead man's avenging soul before it could kill the killer.

Bronze chorus of Waurá women recount a legend in song and dance. In their version, the mythical Amazonian women fled jealous husbands. Following an armadillo tunnel to a distant place, they emerged, made homes, weapons, and new lives independent of men. In reality, Indian women's work leaves scant time for pageantry. The dry season brings the toil of manioc harvest. Implements must be made. The Shipibo of Peru excel at pottery (opposite).

Amazonian women nurse their babies three years or longer. While a Karajá child sleeps at a funeral, cords are tied on its ankles to ward off evil spirits.

distinctive. Foremost among these I would put the myth about the woman who, journeying through the forest, takes a wrong fork in the trail and ends up in the village of the jaguars. Here she is first sheltered and then betrayed by the mother jaguar, and ultimately killed. The woman, made pregnant by her jaguar husband, posthumously gives birth to twins, who turn out to be the sun and the moon. The twins later avenge their mother's death, and after a series of adventures and close calls, finally ascend into the sky.

The tranquility that generally reigns over Indian life is occasionally interrupted by war. Warfare is no longer widespread and intense in Amazonia, but it continues to be practiced by a few tribes. For the Yanomamö, raids and counterraids are a way of life. The aim of these raids is not to take land or prisoners, but to avenge past wrongs and intimidate enemies, perhaps forcing them to flee their village.

Into the 1960s, the Northern Kayapó of central Brazil were formidable warriors, raiding not only each other, but also white settlers who had encroached on their territory. From an early age, a Kayapó boy was trained to be a warrior, leaving his natal house and moving into the men's house. There, besides the martial arts, he was taught the attitudes and demeanor of a warrior. The Yanomamö word *waiteri* and

the corresponding Kayapó word *djokrê* (hard, tough, mean) express the ideal toward which men in these societies are expected to strive.

Cannibalism and headhunting once frequently accompanied war. The Tupinambá of the Brazilian coast were renowned cannibals. One of the earliest accounts of the practice dates back to the 1550s. Hans Staden, a German gunner in the employ of the Portuguese Navy, spent ten months as a prisoner of the Tupinambá. Before he finally escaped, Staden expected daily to be killed and eaten by his captors, and had witnessed the killing and eating of other prisoners. Staden left us a detailed account of the elaborate preparations made for killing a prisoner. The village chief presented the executioner with a decorated club, called *iwera pemme*. With it "the slayer strikes from behind and beats out his brains. The women seize the body at once and carry it to the fire where they scrape off the skin, making the flesh quite white, and stopping up the fundament with a piece of wood so that nothing may be lost. Then a man cuts up the body, removing the legs above the knee and the arms at the trunk, whereupon the four women seize the four limbs and run with them round the huts, making a joyful cry. After this they divide the trunk among themselves, and devour everything that can be eaten." (Continued on page 322)

Young Yanomamö archers practice, aiming toy arrows at targets such as birds (above). In advanced training, tomorrow's warriors blacken their faces and stalk a make-believe adversary. Such play teaches skills used later in hunting and warfare. Though deaths still occur in battles between villages, Indians do not always shoot to kill. Rivals release lesser aggressions in club fights and chest-pounding duels.

OVERLEAF: *Painted bodies gleaming, two Xingu wrestlers vie in a test of strength and skill. The huka-huka matches are a daily ritual in the dry season. Muscle-building armbands worn in preparation for the contest were removed before this bout.*

Several Amazonian tribes prepared trophies from the heads of slain enemies, but the Jívaro of Ecuador were the most famous practitioners of the art. Indeed, these Indians are responsible for the English word "headshrinker," in its original meaning. The Jívaro *tsantsa*, or shrunken head, is no mere trophy or keepsake. Shrinking the head of a slain foe—now rarely, if ever, done—is thought to prevent the *muisak*, or avenging soul, of the victim from killing the slayer.

Preparation of the head begins at once, on the trail. The Jívaro makes an incision up the back of the neck as far as the crown and carefully peels the scalp and the rest of the skin off the skull. Then he stitches it up and soaks it in hot water. When allowed to dry it shrinks to the size of a man's fist. Blackening the head over a smoky fire preserves it from insects. The head may be used later in ceremonies, but its main purpose, driving away the muisak, has already been accomplished.

Intertribal warfare, persisting through the centuries, has accounted for an untold number of deaths. But Indian weapons have never had the range or deadly proficiency of firearms used by outsiders seeking to exploit the resources of Amazonia. Nor have bows and clubs the killing power of diseases; measles, for example, has wiped out entire tribes.

Five million or more Indians lived in Amazonia when Europeans first arrived. Scarcely more than 250,000 of their descendants are alive today, and most of them no longer lead a tribal life. Many of the tribes not actually exterminated have been extensively acculturated. Even a remote Yanomamö village as yet unvisited by white men will have acquired pieces of old machete blades which are set into wooden handles as substitutes for the traditional stone ax.

Though dozens of tribes still survive under conditions essentially aboriginal—villages laid out as in the past, and their social, ceremonial, and religious lives still guided by native custom and belief—the number of such groups is fast diminishing. As the pace of colonization in Amazonia has stepped up, Indian territory has been increasingly invaded and despoiled. Numerous tribes face deculturation or even physical extinction. Whatever their ultimate fate, though, the Indians of Amazonia and their habitat have made enormous contributions—manioc, rubber, tobacco, the hammock, to name only a few—that have influenced world culture.

And they have greatly contributed to ethnology. They have allowed us to draw a vivid and detailed picture of how human groups, using a Stone Age technology, were able to adapt to a tropical forest environment, and ultimately to erect a distinctive culture, full of diversity, richness, and interest.

Between two worlds, a cortege of Shavante prepare to bury a dead child. A suitcase serves as coffin; a Catholic priest performs the rites. But, according to tribal tradition, the grave is round and vertical to receive the corpse feet first. Logs will be placed over the hole, topped by a cloth, a mat, and a mound of fresh earth. At the Shavante village of São Marcos in Brazil's Mato Grosso State, an Indian youth (opposite) serves as acolyte at Mass. The Shavante, in touch with modern value systems, keep a vigorous sense of Indian identity.

THE CHACO INDIANS

Elmer S. Miller

A matron of the Toba tribe sips maté, *the bitter herbal tea drunk ceremonially throughout the Gran Chaco. The host or hostess serves one guest at a time. Then the gourd containing the maté leaves is refilled with hot water and, with its silver straw, passed to the next person.*

Their homeland is called Chaco—Hunting Ground. The Gran Chaco territory, some 300,000 square miles in Paraguay, eastern Bolivia, and northern Argentina, once had prolific animal, bird, and fish life. Here, despite the heavy toll of warfare and alien diseases, about 80,000 Indians survive, the majority with their hunting and gathering culture intact until the middle 1900s.

Europeans found it an inhospitable hunting ground. Those who first attempted to settle the Chaco less than a century ago spoke of it as the "green hell." This parched plain interspersed with forest and scrub suffers some of South America's hottest temperatures: 115° F. on many a sun-seared afternoon. Annual rainfall is a meager 25 inches in the western portion, 50 in the east. Though riverbanks and marshes that dot the area support subtropical vegetation, much of the soil is salt-encrusted, and good water is scarce. Poisonous snakes and nasty insects abounded in colonial days and are still part of the Indians' environment.

Beginning in 1958 and as recently as 1979, I lived for long periods among two of the larger Chaco tribes, the Toba and the Mataco. One day three Toba men and I were walking single file through the forest. Suddenly the man ahead of me stopped, tracing with his eyes the flight of some bees. Excited, he borrowed a machete and followed the bees into the jungle. The rest of us went on to our destination. Two hours after we arrived, the beehunter reappeared—bare-backed and with his shirt tied tightly around his left hand. He had found the bee tree. As he was reaching into the trunk cavity to extract honey, a snake bit his finger. Assuming the worst, that it was a deadly coral snake, he seized the machete and cut off his fingertip before the poison could travel through his body. In time his finger stub healed, but seeing it made me ever aware of the dangers of the seemingly peaceful life around us.

The Chaco peoples traditionally have lived in extended family bands: Parents and children, aunts, uncles, cousins, and grandparents mingled daily. The bands were migratory, moving throughout a recognized territory to exploit the resources there. During summer months, beans of the *algarroba*, or carob, tree served as a staple. These long green pods were eaten raw or ground into meal and *(Continued on page 333)*

Under a spreading algarroba tree, at the forest edge, stands a Toba house. Made of poles plastered with mud, roofed with thatch, it serves mainly for sleeping and shelter when it rains, since family members live in the open. A pot of meat stew simmers over the fire. In the shade stand tables and chairs assembled for a feast honoring visitors; usually, people sit on the ground. A goat from the small flock is butchered (above). Into a blanket partly of homegrown wool a woman weaves bright yarn bought at a store—a mixing of native and borrowed strands typical now of Chaco life.

OVERLEAF: These Indians pick cotton on their own land, but many others work for wages. As open land dwindles, more Chaco Indians take migrant jobs as lumberjacks and farmhands. Women now do field work along with men, a break with traditional division of labor.

Stems of the caraguatá plant provide raw material for the handiwork of women. Separating the fibers with fingernails, they soak, pound, and scrape them, then deftly craft bags, belts, or fishing nets (below). A Toba man (right) grasps a completed net, attached to two flexible poles tied at both ends. Wading into waist-deep water, he will spread the poles apart, allowing fish to enter. Then he lets the poles snap shut, trapping his quarry. Fishing in the Chaco is a seasonal activity, most productive when schools are moving upriver to spawn.

pressed into cakes. Gathering wild vegetables and fruits was women's work. Gathering wild honey—the Toba harvest 14 different kinds—was men's work, along with fishing and hunting. Various species of deer, wild pig, armadillo, partridge, and rabbit supplied protein needs.

As game has become scarce through European overkill and the fencing off of large tracts as private property, Chaco breadwinners have had to work as migrant laborers in lumber camps, sugarcane and cotton fields, and in the 1970s in urban industries. Some groups have settled on small farms, keeping a few sheep and goats, attempting to raise local cash crops to supply their increasing wants, supplementing their diets by traditional means.

Hunting weapons include bows and arrows, spears, bolas, and a few shotguns. Men consider it a virtue to be able to endure long treks with

Fervent sermons, music, and shouting mark Pentecostal church services among the Argentine Toba. Spontaneous dance, along with a rhythmic chittering, begins among the congregation (above) and continues until a dancer falls into a trance, thought necessary to contact the healing spirits. To the Toba, conversion means healing. The revivalist sect readily amassed an Indian flock. Free-form services recall the Feast of Pentecost, when the Holy Spirit descended upon Christ's disciples, conferring the gift of "tongues."

little food or water—the first to request either one is derided as unmanly or weak. When stalking game, hunters camouflage their heads and shoulders and try to approach their prey closely. A good Toba hunter masked with rhea feathers can imitate the bird's movements with such skill that he can often get near enough to kill one with a club. Though it is no longer the principal means of livelihood, hunting is not taken lightly. It is under supervision of the shaman, usually a grandfather of the extended family group.

Once, after seeking the shaman's permission, I was allowed to join a Toba hunting party. I had a 16-gauge pump gun, another man had an old single-barrel 12-gauge, and the remaining two carried bows and arrows. As we trudged across an open field heading toward the forest, a grouse took wing from the grass in front of me and quickly shifted direction to the left and behind me. I whipped my 16-gauge around and with one shot brought the grouse to earth. But when I retrieved my catch, not one of my fellow hunters had a word to say. On the contrary, they were looking off in the distance ignoring me. I found this hard to understand. Unable to control my enthusiasm, I finally blurted out, "What did you think of that shot? Wasn't it a beauty?"

Again the silent treatment. Eventually the man with the 12-gauge said, "What if you had missed?" In other words, I had taken a foolish risk. I came to learn that the Toba count it a crime to wound an animal and not kill it outright. I might have done that, causing the ill will of the animal spirits, and spoiled the hunting luck of the whole group.

In the Chaco world view, animal lords and deceased spirits assist the shamans in keeping balance and harmony, essential for health and well-being. The Toba cosmos has five layers, and all "beings," or spirits, belong to one of the five. Sun, moon, and star constellations have a natural abode in the heavens; lightning, thunder, north wind, and south wind abide in the atmosphere. Humans and most animals belong to the surface of the earth; snakes, frogs, and pumas inside the earth. Water beings belong at the lowest level. A being that moves outside its appropriate sphere causes trouble. When a snake being writhes from inside the earth and reaches the surface, for example, it may enter a person and cause illness. With the aid of a companion spirit, the shaman must return this snake to its rightful place so that health and harmony can be restored. His means of curing traditionally has been to sing a song, blow on the painful spot, and suck out the intruding "object" causing illness.

The teachings of Christian missionaries, both Catholic and Protestant, have done much to break down the Indians' reliance on the supernatural in everyday events. Governments, too, assume it a duty to "bring them into the 20th century." Missions, health clinics, schools, and wage-earning activities inevitably work changes in Chaco society. So far, these contacts have not significantly altered their basic world view, but there are signs that transformations are under way. Amidst well-intentioned, but sometimes misguided, benefactors, aboriginal cultures can survive only by the strongest of will.

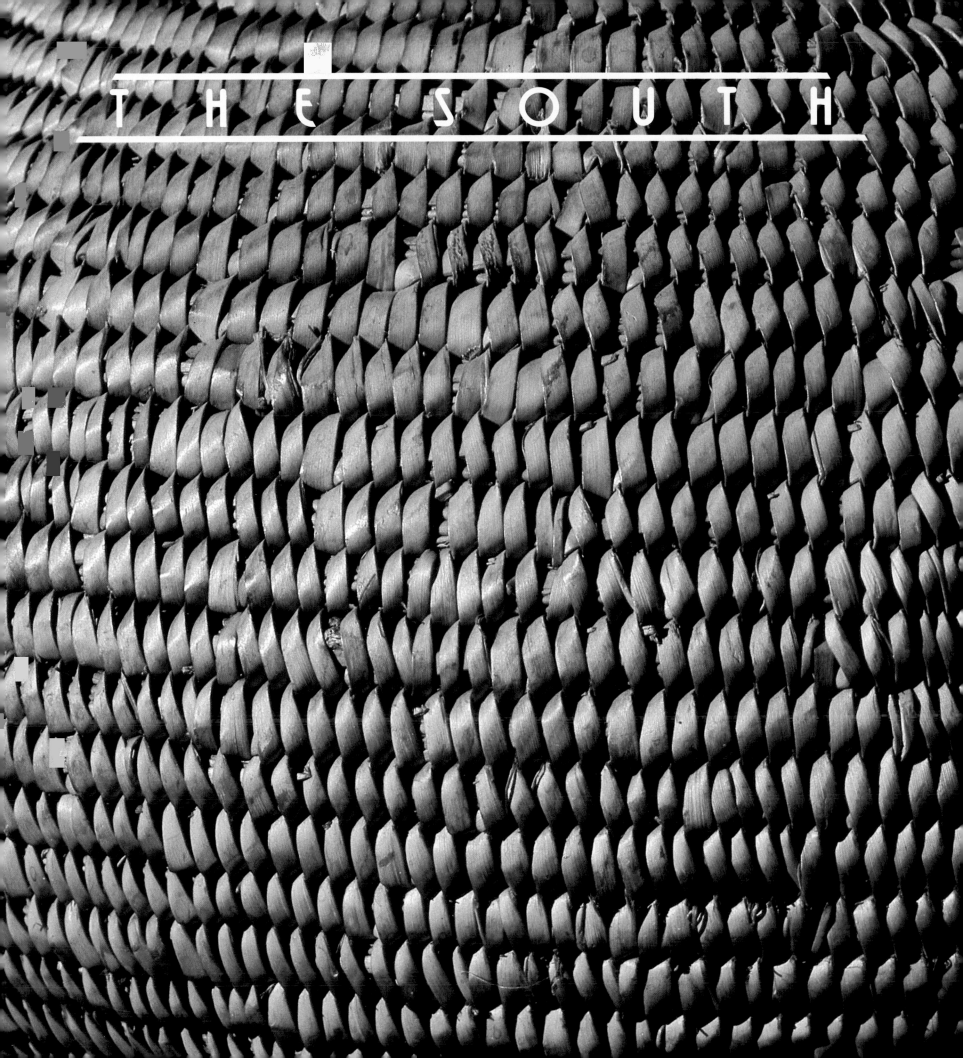

THE SOUTH

*S*kyscraping volcanoes and rolling grasslands, complex Indian societies and Stone Age peoples, highland farmers and coastal gatherers and plains hunters—the wedge-shaped tip of South America embraces a land rich in contrasts. From mighty Aconcagua, the continent's highest peak, the Andes march southward to disappear into frigid waters near the Antarctic Circle. West of the Andes, Mapuche farmers, descendants of indomitable Araucanians in Chile's fertile Central Valley, thrive as one of the largest Indian groups in South America. But east of the Andes only the ghosts of nomadic hunters ride the vast plains that Indians called pampa, meaning "space." They have vanished, along with virtually all the tribes who once inhabited this end of the world. They live on only in the blood of mestizos and in the words of explorers, scientists, and missionaries.

On the first voyage around the world, the intrepid mariner Ferdinand Magellan observed "a land stark with eternal cold" as he sailed through the treacherous strait that bears his name. Indian fires twinkled on every shore, so he called the region Tierra del Fuego, Land of Fire. Even summers could be viciously bitter; two servants with Captain Cook stayed out one summer night and froze to death.

When H.M.S. Beagle anchored off the island in 1832, a seasick young naturalist named Charles Darwin described the squat, red-eyed natives as "man in his lowest and most savage state." He watched a mother nurse her baby as sleet fell on their naked bodies. He saw stunted men, "their hair entangled, their voices discordant, and their gestures violent." Darwin wondered: "Could our progenitors have been men like these?"

The white man's diseases and weapons finally decimated the Fuegians as well as the grassland hunters. Magellan had called these Argentine natives, who wore grass-stuffed moccasins, Patagones, or Big Feet. Though they are no more, the name has stuck to their semiarid homeland—Patagonia. But Mapuche farmers beat back Inca invasions, withstood new diseases, and for several centuries blocked Spanish and Chilean attempts at domination. Ironically, Mapuche heroism inspired the Chileans in their fight for freedom from Spain in the early 1800s.

Left: Sacred Mapuche wooden statue, Chile. Opposite: Mapuche basket, Chile.

HUNTERS AND HARVESTERS OF THE CONE

Tom D. Dillehay

Drums beat a hypnotic tempo as seated men and women sing and chant, and small groups prance and gyrate rhythmically around a sacred altar in the center of the ceremonial field. Men on horseback gallop around the edge of the field, their shouts and the thunder of hoofbeats chasing away evil spirits. I watch partially mesmerized, caught up in the *nguillatun*, a four-day agricultural fertility rite of the Mapuche Indians. It's an early spring morning in a pine forest on Chile's wet coastal strip, and I find it ironic that the friendly people around me are descendants of the legendary Araucanian Indians, an indomitable people whose warriors were so fierce they stopped the Inca's invasion in the mid-15th century, then for the next 350 years defied the Spaniards and Chileans.

I was in Chile to teach anthropology at universities in the heart of Mapucheland, and I had jumped at the chance to participate in this sacred ceremony. Soon I found myself helping Mapuche men cut wooden poles and branches for their family *ramadas*. As the lean-tos rose, the men chatted about the days ahead, the relatives and friends coming from far away, the food and the dancing, and the goodwill to be shared by all. Late that afternoon, rosy-cheeked women brought us bowls of potatoes and horsemeat. As we ate, a crackling fire of fragrant boughs sent sparks and sweet-smelling smoke into the air.

Now the nguillatun is in its last day. Ramadas surround the field. While some Indians dance and perform rituals, others sit on the ground and chant, communing with their ancestors and their gods.

The dancing stops, and the participants feast once more with relatives and friends. The elder men kindle a fire on the altar and place there the meat of a sacrificial goat or sheep. The ritual priest watches over the activities, while the shaman sits immobile, transfixed by some unseen spiritual force. Now the ritual ends, quietly, and the Indians leave, strengthened in their sense of being Mapuche.

The Spanish conquistadores had called the ancestors of these Indians Araucanos, a name perhaps derived from a fruit-bearing tree called the Araucaria, or from the Quechua word *auka*—warrior. Thinking in geographical terms and measuring Indian cultures by their savagery and

Regal in ancient silver, a Mapuche elder profiles a defiant people. For 400 years these "Apaches of South America" fought off Incas, Spaniards, Chileans. The epic poem La Araucana, *first literary masterpiece penned in the New World, recounts Indian might: "And with warfare undiluted, With sheer grit outrocks the earthquake."*

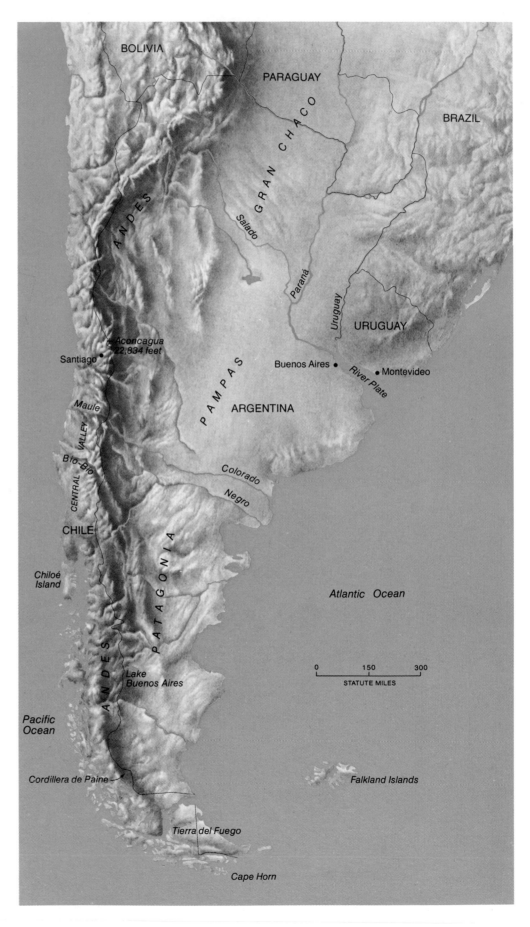

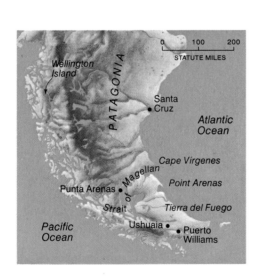

The cone of South America: home of fierce Araucanians west of the Andes and Patagonian tribes on eastern grasslands. Fuegian Indians inhabited the cone's tip, storm-lashed Tierra del Fuego—one of the earth's "most inhospitable" places, Darwin noted.

resistance, the chroniclers identified three Araucanian groups: The northernmost were called the Picunche; the middle group, the Mapuche, lived south of the Bío-Bío River; farther south the Huilliche occupied the territory down to Chiloé Island. The outstanding difference among these groups, as the Spaniards saw it, was the ability of the Mapuche to resist Spanish settlement. The Picunche were quickly defeated and assimilated by the Incas and then the Spaniards. Most Huilliche eventually joined the Mapuche cause, and the story of these two groups became one. Under the leadership of the Mapuche, Araucanian culture and influence expanded eastward across the Andes into the Argentine pampas.

Although today many Mapuche are assimilated into the Chilean way of life, about 200,000 Indians live on more than 2,000 small reservations scattered among numerous towns and estates. Possibly more than any other American Indian group, the Mapuche have fought longer and harder to preserve their identity; they have become one of the largest surviving Indian societies in South America.

In prereservation days the Mapuche followed a semisedentary way of life in tune with the changing seasons. Hunting parties stalked deer, fox, birds, and *guanaco*, a species of wild llama. In summer the Indians gathered an abundance of wild plants and fished lakes and streams. "During the months of February and March," wrote a Spanish chronicler, "the people would line the banks of a river . . . each man was equipped with a long, sturdy cane pole with a pointed, trident-shaped end . . . there were so many fish that the Indians could slap the water, stunning and hooking a fish and bringing it ashore. . . . Within hours they would have enough fish to feed all the people." The Mapuche who lived along the coast dug clams in the inlets and fished the cold waters of the Humboldt Current.

The Araucanians paddled about in plank boats, dugout canoes, and small reed rafts. Chroniclers mention that in some areas llamas served as pack animals. From the Spaniards the Araucanians obtained horses. Today the Mapuche value horses for transportation and also as items of social prestige. Oxen, their only draft animal, are used to till the soil, clear fallen timber, and pull single-axle oak carts.

In the fertile valleys the Mapuche practiced slash-and-burn agriculture. When gardens around the family households wore out, the Indians shifted the plots to a new area. In the past the men cleared the land by girdling trees with stone axes, then burning the downed timber and underbrush. Using crude oar- or shovel-like tools to break up, loosen, and lift the earth, the Mapuche cultivated corn, squash,

OVERLEAF: *Glacier-gouged Cordillera de Paine spikes the southern Andes. In the shadow of snow-enameled flanks once roved hardy Alacaluf Indians. They navigated fjords of the Chilean archipelago in bark canoes, the women diving into icy waters for shellfish.*

341

Ostrich of South America, Darwin's rhea ranges Patagonia's dry plains. Nomadic Tehuelche hunters killed the flightless bird for food, often mixing it with guanaco meat, another staple, to make pemmican. Two-pound rhea eggs were punctured and cooked over coals.

344 potatoes, beans, chili peppers, and *quinoa*, an Andean pigweed.

To a Mapuche, working the fields is not strictly a laborious task; it is also a seasonal event of social pleasure. In areas where modern technology has not been adopted or cannot be afforded, the Mapuche plant and harvest on a communal basis, a practice probably learned from the Incas. A man invites his relatives to come with their hoes, wooden prongs, and shovels. Wrote a Chilean anthropologist: "The men break the ground, the women faithfully following behind them, . . . making holes for seeds with their wooden sticks. When the tasks are over, the group retires to the owner's house, to indulge in lengthy conversation, telling stories of their young ones or how their grandparents used to work the fields . . . all graciously drinking and eating at the expense of the owner."

Now as then, each family farms about three to five acres. Households are scattered over the countryside on low hilltops or gently sloping hillsides within sight of each other. The dispersed nature of the community lends itself to the shifting of agricultural plots every few years. Even in the old days, the Indians kept a good distance from their neighbors, fearing poisoning or witchcraft from evil spirits.

During the long era of warfare the Mapuche installed local *toquis*, or war chiefs, seasoned warriors who were wise and gifted leaders. Evidence suggests that lack of centralized leadership made it much more difficult for Spaniards and Chileans to defeat the Mapuche. Scattered groups had to be tracked down and subdued one at a time.

In times of peace the Mapuche lived in autonomous groups led by an elder, the *lonko*, a practice still followed today. The lonko exercises no real authority; his counsel is followed because he is considered

Mapuche plowmen, following yoked oxen, ready a field for planting. Kinsmen participate in communal labor called mingaco, *a practice employed also to harvest crops, drain marshlands, clear land, repair roads and canals. The Indians live in shaggy pole-and-thatch* rukas; *inside, soot from open fires blackens windowless walls.*

OVERLEAF: *Fog shrouds Mapuche draymen awaiting oxen to trundle their cargo of charcoal to market. Slow to adopt mechanical ways, the Indians transport goods in two-wheeled carts.*

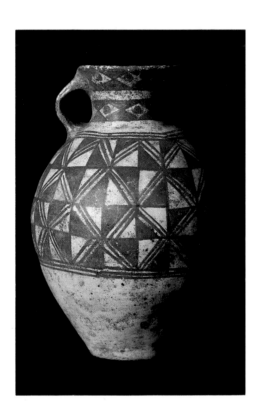

experienced and wise, particularly in matters of economics.

The Mapuche are bound by a strong sense of neighborly welfare, mutual dependence during hard times, and kinship ties. They trace their ancestry through the male line to a common ancestor, the "founder of the lineage." When a young Mapuche woman marries, she resides with a member of her husband's kinship group. Today a monogamous family of parents and children form the Mapuche household, but until the early part of the 20th century, polygyny, or the taking of several wives, was common. I have often heard men speak of their fathers and grandfathers, who were considered rich and powerful because they could support many wives. A Spanish historian described how "The first wife is always the preferred one . . . the other wives look up to her and see her as the true wife of the common husband . . . the first wife directs all the domestic chores. When she says that the fields need to be planted or harvested then the others do it. . . ." Each wife had her own work space within the household and her own hearth to cook food for herself and her children. Each wife also worked her own land and took care of her own animals.

Standing alone in the countryside, the typical Mapuche household consists of an oval-shaped, thatched house called a *ruka*, a corral made of poles and branches, and a small, planked storage bin. The thick, high walls of the ruka insulate against the summer heat and the winter cold. Furnishings are sparse—usually low wooden benches, blankets, beds, woven storage bags, a mill for grinding corn, and a small low table.

Even today the Mapuche are cautious about the outside world. When a visitor approaches the ruka, he is met by barking dogs and curious eyes. Children go outside to look, then run to their mother announcing that someone has come. If the person is familiar, he is invited in to visit and drink *chicha de manzana*, a fermented beverage made from apples. A stranger is greeted politely outside the dwelling and after brief conversation may be asked inside.

Often I joined the household of Antonio Alquipan for a meal. He and I leaned forward on low wooden benches while his wife, Eliana, presided at the fire. She spooned potatoes, beans, and horsemeat—a luxury among the Mapuche—from the pot. We also munched hot peppers, carrots, and bread, and washed it all down with fresh chicha.

We talked in the eating area of the ruka, comforted by the warmth and fragrance of the fire. Antonio wiped his eyes often, as people do in a smoky room, his old hands trembling a bit. Antonio was a small man with broad, powerful shoulders. He had worked the land ever since he was old enough to walk the furrows and plant seeds. He showed me a

Araucanian potters as well as weavers favored geometric patterns typified in this museum pitcher. The Indians used other clay pots for cooking, dropping hot stones in with chunks of meat and vegetables. They ladled the stew into bowls hollowed from tree trunks.

"The people are tall," conquistador Pedro de Valdivia wrote of the Araucanians, "with handsome faces, both men and women." In this family the father grasps a lance, a weapon used against the Spanish. His son plays chueca, *a form of field hockey.*

three-foot-long sling he had twined from a local junco reed. "I remember when I used to walk in the open fields near the river, looking for small round stones, and shooting down water cranes that flew in from the coast." I offered to trade for the sling. He said, "I don't wish to give away this one. I made it when I was a boy, and it is the last one I have. It would be like saying good-bye to the old times that my grandfather had taught me."

Those who do not know the customs of the Mapuche would be impressed by the order and cleanliness of the ruka and by the good behavior of the children. The Mapuche wife, in constant motion, cares for the smaller children, prepares corn cakes and bread, cleans fresh vegetables, and does other domestic chores. When she does sit down, she cleans household utensils or weaves a carefully designed blanket, poncho, or belt of wool, an art the Mapuche learned from the Incas. The smaller children and unmarried girls help her in all her labors.

The Mapuche man heads the household. Men work the fields and take care of livestock; they also carve wooden bowls, tool handles, and children's toys. Under his father's guidance, a young boy learns to plow, feed the animals, and deliver sacks of grain or potatoes to the market.

Mapuche families work hard outside in the summer, tending the fields and the livestock, with little time for social visits away from the reservation. The family spends the rain-drenched winter months at home huddled around the fire. Children listen raptly while adults relate tales of their ancestors. The adults take advantage of these months to instruct the children in etiquette and morals in both the Mapuche world and the Chilean world. Youngsters learn to read and write Spanish at government schools on the reservation.

A ceremonial field flanked by oxcarts bustles with activities of nguillatun, *a traditional Mapuche religious rite. Smoke from fires in the sacred central plaza drifts over bough-covered ramadas. Ritual priests sacrifice sheep or goats, occasionally sprinkling blood on the flames. The festival, held in association with planting or harvesting, usually lasts two to four days and may draw supplicants from several reservations. At altars of effigy posts (left), priests offer prayers to Ngenechan, the supreme being, as well as to lesser gods and spirits.*

The Mapuche Indian's ancient religion pervades his life. He believes in a unity between the living and the dead, between the natural or visible world and the supernatural world. Sickness and death have no natural causes but come from *wekufes*, or evil forces. The evil spirits will do no harm if religious rituals are performed correctly, according to traditional ways. *Nguillatufes*, or ritual priests concerned with restraining evil, represent the people before the deities at ceremonial events. On a daily basis the shaman—usually a woman—is preoccupied with the eternal struggle between good and evil.

The protecting center of the Mapuche world is *wenen mapu*—a supreme celestial land where their deities live. The Mapuche pray to Ngenechan, the supreme being who lives in this land, for food, prosperity, and a long, wholesome life. Another deity, Pillan, resides in the high mountains to the east and controls such catastrophic events as river floods, tidal waves, earthquakes, volcanic eruptions, and drought. He is the omnipresent protector and personifier of the good spirits of the ancestors, especially those of famous lonkos and warriors. In the past the connection between warriors and the supernatural world was bonded by offering the blood of a captured prisoner to the Pillan. One Spaniard wrote, ". . . standing with their knives in hand . . . they would

Step-notched rewe, garlanded with fresh greenery, serves as sacred center pole for Mapuche healing rites. As part of the ceremony a shaman (opposite)— usually a woman—taps a trance-inducing tattoo on a drumhead design depicting the four quarters of the earth. Whistling and shouting, riders led by standard-bearers encircle a nguillatun field to rid it of evil spirits (right).

cut open the chest [of the prisoner] and remove the pulsating
heart . . . then suck the blood from it and blow tobacco smoke on all
parts of the heart . . . saying to Pillan . . . accept this."

But reservation life, coupled with increased efforts to missionize and
modernize the Mapuche, has hastened change and reduced reliance on
traditional ways. Though their numbers are growing, the Mapuche
already live between two cultures, and in the future may belong
entirely to neither. As each year passes, more and more Mapuche learn
to read and write Spanish, while fewer can recount the old tales and
traditions. The proud people of the land of lakes and forests may
eventually succumb to the roar of the tractor and the bustle of town life.

Far south of the Mapuche heartland, the Pacific and the lower Andes
cradle the southern coast and offshore islands of Chile and Tierra del
Fuego. Capt. Allen Gardiner, a 19th-century missionary, described his
first impressions of Tierra del Fuego: "It is a land of darkness, a scene of
savage desolation. Both scenery and climate coincide in character. The
one is gloomy and desolate, the other tempestuous and black." The
landscape—a maze of rockbound channels, islands, narrow fjords, and
rocky headlands—is lashed by cold rains or sleet and shrouded with
clouds and fog. Surf pounds the outer islands, and the winds howl
incessantly. Though the temperature seldom falls below freezing, one
wonders how unsheltered people survived such a hostile climate.

Four Fuegian groups once occupied this harsh terrain. Afoot,
nomadic Ona hunted in the interior of Tierra del Fuego and along the
coast. Using plank or bark canoes, Yahgan and Alacaluf fished the cold
channels, while farther north the few Chono gathered seafood and
hunted along the tortuous waterways of the Chilean archipelago.
Exceedingly primitive, these Indians recognized no chiefs, had no
tribes. They lacked the settled arts of pottery, metallurgy, and weaving.
Each group spoke a distinctive language. A Yahgan dictionary compiled
by an English missionary listed some 32,000 words.

Small migratory bands of Alacaluf and Yahgan lived in wigwams—
beehive-shaped shelters made of poles and roofed with skins or bark.
The air reeked of smoke, rotting whale blubber, and refuse tossed out
the door. Families collected shellfish, fished, and hunted seals,
porpoises, birds, and sometimes guanacos. The Yahgan lowered a bird
hunter from a cliff top on the end of a seal-hide thong; the hunter
seized a nesting bird in both hands and bit the head or neck to kill it.
Alacaluf cormorant hunters blackened themselves with charcoal, hid in
a shelter until the birds had roosted, then caught and killed them by
crushing the skull with their teeth. (Continued on page 360)

A "wretched hovel of sticks and grass,"
Captain James Cook described the
beehive hut of the Haush tribe, Ona
Indians of southeastern Tierra del
Fuego. Here, he noted, dwelled "as
miserable a set of People as are this day
upon Earth." Whites doomed them.

Cradling bow and quiver, an Ona
hunter stands atop a dune and scans for
game—a seal perhaps. When a target
appeared, the bowman dropped his
guanaco-hide cape and took aim with a
glass-tipped arrow. Children learned to
shoot—and dodge—blunted arrows.

Spangled with tufts of down stuck on with grease, a masked man personifies the evil spirit Short to terrorize a young initiate in Ona puberty rites. Onlookers in guanaco robes crowd the hain, firelit lodge of the all-male secret society. Climaxing the ceremonies, Short sham-wrestles the novice and reveals he is not a monster but a relative or friend. The ritual evolved from a legendary battle of the sexes. Revolting against oppressive matriarchal rule, men conspired to massacre witches, then replaced the women's secret councils with their own.

Fur-clad Ona hunter fingers an arrow crafted from yellow barberry wood. He straightened the shaft over fire and smoothed it with stone. Points were flaked from flint, later from glass. Rawhide tips used in games blunt the arrows of disrobed archers (lower left). Hunters carried spare bowstring and points in foxskin bags strapped to the waist. Women favored a guanaco-hide bag or coiled basket (upper left). Thongs fastened their robes of guanaco fur. Men might go naked; in a weather ceremony (opposite), they wore only headbands and moccasins.

These hardy Indians braved the raw, menacing climate clad only in a breechclout or cape usually made from seal or guanaco skins. Rolls of fat covered their short bodies, providing warmth and an energy reserve.

Women paddled the canoes while men sat in the bow scanning for seals and sea otters. In the center of the canoe, a fire was kept burning on piles of sand or turf. Even in the worst weather Alacaluf women dove without hesitation into the marrow-chilling waters to bring up shellfish. A Yahgan baby girl learning to swim would sometimes clamber onto her mother's head to escape the frigid water. On shore the Yahgan piled green wood on campfires to warn those out fishing of intruders. European explorers who saw these columns of black smoke called the region Tierra del Fuego—Land of Fire.

Fuegian Indians typically plucked hair from the body and face but not the hair on the scalp, which they combed with porpoise jawbones. The Yahgan reportedly tried to pull the beards off visiting French scientists in 1883, so puzzled were they by the hairy growth. Fuegians sometimes painted their faces and bodies; the Yahgan used red to indicate happiness, black for sadness, and white for anger.

Ona hunters camouflaged their bodies, bows, and quivers with yellow clay to resemble dried grass or with chalk to match the snow. Duck hunters, blackened with charcoal and carrying flaming torches, waded into the water and caught the dazzled birds, then drowned them or wrung their necks. If the Ona found a stranded whale, a great delicacy, they would preserve it by burying it in the ice-cold sand.

The Ona devoured everything edible. Besides guanacos, their principal meat source, they ate foxes, seals, geese, eels, mussels, a small burrowing rodent called the tuco-tuco, a variety of roots, bulbs,

Tehuelche toldo, *sewn guanaco skins stretched between stakes, frames family members. Standing tall, the Indians were "giants" to Magellan's crew in 1520. "Their height appears greater than it really is," Darwin later observed, "from their large guanaco mantles, their long flowing hair, and general figure." Tehuelche families banded together to enforce territorial hunting rights. Trespassers risked war unless they were granted entry by a band's headman (opposite). He exhorted his people in battle but had no authority to settle family disputes.*

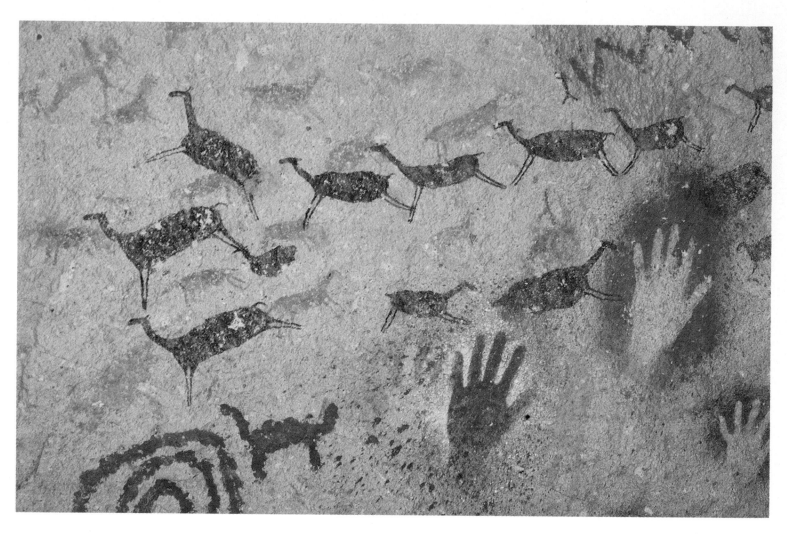

Tehuelche handprints stenciled on cave walls in Argentina's Cueva de las Manos, near Lake Buenos Aires, seem to reach for bounding guanacos. Depicting perhaps some long-ago roundup, the graffiti evoke a 19th-century hunt on a Patagonian plain (foldout). Shouting horsemen ride in pairs from different directions, driving animals to a field ringed by signal fires. Lead riders swing bolas at the necks of ostrichlike rheas and the legs of guanacos. Trailing horsemen lasso pumas and club hobbled animals. The guanaco, said to have "the neigh of a horse, the wool of a sheep, the neck of a camel, the feet of a deer, and the swiftness of the devil," provided the Indians with meat, clothing, and shelter. From its thighbone they fashioned a primitive flute.

seeds, and berries, and even tree fungus and sap.

According to Ona legends, many mountains had once been human beings and should be treated with respect. If rudely pointed at, the peaks might cloak themselves in clouds and send downpours. Among Chono taboos, looking at flying parrots might lead to bad weather; throwing kelp or shellfish on the fire would cause rough seas.

The Ona believed that women had once ruled by means of cunning and witchcraft; then men wrested control from them after a wholesale massacre and founded a secret society that met in large ceremonial wigwams. To terrorize the women and keep them away from lodge meetings, the men impersonated supernatural, women-hating creatures. Women could, however, join in the push-me-down dance recalling the days of female rule. The men pretended to be crippled and let the women "knock them down dead."

An Ona man might obtain a wife by wooing, by killing her husband or father, by kidnapping, or by arranging parental agreements. Although there was no marriage ceremony, at the time of possession the wife sometimes put up a good fight—and the bridegroom appeared later with a scratched face, black eye, or bites. If a man took a second wife, she was often the younger sister of the first.

An Ona mother wrapped her newborn baby in foxskin and tied a dark red eyeshade of guanaco hide above its eyes. When an infant cried continuously, an impatient mother might suddenly scream into each ear. Yet to spare a baby the shock of drinking icy water, she would warm it in her own mouth. A ladderlike framework stuck in the ground held the baby upright, safe from dogs and accidents.

Ona men, clad only in waterproof moccasins and a lengthy robe of guanaco hide, slept in freezing temperatures with their bare legs exposed. Even during the winter, everyone took shelter under a windbreak of skins, and children often went naked.

The advent of the white man brought the eventual extermination of the Fuegian groups. European diseases and the sheep rancher's rifle decimated their numbers during the last half of the 1800s. Professional hunters received a bounty for the ears of Indian men, women, or children. Today these aboriginal societies have disappeared, leaving only a few mestizos acculturated to the white man's world.

North of Tierra del Fuego, Patagonia unfolds east of the Andes. Dry southern plateaus flatten into the pampas, the grasslands to the north. Sparse in population but rich in animal life, the prairies formed the homeland of the Puelche and Tehuelche Indians.

Dependent primarily on hunting, these Indians of the grasslands stalked guanacos, small game, and rheas. Hunters used young, tame guanacos as decoys or camouflaged themselves with rhea feathers. Each band, headed by a chief, claimed its own hunting grounds. Trespassing on another band's area would lead to war, so it was customary for a stranger, before entering foreign territory, to send three smoke signals and wait for a reply. During the 18th century most of the plains tribes

OVERLEAF: *Yahgan bodies glisten in torchlight as they come ashore after a day of fishing and gathering mollusks. Despite frigid Cape Horn weather, the Indians required little clothing other than a pubic covering of bird skin. They adapted to cold naturally, having large blood vessels near the skin to channel body heat to arms and legs. Greasing the skin helped the Indians endure the harsh environment. In a Yahgan's canoe, fabricated from strips of bark, smoke curled from a sod fireplace. Flames were never allowed to die out. On shore glowed Indian campfires, once beacons to the explorer Magellan.*

367

Poised like an Olympic javelin thrower, a Yahgan hunter (opposite) aims his spear. Barbs as sharp as shark's teeth impaled fish. With a sling he stoned birds. The Yahgan lived in domed wigwams roofed with grass in summer (below), sealskins in winter.

acquired horses. Quickly mastering the art of horsemanship, the Indians tirelessly pursued guanacos with spears and whirling bolas and began raiding isolated white settlements.

Continuously feuding with each other, the Puelche wore horsehide armor and fought with lances at close range rather than with bows and arrows from a distance. Mounted bands carried their horsehide-covered huts with them. Commoners wore horsehide robes, while prominent individuals cloaked themselves with guanaco, otter, or fox skins.

The Tehuelche, tall and dark skinned, wore shoulder-length silver earrings, conical hats, and loose guanaco-skin cloaks decorated with colorful geometric designs. They painted themselves with a mixture of grease and red earth or charcoal. Always on the move, they lived in large communal tents facing downwind. In front a fire burned constantly—in the day for cooking, at night for warmth and scaring off wild animals. When a young man negotiated a marriage contract with a girl's father, he specified how much he would pay in horses, rhea feathers, or guanaco hides. Once the arrangements were made, he could not speak to the girl until their wedding day.

Like their brothers in other parts of South America, these plains Indians resisted European colonialism. As immigrants flooded the frontier, the Indians retaliated; in one massive raid, 2,000 braves took 200 captives and 20,000 head of cattle. But in 1879 an Argentine general with an army of 8,000 overran the pampas and wiped out the Puelche. In other campaigns the government subdued the Tehuelche and marched them to Buenos Aires, where the men were forced to join the army. Women and the aged were placed in institutions. Urban families adopted the children. The white man took a terrible toll, leaving only a scattered population of mixed-blood descendants.

As early as the 17th century, renegades of mixed Iberian and Indian blood roamed the grasslands. Known as gauchos, these cowboys hunted the "wild" cattle that had escaped from the Spaniards' grazing lands. The feral herds supplied food as well as hides and tallow for sale in the markets. When authorities attempted to regulate the slaughter of open-range cattle, many renegades resisted. Thus, violence became an aspect of gaucho culture that later played an important role in the upheavals of the region and transformed the gaucho from outlaw to hero. In the early 1800s free-roaming gauchos fought alongside Gen. José de San Martín for Argentina's independence from Spain.

The gaucho was easily recognized by his rugged dress and hunting bolas, his knives and lassos, his barbecued meat and bitter herb tea, and his special brand of folk poetry and music. Eventually his dependence upon the wild cattle depleted the herds, and the gauchos shifted to cattle raising. Today remnants of the old gaucho population have come to be identified with the way of life of the ranch hand or cowboy; and their romantic traditions, which in part grew out of the nomadic Indian existence, are remembered in folk music and dance, poetry, novels, and legends. The ghosts of the vanished plains Indians ride on in the gauchos of South America.

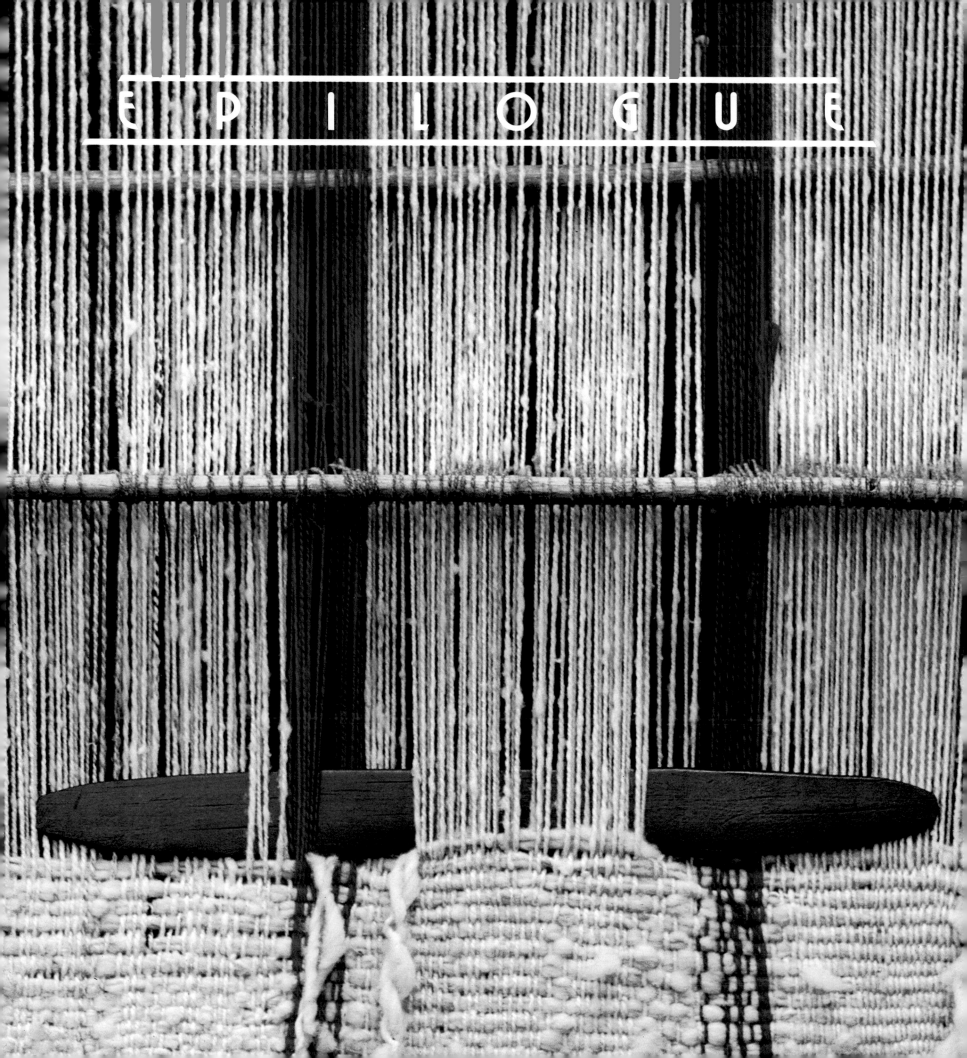

EPILOGUE

CHALLENGE OF THE PRESENT

David Maybury-Lewis

Half-woven Mapuche textile from Chile symbolizes the fabric of ancient cultures that Indian groups strive to preserve in a fast-changing world. In that struggle to maintain identity, acculturation may unravel centuries of tradition. More immediate is the direct clash of cultures. Of several hundred known Brazilian tribes, for example, more than half have vanished since the Conquest.

The two Shavante men were impeccably dressed in white shirts and dark slacks. They were lecturing a group of specialists from Brazil's Indian Service on the problems of development in Indian areas and in Shavante country in particular. They were, I reflected, as eloquent and forceful in Portuguese as their elders had been in their own tongue when I had lived with their people two decades previously. At that time the Shavante spoke no outside language, for they had little contact with the outside world. They roamed the high savannas of central Brazil, hunting and gathering and avoided by Brazilian backwoodsmen who feared their warlike reputation. I remembered trekking with them for days on end through plains and jungles so featureless to me that I lived in constant fear of getting lost. I remembered their feeling for the beauty they saw in that land and their appreciation for the bounty which they knew how to gather from it. I remembered the messengers catching up with our band, bringing news of the others, including my wife and son, and their graphic pantomime of how our child was learning to walk. . . .

"Do you remember this man?" My thoughts were interrupted by one of the Brazilians who was pointing me out to the Shavante. "He lived among your people many years ago."

The Shavante stared at me. Then one of them remarked slowly: "Yes, I remember you. You came with your family and spoke our language well. But . . ." he added, devastatingly, "I did not recognize you, for your hair was black then."

And you, I thought to myself, were a young boy then, chasing wild pigs across the savannas.

In the meantime the frontier finally caught up with the Shavante. Their forefathers had fought the Portuguese in colonial times, and then their people moved westward as more and more settlers pressed in on their lands near the Tocantins River. They migrated across the Araguaia River and settled in their present territory along another river, which came to be known by the Brazilians as the River of Deaths. There they had remained undisturbed for over a century. It was there that I had shared their traditional way of life with them, and that is where they are

374 today. Only today they are hemmed in once again by the ranchers and settlers who have come pouring in as a result of the push to the west, a push that has been gathering momentum in Brazil ever since the building of the new inland capital of Brasília in the 1950s.

The Shavante no longer live as nomadic hunters and gatherers. They have settled down to farming and are as skilled with tractors (if they can get them) as they once were with bow and arrow. Yet the essence of their old way of life, their language and their customs, is still maintained in their villages. The men still meet at dusk and make eloquent speeches to the council, but nowadays many of them also travel to Brasília to use their eloquence in defense of Shavante lands—not the vast hunting territories over which they once roamed, but the much-reduced lands which they now farm. Yet even these are not guaranteed to them under Brazilian law. So the Shavante once more face the dismal prospect of having to move on or to stand and fight. Only this time there is a third option of which they are uncomfortably aware. They could lose their lands and disappear like human flotsam into Brazilian society.

The Shavante, and lowland tribal peoples such as the Yanomamö, are merely recent examples of Indian groups affected by a process that has been going on since the arrival of the Europeans in the Americas. The Europeans were looking for wealth. They hoped to find it in gold and precious stones, but failing that they sought to produce it in the New World or rather have somebody produce it for them. For this purpose they needed Indian labor or Indian land or both. The Spaniards found large settled Indian populations in Mexico, Central America, and the high Andes that could be put to work for their new masters. The Portuguese, on the other hand, found eastern South America relatively sparsely inhabited. After a while they discovered it was easier to import blacks from Africa to work their plantations rather than bother with the wild and recalcitrant Indians.

So the Indian peoples who lived near the Atlantic coast were deprived of their lands and most of them died out. The reasons for this are depressingly familiar. They were decimated by Old World diseases. If they were friendly to the whites, they were invariably exploited or expelled by settlers who came later—sometimes even by the very people they had befriended. If they were hostile, this was usually considered sufficient reason to wage a war of extermination against them. The settlers wanted the land at all costs and the Indians were forced out, often facing starvation as they abandoned their plantations and their hunting and fishing grounds.

Undeterred by balsa lip plug, Chief Rauni of Brazil's Txukahamai tribe chats over a government agent's two-way radio. In 1971 his reluctant agreement to move his people provoked an internal conflict in which seven people died—a twentieth of the tribe.

The pressure on highland Indians has been equally relentless. Under the Inca Empire, for example, the people had to work for the Inca and contribute in this way to maintenance of the emperor and the priesthood. In a bad year their labor produced less and the Inca suffered along with his people. The Spaniards replaced the Inca and required the system to produce tribute in kind for them. In a bad year, however, the tribute was not reduced, so the Spaniards' income did not suffer, but the people who produced it were impoverished.

As the population of the highland regions declined, due to malnutrition and epidemics, it became progressively harder for the Indians to maintain tributary payments to their Spanish overlords. The despair produced by this extortionate system exploded in the middle of the 18th century in the uprising led by a well-educated Indian called José Gabriel Condorcanqui. He took the name of Tupac Amaru, the last Inca who held out against the Spaniards, and led a revolt that took control of central Peru. He was captured and executed, but a series of Indian uprisings erupted throughout the Andean region—in Colombia, Ecuador, Peru, Bolivia, and Chile, all in his name.

These revolts had parallels in Mexico where the Maya of the Yucatán Peninsula almost drove the white men into the sea in 1847. The Indians were forced back into the jungles of eastern Yucatán, but they held out there in what was virtually an independent Maya state until the end of the century. As late as the 1880s the Yaqui of Sonora fought a full-scale war against Mexico.

In these rebellions the Indians felt driven to make a last-ditch stand in defense of their way of life. To borrow a phrase from Hamlet, they felt the times were out of joint, and they fought desperately to set them right again. The revolts were eventually crushed, but the times are still out of joint for most of the Indian peoples of the Americas.

In fact, the pressures on them are now increasing. Something like a second conquest is taking place as the nations of the hemisphere hungrily search for new resources in areas previously ignored and sometimes hardly explored. New frontiers are opening up, bringing boomtowns run by gunmen who live by the creed that the only good Indian is a dead Indian. Efforts to protect the Indians have often been halfhearted, for frontiers are difficult to police, and governments tend to be more interested in opening up remote areas than in protecting the "savage" Indians whom they hardly recognize as fellow citizens.

The fate of these Indians who are being shot on the ground or bombed from the air to clear the way for development has been just cause for concern in the world press. But the plight of long-settled

Cuna woman mixes old and new ways as she stitches a blouse at the home of a missionary in Panama. She sews the reverse-appliquéd mola by hand but uses a sewing machine to attach other pieces. Sale of molas, popular with tourists, supplements family income.

A 19-year-old girl (opposite) who is part Indian adjusts a television set at an assembly plant in Manaus, Brazil. Cultures and bloodlines have long mingled at this river port where the Rio Negro meets the Amazon. It once served as the rubber capital of South America.

Indian peoples is often only a little less desperate. They are no longer tied to the land in colonial forms of serfdom, nor forced by law to work in the mines. But other ways have been found to appropriate their land and their labor. The main one is to deny them legal title to the land they have always occupied. After Guatemala became independent in 1839, for example, the state took over the church lands that the Indians had traditionally used and awarded them to large landowners. Later, during the coffee boom at the end of the 19th century, it allocated more Indian land to outsiders to use for cash crops. The Indians were thus forced to work on the plantations, since they could not feed themselves from their own plots. Finally, in the 1930s, the Vagrancy Law required all Indians to work 150 days a year for a landowner, thus completing the expropriation of both their land and their labor.

   As a result of such policies, there are areas like the municipality of Panzós where less than 3 percent of the population owns more than 65 percent of the land, while the majority of the Indians are sub-subsistence farmers or landless rural laborers. It was to the town of Panzós that 700 Kekchi Indians came on May 29, 1978, to hold a demonstration and present a letter to the mayor asking for consideration of their land claims and for protection against further

evictions. They were met by the army, which shot down more than 100 of them. Others drowned as terrified men, women, and children tried to escape by swimming across the Polochic River.

The Panzós massacre shows the lengths to which an administration will go to keep the Indians in their place, but the conditions that produced it are not confined to Guatemala. For example, in the Cauca Department of Colombia similar pressure by large landowners on the smallholders, both Indian and non-Indian, has led the Indians to form an organization known as CRIC (the Regional Indian Council of Cauca). Since 1971 CRIC has legally re-claimed 37,000 acres of arable land for the Indians at 50 different places. It has established 40 cooperatives and a number of bilingual education programs.

All of this activity has provoked reprisals. Leaders of CRIC have been murdered, others imprisoned, and the organization has been accused of being in league with guerrillas seeking to overthrow the government. Rural unrest has been chronic in Colombia ever since the unhappy years referred to quite simply as the time of *la violencia*, but CRIC insists that it wants nothing to do with the various competing guerrilla organizations. Its motto is "Unity, Land, and Culture" and it insists that it will defend all three against the state, against the missionaries, and against the revolutionaries too.

There are those who argue that Indians could solve their problems by turning their backs on their own culture, in effect by ceasing to be themselves and joining the mainstream of the country they live in. Such proposals are extraordinarily insensitive. Few of us have any idea of what it means to be told to rid ourselves of our way of life, our language, our way of thinking, our religion, of everything that gives our existence its meaning. Most of us would consider such deprogramming as cruel and inhuman punishment. Moreover, Indians who do abandon their own culture are not usually permitted to blend into their nations as solid citizens. They are more likely to be cast adrift as rootless laborers in a society which despises them.

Yet the "deculturation" of Indian peoples is still official policy in many countries. It lay, for example, behind the Brazilian government's proposal to "emancipate" the Indians in 1978 by abolishing the status of Indian—and the legal protections that went with it—in order to merge the Indians with the majority population. The law was shelved when a storm of protest, led by the Indians themselves, pointed out that the repeal even of unsatisfactory laws that offered some protection to Indian peoples would lead to the loss of their lands and the final destruction of their traditional way of life.

Campa child in eastern Peru is not writing "Jane" but a word in her native tongue. Classes at the bilingual school begin in Campa, but by the third grade are mostly in Spanish. Dozens of Campa families, once widely scattered in the jungle, now cluster around the school.

Guajiro girls (opposite) bless themselves before a meal at a Catholic mission school on Colombia's Guajira Peninsula. Founded half a century ago, the school provides elementary grade training for hundreds of children. How many return to their villages is unknown.

It is precisely their own way of life that most Indian peoples in the Americas are struggling to protect, and this usually means defending the right of their communities to hold land in common. So in Paraguay the major national Indian organization, the Association of Indian Peoples (API), and the major Indianist group supporting their cause, the Paraguayan Association of Indianists (AIP), have long been pressing for the passage of a law that would enable Indian communities to gain legal title to lands they hold in common.

Meanwhile in Chile the government has passed a statute which, in spite of all proposed modifications, would lead to the eventual breakup of Indian lands into individual holdings. The law was bitterly opposed by the people it will affect, the Mapuche Indians, who make up about 3 percent of Chile's population. They are the descendants of the famous Araucanians who fought the conquistador Pedro de Valdivia to a standstill and inspired epic poems in Spain. For centuries they have maintained their ethnic identity, based on their ties to the land. Their traditional lands have been whittled away, but the Mapuche have survived every adversity. The Mapuche are quick to perceive that the new law, which would eventually do away with Indian lands altogether, will consign them to oblivion as a people.

Such measures that threaten the final destruction of the way of life of entire Indian peoples come wrapped nowadays in the rhetoric of development. But development in Indian areas rarely brings much benefit to the Indians. The construction of hydroelectric works along Paraguay's border with Brazil has produced a boom in eastern Paraguay, but so far the effects of this have been to squeeze Indians off their lands. Again and again the modernization of agriculture has meant that Indian lands are taken so that other people can produce cash crops. The modernization the Chilean government is encouraging in Mapuche country will be based on agribusiness and a tourist complex in which the Mapuche have no part.

The exclusion of Indians from the fruits of development on their own land is sometimes defended on the grounds that they are culturally and temperamentally unsuited to participate in a modern economy. That is why Indians particularly resent being portrayed as a picturesque part of their country's heritage, for this implies that they and their way of life are quaint survivals from the past which have no place in the future.

Yet over the centuries Indian societies have shown a remarkable capacity to adjust to shattering changes while keeping their own sense of identity intact. Indians do not cease to be Indians when they abandon their bows and arrows, any more than Americans ceased to be

Maya medic practices basic dentistry on a patient in Chiapas, Mexico. Clinics staffed by Indians often provide the only non-traditional medical care that is sensitive to the cultural values of people in the remote areas of Middle and South America.